Creating and Changing Layers with a Dialog Box

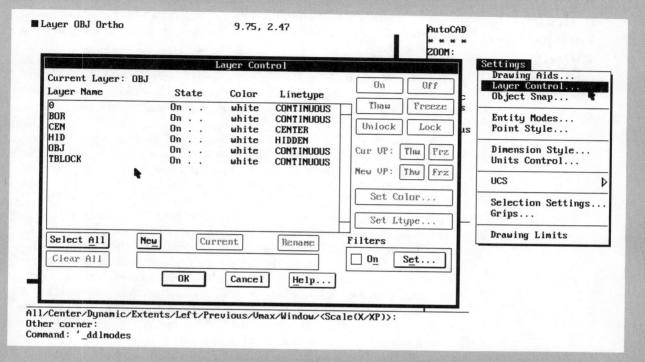

1. Move the cursor to the top of the screen. When the menu bar appears, highlight the menu title Settings and press the pick button to pull down the menu.

2. Move the cursor down the menu to highlight Layer Control and press the pick button.

3. You can now create and freeze layers as well as select the current layer. You can also rename and change the color and linetype of a layer.

Computer users are not all alike. Neither are SYBEX books.

We know our customers have a variety of needs. They've told us so. And because we've listened, we've developed several distinct types of books to meet the needs of each of our customers. What are you looking for in computer help?

If you're looking for the basics, try the **ABC's** series. You'll find short, unintimidating tutorials and helpful illustrations. For a more visual approach, select **Teach Yourself**, featuring screen-by-screen illustrations of how to use your latest software purchase.

Mastering and **Understanding** titles offer you a step-by-step introduction, plus an in-depth examination of intermediate-level features, to use as you progress.

Our **Up & Running** series is designed for computer-literate consumers who want a no-nonsense overview of new programs. Just 20 basic lessons, and you're on your way.

We also publish two types of reference books. Our **Instant References** provide quick access to each of a program's commands and functions. SYBEX **Encyclopedias** and **Desktop** References provide a *comprehensive reference* and explanation of all of the commands, features, and functions of the subject software.

Sometimes a subject requires a special treatment that our standard series don't provide. So you'll find we have titles like **Advanced Techniques**, **Handbooks**, **Tips & Tricks**, and others that are specifically tailored to satisfy a unique need.

We carefully select our authors for their in-depth understanding of the software they're writing about, as well as their ability to write clearly and communicate effectively. Each manuscript is thoroughly reviewed by our technical staff to ensure its complete accuracy. Our production department makes sure it's easy to use. All of this adds up to the highest quality books available, consistently appearing on best-seller charts worldwide.

You'll find SYBEX publishes a variety of books on every popular software package. Looking for computer help? Help Yourself to SYBEX.

For a complete catalog of our publications:

SYBEX Inc.
2021 Challenger Drive, Alameda, CA 94501
Tel: (510) 523-8233/(800) 227-2346 Telex: 336311
Fax: (510) 523-2373

SYBEX is committed to using natural resources wisely to preserve and improve our environment. As a leader in the computer book publishing industry, we are aware that over 40% of America's solid waste is paper. This is why we have been printing the text of books like this one on recycled paper since 1982.

This year our use of recycled paper will result in the saving of more than 15,300 trees. We will lower air pollution effluents by 54,000 pounds, save 6,300,000 gallons of water, and reduce landfill by 2,700 cubic yards.

In choosing a SYBEX book you are not only making a choice for the best in skills and information, you are also choosing to enhance the quality of life for all of us.

This Book Is Only the Beginning.

The ABC's of
AutoCAD® Release 12

ALAN R. MILLER

SYBEX®

San Francisco
Paris
Düsseldorf
Soest

Acquisitions Editor: Dianne King
Editor: Armin Brott
Project Editor: Kathleen Lattinville
Technical Editor: Kurt Hampe
Word Processor: Ann Dunn
Chapter Art and Layout: Charlotte Carter
Screen Graphics: John Corrigan
Desktop Publishing Specialists: Dina F Quan, Stephanie Hollier
Proofreader: R.M. Holmes
Indexer: Ted Laux
Cover Designer: Archer Design
Cover Photographer: Mark Johann
Photo Art Direction: Ingalls & Associates
Book design based on a design by Amparo del Rio.
Screen reproductions produced with Collage Plus.

Library of Congress Card Number: 92-61600
ISBN: 0-7821-1038-X

Manufactured in the United States of America
10 9 8 7 6 5 4 3

ACKNOWLEDGMENTS

I am sincerely grateful to Kathleen Lattinville, project editor of this book, to Armin Brott for his skillful editing, and to Kurt Hampe for his technical review. I would also like to acknowledge the helpful feedback I have received from my students at the New Mexico Institute of Mining and Technology.

Contents at a Glance

Introduction xiv

CHAPTERS

1 AutoCAD Fundamentals   1
2 Starting a Border Template for Your Drawings   9
3 Adding a Title Block to the Border Drawing   25
4 Drawing Lines and a Circle   48
5 Selecting Objects   64
6 Trimming and Extending   81
7 Drawing a Pulley   102
8 Drawing Three Views of a Bracket   130
9 Drawing the Flange   167
10 Dimensioning the Bracket   193
11 Dimensioning the Flange   218
12 Introduction to Drawing in Three Dimensions   234
13 Paper Space: Separating
    the Model from the Drawing   269

APPENDICES

A Installing AutoCAD   290
B AutoCAD Commands   298

Index 301

INTRODUCTION . . . . **xiv**

CHAPTERS

Chapter 1

AUTOCAD FUNDAMENTALS   **1**

Technical Drawing Conventions Used in This Book . . . 2
Getting Help 2
    Getting Help for a Specific Command 3
Working with the Drawing Editor 4
    The Drawing Cursor and the Coordinate Readout . . . 4
Using Cartesian and Polar Notation 5
    Cartesian Notation 5
    Polar Notation 7

Chapter 2

STARTING A BORDER TEMPLATE FOR YOUR DRAWINGS   **9**

Starting AutoCAD 10
Setting Up the Drawing Area 11
    Setting the Number of Displayed Digits 12
    Changing the Drawing Limits 13
Using AutoCAD's Grid System 15
    Turning On the Grid 15
    Positioning the Cursor Precisely with Snap Mode . . 16
    Changing the Grid Spacing 17
    Changing the Snap Spacing 18
Turning Off the Coordinate Icon 18
Adjusting the Drawing Scale 19
Drawing a Line with the Line Command 19
Widening Border Lines 22
Saving Your Border Template 24

Chapter 3

ADDING A TITLE BLOCK TO THE BORDER DRAWING   **25**

Checking Your Drawing Time 26
Creating Layers 26
Moving the Border to Its Own Layer 27
Creating a Layer for the Title Block 28
Creating a Title Block 30
   Drawing the Title Block Border 30
Enlarging the Title Block with the Zoom Command . . 32
   Drawing Interior Lines 32
Using AutoCAD Typefaces 35
   Selecting the Typeface 36
Filling in the Title Block 38
   The Company Name 38
   Writing the Drawing Title 40
   Changing to the Simplex Font 42
   Writing Your Name 42
   Completing the Title Block 43
Plotting Your Drawing 45
Saving the Completed Border Template 47

Chapter 4

DRAWING LINES AND A CIRCLE   **48**

Beginning a New Drawing 49
Verifying the Drawing Name 50
Making Changes to Text 50
   Making Changes with the Ddedit Command . . . 51
Viewing the Entire Drawing 52
Drawing a Line with the Line Command 53
   Drawing an Attached Line Segment 56
Drawing an Angled Line 57
Erasing Lines with the U Command 59
   Redrawing an Erased Line 60
   Completing the Line Command 60

Using U and Redo after a
Command Has Been Completed 61
Drawing a Circle with the Circle Command 62
Saving Your Work Automatically 63

Chapter 5

SELECTING OBJECTS   **64**
AutoCAD Selection Methods 65
Selecting by Pointing 67
Selecting Previously Selected Items 69
Selecting Previously Drawn Items 70
Selecting with a Regular Window 71
Removing Objects from the Selection Set 73
Adding Objects to the Selection Set 75
   Removing the Most Recently Added Object 75
   Selecting with a Fence 75
Selecting with a Crossing Window 76
   Selecting with a Polygon 78
Undoing the Previous Command 79
   Centering the Circle 79

Chapter 6

TRIMMING AND EXTENDING   **81**
Using the Change Command 82
   Making Lines Horizontal
   with the Change Command 84
Making Precise Connections
with the Osnap Options 86
   Using the Osnap Screen Menu 86
   Using the Osnap Cursor Menu 87
Duplicating Objects with the
Copy Command 88
   Establishing the Displacement 88
Rotating an Object 89

Moving Objects within a Drawing 91
The Break Command 93
Using the Trim Command 94
   Trimming Lines 95
Using the Extend Command 97
Breaking the Circle 98
Trimming the Circle 100
   Plotting the Drawing 101

Chapter 7

DRAWING A PULLEY   **102**

Beginning a New Drawing
with the Border Template 103
Drawing Two Connected Circles 103
Turning On Tangent Osnap Mode 105
Drawing Tangent Lines with the Tangent Option . . . 106
   Turning Off Tangent Osnap Mode 108
Rotating the Drawing 109
Elongating an Object with the Stretch Command . . . 110
Enlarging the View of an
Object with the Zoom Command 113
Drawing a Concentric Circle 114
Drawing Tangent Circles 115
Making Multiple Copies with the Array Command . . 116
   Making a Polar Pattern 117
Drawing an Arc 118
Drawing a Wedge 122
   Replicating Objects with the Mirror Command . . . 123

Chapter 8

DRAWING THREE VIEWS OF A BRACKET   **130**

Starting the Bracket Drawing
with the Border Template 132

Loading the Hidden and Center Line Types 132

Creating the Hidden and Center Layers 133

Setting the Line Type for
the Hidden and Center Layers 134

Updating Your Border Drawing Template 135

Drawing the Top View 136

Drawing a Circle 136

Drawing the Rest of the Perimeter 136

Trimming the Left Edge of the Circle 138

Drawing Two Concentric Circles of the Boss 139

Copying the Vertical Line 140

Drawing the Short Horizontal Lines 140

Drawing the Front View 141

Drawing the Perimeter of the Front View 142

Drawing the Boss in the Front View 143

Drawing the Right View 144

Drawing the Square Outline of the Right View 144

Using the Explode Command 146

Adding Three Lines to the Top of the Right View . . 148

Drawing the Boss in Right View 149

Adding a Semicircular Arc to the Right View 151

Adding Two Arcs with the Fillet Command 152

Drawing Hidden Lines 154

Changing Layers with a Dialog Box 155

Drawing Two Vertical
Hidden Lines in the Front View 155

Drawing a Horizontal
Hidden Line in the Front View 156

Drawing the Vertical
Hidden Lines in the Right View 157

Changing the Scale of the Line Type 158

Widening the Object Lines of the Bracket 159

Changing to Layer OBJ 159

Changing Lines to Polylines 159

Plotting the Bracket 165

Chapter 9

DRAWING THE FLANGE   **167**

Starting the Flange
Drawing with the Border Template 168
Drawing the Top View 169
    Drawing the Three Circles 169
    Converting a Circle to an Arc 172
    Replicating the Circle Opening 176
Drawing the Front View 182
    Outlining the Front View 182
    Adding the Interior Lines 183
    Creating the Hatch Layer with a Dialog Box 186
    How to Add Section Lines with a Hatch Pattern . . 187
Widening the Top View Lines 189
Completing the Drawing 191

Chapter 10

DIMENSIONING THE BRACKET   **193**

Principles of Dimensioning 194
Continuing with the Bracket Drawing 195
Speeding Up Text Regeneration 196
    Speeding Up Regeneration with Qtext 196
    Speeding Up Regeneration by Freezing a Layer . . . 197
    Changing the Font with the Style Command 198
Adding Centerlines to the Front View 199
Dimensioning the Front View 201
    Creating the Dim Layer with a Dialog Box 202
    Starting the Dimension Command Mode 202
    Specifying a Vertical Dimension 203
    Specifying a Horizontal Dimension 204
Dimensioning the Top View 206
    Dynamic Zooming to the Top View 207
    Dimensioning the Top Edge 208
    Establishing the Form of Crossed Centerlines . . . 208

Dimensioning a Radius 209
Dimensioning Two Diameters 210
    Extending the Centerline 211
Dimensioning the Right View 213
    Dimensioning the Corner 213
    Adding Centerlines to the Slot 214
    Dimensioning the Slot 214
    Extending the Vertical Centerline 215
    Completing the Drawing 217
Plotting the Drawing 217

Chapter 11

DIMENSIONING THE FLANGE · 218

Dimensioning the Flange Drawing 219
    Specifying a Vertical
    Dimension for the Front View 220
    Specifying a Horizontal
    Dimension for the Front View 221
    Dimensioning the Top View 222
    Adding a Centerline to the Front View 232
    Plotting the Drawing 233

Chapter 12

INTRODUCTION TO DRAWING IN THREE DIMENSIONS · 234

Starting the Cube Drawing 236
    Setting the Drawing Limits 236
    Dividing the Screen into Four Viewing Ports 237
    Setting Grid and Snap in Each Port 238
    Changing the Viewpoint in Each Port 239
Drawing in the Z Direction 242
    Loading the Autolisp
    Solids Program from the Dialog Box 242
    Adding Text for Orientation 244
Drawing Outside the Plane of the Ucs 247

The Wrong Way 248
The Right Way 249
Erasing the Two Lines 249
Changing the Location of the Ucs 250
Translating the Ucs 251
Moving the Ucs Icon to the New UCS Origin 251
Rotating the Ucs Relative to the WCS 252
Drawing a Circle on the Front Face 253
Drawing a Circle and Cone on the Right Face 255
Moving the Ucs to the Right Face 255
Drawing a Circle on the Right Face 256
Drawing a Cone on the Right Face 258
Drawing a Torus on the Back Plane of the Cube 261
Moving the Ucs to the Back Plane 261
Drawing the Torus 262
Drawing a Dome on the Top of the Cube 264
Moving the Ucs to the Top of the Cube 264
Drawing the Dome 265
Returning to World Coordinates 266
Completing the Drawing 267

Chapter 13

PAPER SPACE: SEPARATING THE MODEL FROM THE DRAWING   **269**
Starting the Combined
Model Space, Paper Space Drawing 271
Erasing the Border and
Title Block from Model Space 272
Creating a Layer for Drawing in Paper Space 273
Changing to Paper Space 274
Adjusting Paper Space 275
Inserting a Border and Title Block 276
Adding View Ports to Paper Space 278
Checking the New View Port 280
Copying the View Port 280

Changing the Viewing Direction for the New Ports . . . 282
   Changing the Viewing
   Direction for the Upper-Right Port 283
   Changing the Viewing
   Direction for the Lower-Right Port 283
   Changing the Viewing
   Direction for the Lower-Left Port 284
Resizing and Deleting a View Port 285
Plotting the Paper Space Drawing 286
   Hiding Details in Two Ports 287
   Hiding the Port Boundaries 287
   Plotting the Drawing 288

APPENDICES

Appendix A
INSTALLING AUTOCAD

290

Appendix B
AUTOCAD COMMANDS

298

INDEX 301

I N T R O D U C T I O N

f you have never used AutoCAD before and want to learn now, this book is for you. If you've been frustrated while trying to learn AutoCAD from other books, this book is for you. *The ABC's of AutoCAD Release 12* explains both the basics and the fine points of the program and every chapter has clear explanations and examples. This book contains numbered, easy-to-follow exercises that will get you up and drawing with AutoCAD almost immediately.

About This Book

This book will teach you how to use AutoCAD on IBM PC compatible or Sun Microsystems computers. No previous experience with AutoCAD is required, because all the terminology and basic procedures are explained with the beginner in mind. Even if you are an experienced AutoCAD user, you will find helpful tips throughout the book that will help you use AutoCAD more effectively.

Chapter 1 discusses some of the most important things you'll need to know before starting to use the program. Topics such as technical drawing conventions, Cartesian and Polar notation, and how to get help are covered.

In Chapter 2, you will use AutoCAD to start a prototype drawing which will then be used for all the exercises in this book.

You will establish your drawing limits and draw a border. In Chapter 3, you will add a title block (with your company or school name, drawing title, your name, etc.) to the template.

In Chapters 4, 5, and 6, you will begin drawing lines and circles, and, using a variety of AutoCAD commands, you will learn how to select items, make precise connections, and recover from mistakes.

In Chapter 7, you will create another drawing and explore more useful AutoCAD features. In Chapter 8, you will create three views of a bracket, and in Chapter 9, you will draw two views of a flange, complete with hatching. In Chapters 10 and 11, you will add dimensions to the bracket and flange.

Chapter 12 will introduce you to drawing in three dimensions, and in Chapter 13, you will use Paper Space to separate the construction of the model from the construction of the drawing created in Chapter 12.

If you have just bought AutoCAD and haven't installed it on your computer, begin with Appendix A, which will guide you through the installation process. Finally, Appendix B provides an alphabetical list of the most command AutoCAD commands.

Conventions Used in This Book

In the beginning of each section of this book, you will be given some general information in standard paragraph format. This information is often followed by a series of numbered steps. In some instances, you will be asked to type a command or to supply some information. To avoid confusion, I've devised a few standard conventions I'll use throughout this book.

GIVING COMMANDS TO AUTOCAD

When AutoCAD wants you to take some action, it will display a prompt (the most common one is **Command:**) on the bottom line of your screen. You can respond by giving a command from the keyboard.

You will tell AutoCAD to execute your command by pressing *either* Enter *or* the spacebar. In this book, I have used Enter and spacebar interchangeably.

If you don't want to use the keyboard, you can give commands to AutoCAD by using the buttons on your mouse.

When you are to type something at the computer, what you are to type is set off in a different typeface for easy reference. Here's an example:

1. Give the **Zoom** command with the **w** (for Window) option.

This means that you type the word **zoom** and press either the spacebar or Enter. You then press the letter **w** and press Enter or the spacebar again. I will occasionally remind you that you need to press the spacebar or Enter.

AutoCAD's prompts, such as **Command:**, are highlighted in the same way.

AUTOCAD ABBREVIATIONS

Generally, AutoCAD commands are ordinary English words such as Change, Copy, and Plot, and are fully spelled out. In addition, several commands can be abbreviated. These are:

A for Arc

C for Circle

E for Erase

L for Line

LA for Layer

M for Move

P for Pan

PL for Pline

R for Redraw

Z for Zoom

Of course, if you wish, you can still spell out the complete command. However, pay special attention to the U command—although it is only one letter long, it is *not* an abbreviation. The U command is used to undo the previously given command.

USING CONTROL CHARACTERS

Pressing Enter or the spacebar and clicking the mouse are not the only ways to execute AutoCAD commands—in some cases, you will need to use *control characters*. Control characters consist of two keys (the control, or Ctrl, key and another key) and are represented in this book by the ^ symbol followed by a letter or other symbol—for example, **^G**. To use a control character, first press Ctrl, then, *while still pressing Ctrl,* press the other key. Remember: when using a control character, *do not* press the Enter key to execute the command.

THE FUNCTION KEYS

There are several commands which are given by pressing function keys. Unfortunately, the function key numbers are not the same for all computers. Therefore, I have devised a way to give the three most common function key numbers at the same time. Here's an example:

1. Turn on the grid with **^G** (**F7/F3**).

   This means that the grid can be turned on by either typing **^G**, **F7** if you have an IBM PC or compatible, or **F3** if you have a Sun computer.

The most common function keys you will be using are:

^G (**F7/F3**) for the grid.

^O (**F8/F4**) for Ortho mode.

^B (**F9/F5**) for Snap mode.

Toggle Keys

The grid, Snap, and Ortho function keys are *toggles*. This means that the same keystroke alternately turns the specific function on and off, just like a light switch.

GIVING COMMANDS WITH A MOUSE

Throughout this book, you will use your mouse to tell AutoCAD where and what you want to draw. In addition, the mouse can be used (instead of the keyboard) to give commands. To do so, move the cursor to the menu on the right edge of the screen, highlight the desired item, and click the left mouse button. I will refer to the left mouse button as the *pick* button. In addition, you can start other AutoCAD commands by highlighting the menu bar at the top of the screen and using the pull-down menus. (See the inside front and back covers for examples.) The third button (or Shift + button 2) gives you the cursor menu. Whether you choose to type your commands or use the mouse, you can repeat the previous command either by her clicking the second mouse button, or by pressing Enter or the spacebar.

If you type quickly, you will probably find that it is much faster to type a command than to select it from a screen menu. To execute many commands, you often need only type one word instead of having to select a series of items from a sequence of menus.

Other Types of Digitizers

While the most common digitizer is a mouse, many other digitizers can be used with AutoCAD. These include the trackball and the tablet—the most sophisticated digitizer of all.

The AutoCAD Cursor

When you move your mouse, a cursor or reference symbol moves on the video screen in accord with your mouse. The *drawing cursor* is a pair of crossed lines—one horizontal and one vertical—which extend to the four edges of the drawing area.

When AutoCAD wants you to select an object on the screen, the drawing cursor changes into a small square. This square is called the *selection cursor* or *pick box* because, in order to select an item, you must move the cursor over a part of the object and press the mouse pick button. When selecting objects with a window, the cursor will initially disappear. It will then reappear as a rectangle which grows or shrinks as you move your mouse.

On the other hand, when you point to a specific part of an object, the regular drawing cursor does not disappear. In this case, a box is superimposed over the crossed cursor lines. This box, which is larger than the selection box, is called a *target cursor* or *target box*.

Throughout this book, I first select a command such as Erase or Move, then I select the items to be erased or moved. However, when the target cursor is displayed, you can reverse this procedure. In other words, you can first pick the objects, then select the command. When you select the objects first, small boxes appear at several points on the object you selected. If you accidentally get these boxes, press **^C** twice.

The Prototype Drawing

When you first start AutoCAD, the program begins with a prototype drawing called ACAD, which is the default drawing. In Chapter 4, you will change this default to the BORDER drawing you will create in Chapters 2 and 3. From then on, you will always begin a new drawing with your BORDER drawing.

If you are working on your own computer, or if you are on a network, you will want to retain the new default. However, if you are using someone else's computer, you might want to change back to the original ACAD prototype default when you are through with your drawing.

1 CHAPTER

FEATURING

Technical drawing conventions

Getting Help

Working with the Drawing Editor

▼

AutoCAD Fundamentals

By the time you finish this book, you will have mastered the basics of one of the most important tools available to engineers and architects today. But, before we look at how AutoCAD works, let's go through some of the important information you'll need to know.

Technical Drawing Conventions Used in This Book

Throughout this book, we will follow the conventions of engineering rather than those of architectural drawing. Nevertheless, the process of using a computer for computer-aided design (CAD) will be similar for both disciplines.

Engineering drawings usually show three views of the object they represent: front view—as seen from the front, right view—as seen from the right side, and top view—as seen directly from above. On the drawing itself, the right view is shown to the right of the front view while the top view is above the front view. This arrangement of views is called *orthographic projection*. However, as more and more engineers use CAD systems to design objects in three dimensions and then use the information in the database to produce the object directly, traditional three-view orthographic drawings may soon be needed only rarely.

Getting Help

There are over one hundred commands in AutoCAD, many with several options. You can see that it might be easy to get confused. Fortunately, AutoCAD provides the Help command to give you details about particular commands. Help can also show you a list of the names of all the commands—just in case you've forgotten the exact name or the spelling of a particular one. Let's see how Help works.

1. Make sure the **Command:** prompt is displayed. If not, press ^C.

2. Type **help** or **?** and press the spacebar. The Help dialog box appears.

3. You can now type the name of any command and press Enter to learn more about that command. But instead, move the cursor to the Index box and click the left mouse button. The Help Index dialog box appears with a vertical listing of the AutoCAD commands. A list of the most useful commands is found in Appendix B.

4. Type the letter **m** to see the commands that begin with that letter.

5. Position the cursor over the word Move and press the left button to highlight that command.

6. Click on the OK box to learn about the Move command.

7. Click on the OK box to complete the Help command.

GETTING HELP FOR A SPECIFIC COMMAND

You have just learned how to get help in general. Sometimes, however, you may need help with a specific command—after you have already started it. You can start the Help command while you are in the middle of another command, by prefacing the word Help with an apostrophe. Let's see how to do that.

1. Check that the **Command:** prompt is displayed. If not, press **^C**.

2. Give the **Line** command (or its abbreviation **L**) and press Enter.

3. The **From point:** prompt should now be showing.

4. Type **'help** (or **'?**) and press Enter. The Help dialog box appears with a brief description of the **From Point:** prompt of the Line command.

5. Click on the OK box to complete the Help command and return to the Line command.

6. Press **^C** to cancel the Line command.

Working with the Drawing Editor

AutoCAD can display one of two screens: the drawing editor (or graphics) screen and the text screen. The drawing editor screen is the one you'll see most often. Sometimes, however, when giving you a large amount of information, AutoCAD will automatically change to the text screen. After you have read the information, you can return to the drawing screen by pressing F1. (On the Sun computer, both screens are displayed at once.)

Most of the graphics screen will be used for drawing. There are, however, three other important regions of the drawing editor. The area along the right edge of the screen shows a menu of other menus and commands you can select using the mouse. The second region, called the *status line,* runs along the top line of the screen and provides additional important information. The third region consists of the bottom three lines of your screen. This is where AutoCAD displays its prompts and your responses to those prompts.

THE DRAWING CURSOR AND THE COORDINATE READOUT

Move the mouse and watch the *drawing cursor* (a pair of crossed lines) move on the screen. As you move left or right, the cursor moves left or right correspondingly. Similarly, if you move the mouse away from or toward yourself, the cursor moves upward or downward on the screen. The drawing cursor tells AutoCAD exactly where you want to draw. At any given moment, the drawing cursor's exact position on the screen is shown on the *coordinate readout* (part of the status line at the top line of the screen.)

To see how cursor movement affects the coordinate readout, try this exercise.

1. Look at the status line, just to the right of the center. You should see two numbers, separated by a comma.

2. Move your mouse upward and to the right.

3. Watch the coordinate display as you move your mouse. If the coordinates did not change, type **^D**. (Or, you can press **F6** on an IBM PC compatible or **F2** on a Sun.)

Using Cartesian and Polar Notation

At this point, you may be wondering what exactly the coordinate readout is telling you. In order to understand completely, it will help if you're familiar with both *Cartesian* and *Polar* notation. Let's talk about Cartesian notation first.

CARTESIAN NOTATION

Simply put, Cartesian notation is a rectangular coordinate system established to locate items precisely in a drawing. There is a horizontal or X-axis and a vertical or Y-axis. The two axes are *orthogonal* or perpendicular for orthographic projection, and intersect at the *origin* (initially located in the lower-left corner of the screen.) Each point on the drawing is identified in the coordinate system by a pair of numbers, separated by a comma, which gives the X and Y distances as measured from the origin. The horizontal X numbers increase as they move to the right and the vertical Y numbers increase upward. The coordinate position of the origin is 0,0.

As an example, consider the two points, A and B, shown in Figure 1.1. The coordinate position of point A is 2,1 because it is located at an X distance of 2 and a Y distance of 1 from the origin. The coordinate position of point B is 6,4 because it is located at an X distance of 6 and a Y distance of 4 from the origin. (In a graph, coordinates are sometimes enclosed within parentheses.)

We can define a straight line by the coordinates of its two end points. For example, we might draw a line from point A at coordinate location 2,1 to point B at coordinate position 6,4 as shown in Figure 1.2. This is called an absolute Cartesian reference because both ends are identified absolutely with reference to the coordinate system.

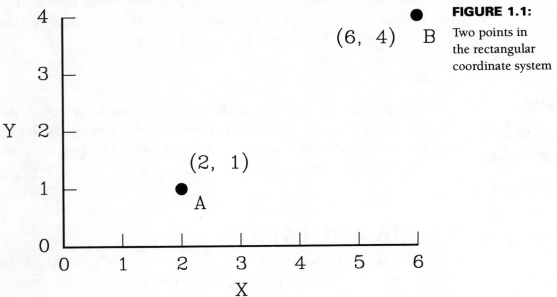

FIGURE 1.1:

Two points in the rectangular coordinate system

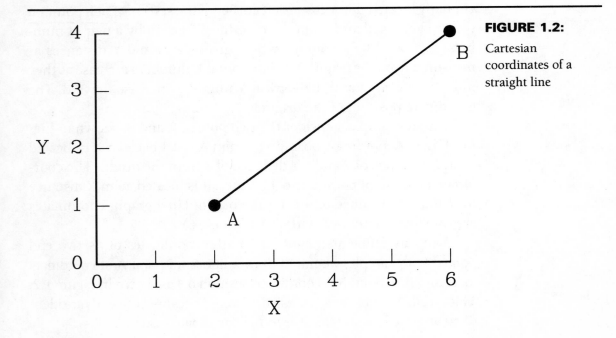

FIGURE 1.2:

Cartesian coordinates of a straight line

Sometimes, however, it will be moᵣe convenient to give the coordinates of the second point relative to the first point, rather than to the coordinate origin. In the presᵉnt example, the second point has the relative coordinates 4,3 because the X distance between the points (6-2) is 4 and the Y distance between the points (4-1) is 3. Putting the at-sign (@) in front of the numbers indicates you are using relative numbers. Thus, the relative distance 4,3 is shown in AutoCAD as @4,3.

POLAR NOTATION

A variation of the relative reference system is known as *Polar* notation. With this method, you give a relative radial distance and an angle from the horizontal. In Figure 1.2, the length of the line is 5. Therefore, the second point has a relative polar location of 5 at the angle 37 degrees as shown in Figure 1.3. This polar coordinate is displayed as **5<37**. Type this polar reference as **@5<37**.

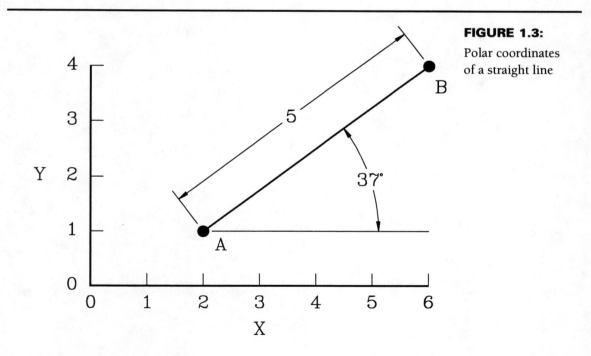

FIGURE 1.3:

Polar coordinates of a straight line

Thus, with Polar notation, the direction to the right (the east or 3 o'clock orientation) is an angle of zero, while straight up (the north or 12 o'clock orientation), in the direction of the Y-axis, is an angle of 90 degrees. The direction to the left is 180 degrees (9 o'clock), while the direction downward (6 o'clock) is both 270 degrees and −90 degrees. (A negative angle simply indicates that the angle is measured clockwise.)

Starting a Border Template for Your Drawings

n this chapter, you will actually start working with AutoCAD. You'll learn how to give commands and how to set up your drawing area. You'll explore the grid system and AutoCAD's Snap mode. You will then start creating a border template for a Size A drawing which you will use for all your other drawings. (We'll finish the template in Chapter 3).

If you are using this book in a CAD class, the border template will identify and distinguish your drawing from those of other students. The complete border template, described in this chapter and Chapter 3, can be drawn in one to two hours and most likely would be the first assignment in a CAD class.

In this chapter, we will be working with the following AutoCAD commands:

- Status (to check the status of your drawing screen)

- Limits (to establish the drawing size)

- Snap mode (to locate a position precisely)

- Grid mode (to display an array of dots)

- Ddunits (to change the way numbers are displayed)

- Line (to draw a line)

- Pedit (to change a polyline)

- Qsave (to save an intermediate version of a drawing)

- End

Let's get started!

Starting AutoCAD

AutoCAD must be properly installed and configured before it can be used. If you have not yet done this, go to Appendix A.

- If AutoCAD is properly installed on your computer, you will be able to start from the DOS **C>** prompt by simply typing **acad border**. (The word *acad* starts AutoCAD while *border* will be the name of your first drawing.)

If you are running a network version of AutoCAD, you will see a login window on the screen identifying you and your organization. Press Enter to continue.

You will now see the drawing editor screen as shown in Figure 2.1. You're ready to begin!

```
■ Layer 0                6.9503,4.4891        AutoCAD
                                              * * * *
                                              ASE
                                              BLOCKS
                                              DIM:
                                              DISPLAY
                                              DRAW
                                              EDIT
                                              INQUIRY
                                              LAYER...
                                              MODEL
                                              MVIEW
                                              PLOT...
                                              RENDER
                                              SETTINGS
                                              SURFACES
                                              UCS:
                                              UTILITY

                                              SAVE:




Loaded menu E:\ACAD\SUPPORT\ACAD.mnx
AutoCAD Release 12 menu utilities loaded.
Command:
```

FIGURE 2.1:

The AutoCAD drawing editor screen

Setting Up the Drawing Area

Before beginning your prototype drawing, you will want to set up the drawing area. In the sections that follow, you will learn how to set and change the display precision, the size of the drawing area, and the grid spacing.

Take a look at the bottom line of your screen. It should show the word **Command:** (called the **Command:** prompt.) Whenever you see the **Command:** prompt, you will know that AutoCAD has completed the previous command and is waiting for another. If the **Command:** prompt is not displayed, type **^C** to terminate the previous command.

When you create a technical drawing by hand, you must first select a scale. When drawing with AutoCAD, however, you will always draw in full scale—even though the image displayed on the screen may be the entire drawing or only a part of it. Later, when you make a plot of the drawing, you will simply choose the appropriate scale to fit the size of the paper. In addition, you can plot the entire drawing or only a part of it.

Since the next three AutoCAD commands display more lines of text than will fit on the bottom of your screen, AutoCAD will automatically change to the text screen. After you have read the information, press **F1** to return to the graphics screen. If you need to reread the information, press **F1** again.

SETTING THE NUMBER OF DISPLAYED DIGITS

Although AutoCAD initially displays numbers with four digits past the decimal point, all numbers are internally accurate to 14 decimal places. Using the Ddunits command you can easily change the number of displayed digits to suit your need for display precision. Let's try it now.

1. Give the **Ddunits** command and press the spacebar. The Units Control dialog box appears.

2. Move the cursor to the input box (just below the word Precision) and press the pick button.

3. Move the cursor into the new menu and click on 0.00.

4. Click on the OK box. AutoCAD will now display numbers with only two digits past the decimal point. Of course, AutoCAD's internal precision has not been changed.

5. Move the cursor and notice that the coordinate readout on the status line now shows only two digits past the decimal point.

CHANGING THE DRAWING LIMITS

The size of the drawing area is established by AutoCAD variables known as the *minimum* and *maximum coordinates,* which are initially set at (0,0) and (12,9). This means that the lower-left corner of your drawing is 0,0 and the upper-right corner is 12,9. You can, however, change these coordinates whenever you wish.

In this section, you will examine the drawing limits and change them to (0,0) and (11,8.5)—the dimensions of a Size A drawing when full scale. But first, let's take a look at your drawing setup by using the Inquiry menu.

1. Move the cursor to the far right edge of the screen, into the menu area. Notice that the cursor shape changes to a rectangle.

2. Move the cursor up the right edge of the screen. Notice that the word at the cursor location is highlighted.

3. If the word INQUIRY does not appear on the menu, highlight the word AutoCAD, and click the left mouse button.

4. Move the cursor to highlight the word Inquiry and click the pick button. The root menu changes to the INQUIRY menu.

5. Move the cursor to the word Status and click the pick button again.

This command does two things. First, it automatically switches to the text screen. Second, it displays information about your drawing screen and about your computer. (Notice that you had to pick two items from the screen menu: Inquiry and Status. From the keyboard, you would only have had to type one word—status—to get the same results.)

Your screen should look like the one in Figure 2.2. The first line gives the name of your drawing and how many entities (items) it has.

```
0 entities in BORDER
Model space limits are X:    0.00  Y:      0.00  (Off)
                       X:   12.00  Y:      9.00
Model space uses       *Nothing*
Display shows          X:    0.00  Y:      0.00
                       X:   12.49  Y:      9.00
Insertion base is      X:    0.00  Y:      0.00  Z:      0.00
Snap resolution is     X:    1.00  Y:      1.00
Grid spacing is        X:    0.00  Y:      0.00

Current space:         Model space
Current layer:         0
Current color:         BYLAYER -- 7 (white)
Current linetype:      BYLAYER -- CONTINUOUS
Current elevation:        0.00  thickness:       0.00
Fill on  Grid off  Ortho off  Qtext off  Snap off  Tablet off
Object snap modes:     None
Free disk: 9322496 bytes
Virtual memory allocated to program: 3436 KB
Amount of program in physical memory/Total (virtual) program size: 58%
Total conventional memory: 436 KB     Total extended memory: 4260 KB
-- Press RETURN for more --
```

FIGURE 2.2:

The Status command from the Inquiry menu shows information about the drawing screen

The second and third lines give the limits of your drawing area:

Model space limits are X: 0.00 Y: 0.00 (Off)
X: 12.00 Y: 9.00

These displays tell you that the drawing has a width of 12 units (in the X direction) and a height of 9 units (in the Y direction). That is, the lower-left corner is at location (0,0), the coordinate origin, and the upper-right corner is at coordinate location (12,9). You will, of course, want to enlarge these limits when drawing large items.

The word (Off) means the limits check is off. When the limits check is *on*, AutoCAD will not allow you to draw outside the limits. You can turn on the limits check with the Limits command. In this book, however, we will leave the limits check off.

6. If instructed to do so, press Enter to see the next screen. Then press F1 to return to the drawing screen.

7. To change the limits, give the **Limits** command and press the spacebar. AutoCAD responds with

ON/OFF<Lower left corner><0.00,0.00>:

which shows the current coordinates for the lower-left corner. The values enclosed in angle brackets are the current ones.

8. Press the spacebar to accept the current value. AutoCAD then displays the current coordinates for the upper-right corner and waits for you to enter new values.

9. Type **11,8.5** (no spaces) and press Enter to change the upper-right corner.

10. Give the **Status** command and press the spacebar. Check the second and third lines to see that the drawing limits are correct.

11. Press Enter to see the rest of the information.

12. Press **F1** to return to the drawing screen.

Using AutoCAD's Grid System

In the previous section, you changed the size of the drawing area. Each part of your drawing can be precisely referenced to the origin through a rectangular grid system. *Grid points* are the dots that appear at regular intervals in both the horizontal and vertical directions. The grid points are like mile markers on a highway because they help you locate a desired position. Grid points have a default spacing of one unit, but this can be easily changed. The grid appears only on your screen. It is not stored in the database and will not show on a printout. You can turn the grid display on and off as needed.

TURNING ON THE GRID

In this section, you will turn on the grid system and learn how to move the cursor from one point to another.

1. Turn on the grid by typing **^G** or the Grid function key (**F7** for IBM PC compatibles/**F3** for Sun terminals).

The Grid function key is a toggle key, enabling you to switch the grid on and off as needed. You also can turn on the grid by giving the **Grid** command with the **on** option. This, however, takes a little longer. When the Grid mode is on, an array of dots appears on the drawing screen.

2. Move the mouse and try to position the cursor precisely at the coordinate location **3.00,3.00**. Notice that it is very difficult to move the cursor to exactly that location. In the next section you will learn how to position the cursor precisely at a specific grid point.

3. Move one grid point to the right and notice that the first number of the coordinate readout, the horizontal value, has changed by 1 because the grid spacing is one unit.

POSITIONING THE CURSOR PRECISELY WITH SNAP MODE

You saw in the section above that it is difficult to position the cursor precisely. To help you with this task, AutoCAD can lock the cursor onto the grid system. Then, when you draw an object, the cursor can stop precisely at a specific grid point. This feature is known as Snap mode because as you move the mouse, the cursor jumps or snaps from one grid point to another.

Let's see how Snap mode works.

1. Move the mouse and notice that the cursor moves smoothly on the screen.

2. Move the cursor near coordinate position **4.00,3.00**, but don't try to position it exactly.

3. Turn on Snap mode by pressing **^B** or the Snap function key (**F9** for IBM PC compatibles/**F5** for Sun terminals).

The Snap function key is a toggle key, enabling you to switch the Snap mode on and off as necessary. When the Snap mode is on, the word

Snap appears on the top line of the screen. The coordinate readout will now show precisely **4.00, 3.00**.

4. Move the cursor to the right several grid points. Notice that the cursor now snaps from one grid point to the next.

5. Turn off Snap mode (see step 3 above).

6. Check the top line of the screen to see that the word Snap has disappeared.

CHANGING THE GRID SPACING

As you have seen, the cursor is automatically positioned to the grid points when Snap mode is on. Grid spacing and Snap spacing, however, can be different.

1. To change the Grid spacing, give the **Grid** command and press the spacebar. AutoCAD responds with

Grid spacing (X) or ON/OFF/Snap/Aspect <0.00>:

Notice that options given for the Grid command show a mixture of upper- and lowercase letters. When you type an option, you can abbreviate it by typing only the uppercase letters given in the response. (While you cannot abbreviate Grid, you can abbreviate many other AutoCAD commands).

2. Type **0.5** (you can omit the zero) and press the spacebar to change the grid spacing to 0.5. Notice that the grid is now denser. Since the point spacing was reduced in both the X and Y directions, there are four times as many points as before.

3. Move the cursor to coordinate position **3.50,3.00**. Now, move the cursor to the next grid point. Notice that the coordinate location is **4.00,3.00**. This confirms that the grid spacing is 0.5.

4. Turn Snap mode back on and check for the word Snap on the status line.

5. Take a look at the coordinate readout as you move the mouse to the right until the cursor snaps to the next point. Notice that the X value increases by 1 rather than 0.5. This is because the Snap spacing is still set to 1.0.

CHANGING THE SNAP SPACING

The default snap spacing is 1, but since the drawings you will create later in this book use measurements that are multiples of 0.5, it will be convenient to set the snap spacing to 0.5, too.

1. To change the snap spacing, type **snap** and press the spacebar. AutoCAD responds with

Snap spacing or ON/OFF/Aspect/Rotate/Style <1.00>:

to show you what options you can select. <1.00> is the current spacing.

2. Type **0.5** (you can omit the zero) and press the spacebar to change the snap spacing to 0.5. Notice that Snap mode has been turned back on automatically.

3. Move the mouse and see that the cursor snaps in 0.5 steps.

Turning Off the Coordinate Icon

You can see from Figure 2.1 that there is an L-shaped icon in the lower-left corner showing two arrows at right angles. One arrow, labeled X, points to the right. The other arrow, labeled Y, points upward. This symbol is called the *user coordinate system icon* or *UCS Icon* for short. It shows where two-dimensional objects are to be drawn when you are working in three dimensions. You can reorient the icon to draw in a different direction.

In the default position, the coordinate icon is called the *World* icon, and a letter W appears on it. If you move the icon, however, the W disappears. Since you will be drawing in only two dimensions until Chapters 12 and 13, let's turn off the icon until then.

1. Type the **Ucsicon** command and press the spacebar.

2. Type **off** (or simply **of**) and press Enter.

The icon has disappeared from the screen. You can turn the icon back on by giving the **Ucsicon** command again with the **On** option.

Adjusting the Drawing Scale

Before moving on, let's adjust the scale on the screen for the limits you have specified.

■ Give the **Zoom** (or **z**) command with the **a** (for All) option. This changes the scale of your drawing to show just the drawing area defined by your Limits command.

Congratulations. Your drawing area is set up and you are ready to make an AutoCAD drawing.

Drawing a Line with the Line Command

In this section, you will draw a border around your drawing by giving the Line command. You draw a line by marking the two end points. You can mark a point by snapping to a grid point or by typing the coordinates from the keyboard.

1. If the grid is off, turn it on.

2. Check the status line. If the word Snap does not appear, turn Snap mode on.

3. Type the **Line** (or **L**) command and press the spacebar to start the Line command. With this command, you can draw a sequence of connected lines.

4. Move the cursor to the lower-left corner of the screen. The coordinate display will read **0.00,0.00**.

5. Move one grid point up and one to the right from the lower-left corner. When the cursor snaps to the point, make sure the coordinate display shows **0.50,0.50**.

6. Now, click the pick (the left) mouse button to mark the beginning of the first line.

7. Turn off Snap mode.

8. Move the cursor upward and to the right of the first point as in Figure 2.3.

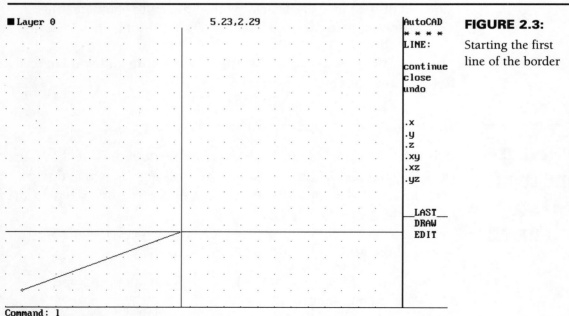

FIGURE 2.3:

Starting the first line of the border

9. You are now going to draw a border that is half an inch inside the limits. Therefore, since the horizontal limit is 11, this line will have a length of 10. Type the relative position **@10,0** (no spaces) and press the spacebar. As you learned previously, this is a relative reference from the previous point. In other words, the line has a length of 10 in the X direction and 0 in the Y direction. The line appears along the bottom of the screen and stops at the next-to-last grid point. Another line connects with the cursor. Notice that the bottom line of the screen shows **To point:** rather than the usual **Command:** prompt. This means that even though you just drew a line, the Line command is still active. If the **Command:** prompt appears on the bottom line, you have inadvertently completed the Line command by pressing Enter. If this has happened, press the Enter key twice to restart the Line command and connect up with the previous line. Because the Line command is still active, you can add another line to your first line. Let's do that now.

10. The second line will go along to the right edge of the screen. Check that Snap mode is off before moving the cursor.

11. Move the mouse so the cursor goes straight up to the next-to-last grid point. Notice that a new line connects the end of the previous line to the cursor. This is sometimes called a *rubber-band* line because it stretches or shrinks as you move the cursor. The coordinate position should read approximately **7.5<90** to show a line that is 7.5 inches long at an angle of 90 degrees. However, if the coordinates are Cartesian press ^ **D(F6/F2)** twice to change the display to Polar mode.

12. Turn on Snap mode and move the mouse a little until the cursor snaps to the grid point. The cursor will show exactly **7.50<90**.

13. Press the pick button to draw the second line segment.

14. Turn off Snap mode.

15. Move the cursor downward and a little to the left.

16. Type the relative Polar coordinate **@10<180** (no spaces) and press the spacebar. This specifies a line that is 10 inches long to the left (180 degrees) of the previous point. Alternatively, you can type **@-10,0**. Make sure that a line appears across the top of the screen.

17. You can draw the fourth line of the border by moving the mouse or by typing the coordinate. This time, however, there is still an easier way. Type **c** (for Close) and press the spacebar to complete the border and finish the Line command. Notice that AutoCAD automatically drew the final line segment. The **Command:** prompt should appear on the bottom line of your screen.

Widening Border Lines

In this section, you will widen the border lines by changing them to *polylines*. A polyline is similar to a regular line except that it can have width. It can also combine several lines into a single entity. To change a line to a polyline, you will use the Pedit (for polyline edit) command. (Pedit is pronounced P-edit.)

1. Give the **Pedit** command and press Enter to start the polyline editor.

2. AutoCAD responds with the **Select polyline:** prompt, and the drawing cursor changes to a small box. This is called a *selection cursor* or *selection box,* because you select an item you have drawn by placing the box over it. Move the selection box near the middle of the lower border line. Be sure the box straddles the line. Click the pick button to select the line. Move the cursor up a little and notice that the selected line becomes spotty.

AutoCAD tells you the line you have selected is not a polyline and asks whether you want to convert it to one.

3. Click the second mouse button or press Enter to accept the default value of Y for Yes. The line you marked is then converted to a polyline and changes back to its former appearance. The crossed lines of the drawing cursor return.

4. To change the width of the new polyline, type **w** and press the spacebar.

5. Type the value **0.03** and press the spacebar. Notice that the bottom line becomes wider.

6. To automatically convert the remaining lines to polylines, connect them to the first line and widen them. Then, type **j** (for Join) and press the spacebar. The cursor changes back to a selection box. (Do not individually convert these lines to polylines.)

7. Move the selection box over the right border line and press the left mouse button. This line becomes spotty.

8. Move the cursor over the top line and press the left button. It too becomes spotty.

9. Position the cursor over the left line and click the left mouse button.

10. Press Enter or the second mouse button to complete this step. The three other lines are also widened, matching the first line.

11. Click the second mouse button or press Enter to complete the Pedit command.

Saving Your Border Template

Now that you've worked so carefully to set up your drawing, let's spend the next few moments learning how to protect it from accidental loss. For example, if the electricity should fail at this point, you would lose all your work because it has not yet been saved on a disk. To avoid such a loss, you should save your work with the AutoCAD Qsave command every 10 or 15 minutes. It's very simple and, if there's an accident, you won't lose much work. Let's do it now.

- Give the **Qsave** command and press the spacebar. A copy of your drawing has been saved to disk.

Now that you have saved your work, you might want to take a break before completing the border drawing in the next chapter. If you will be continuing in a few minutes, leave AutoCAD and the computer running. If you want to quit for a longer time, give AutoCAD the **End** command.

3 CHAPTER

FEATURING

**Creating layers
Writing text
Plotting the
drawing**

▼

Adding a Title Block to the Border Drawing

n this chapter, you will complete the border template you began in Chapter 2. You will add a title block and write the company or school name, title, your name, and date. You will then save the drawing so you can use it as the starting point for all other drawings in this book.

In this chapter, you will use the following AutoCAD commands:

- Time (to check how long you have been working on the drawing)

- Pline (to draw a wide line)

- Layer (to create new layers)

- Change (to change an object's layer)

- Array (to create equally spaced copies)

- Perpendicular Osnap option

- Nearest Osnap option

- Midpoint Osnap option

- Dtext (to add text)

- Ortho mode (to force orthogonal alignment)

- Plot (to plot a drawing on the printer)

Checking Your Drawing Time

If you left AutoCAD at the end of the previous chapter, start it up again and load your border drawing by giving the command **acad border**. The work you have done so far on the border template should have taken you 30–60 minutes. To verify the amount of time you actually spent, follow these steps:

1. Give the **Time** command. Notice that AutoCAD changes to the text screen and displays three dates and times—the current date and time, the time you started the drawing, and the time you last saved the drawing. The total time you have been working on the drawing and the time since the last Qsave command are also given.

2. Press Enter to terminate the Time command.

3. Press **F1** to return to the drawing screen.

Creating Layers

AutoCAD allows you to organize your drawings on more than one *layer,* or level. It may be helpful to think of these layers as transparent overlays. You can create as many different layers as you need and use different layers for different concepts. For example, you will use separate layers for the border, the title block, regular objects, dimensions, hatch lines, and so forth. Furthermore, you can turn off individual layers so they won't show or plot. You can also display each layer in a unique color. Using layers helps organize your drawing and makes modifications easier.

Look at the status line of the drawing screen. Notice that the words *Layer 0* appear in the upper-left corner. So far, your work has all taken place in Layer 0 because that is AutoCAD's default layer. You will, however, want to create your own layers and give them meaningful names. You will now create layers named BOR (for the border) and OBJ (for object lines). Later, you will move the border to its own layer.

1. Give the **Layer** command (you can abbreviate it to **La**). AutoCAD responds with

   > **?/Make/Set/New/ON/OFF/Color/Ltype/Freeze/Thaw/ LOck/Unlock:**

2. Type **n** (for New) and press the spacebar.

3. At the **New layer name(s):** prompt type **bor,obj** (no spaces) and press Enter.

4. Press Enter to complete the Layer command. You have just created two new layers—BOR and OBJ.

Moving the Border to Its Own Layer

To move the border to its own layer, follow these steps:

1. Give the **Change** command. The cursor changes to a selection box.

2. Place the selection box over one edge of the border and click the left mouse button. All four lines of the border become spotted because they are now one entity, a polyline.

3. Click the second mouse button or press Enter to complete the selection step. The crossed lines of the drawing cursor reappear. AutoCAD's response is the following: **Properties/<Change point>:**

4. Type **p** (for Properties) and press Enter. AutoCAD's response is **Change what property (Color/Elev/LAyer/LType/Thickness) ?**

5. Type the option **La** (for Layer) and press the spacebar. Reminder: you can enter abbreviated AutoCAD options by typing only the uppercase letters in the prompt.

6. AutoCAD responds with the **New layer <0>:** prompt, showing that the selected item is currently on Layer 0. Type **bor** and press the spacebar to move the border to layer BOR.

7. Press Enter to complete the Change command.

You have just moved the border to the new layer BOR. As you can see from the top line of the screen, however, Layer 0 is still current. Using the Change command, you can move items from one layer to another even if neither layer is current.

Creating a Layer for the Title Block

You will now create a layer for the title block, make it current, and draw the title block on it. As you have seen, you can do this by typing the Layer command. This time, let's use a dialog box instead.

1. Move the cursor to the top line of the screen to get the menu bar with its menu titles.

2. Move the cursor to highlight the menu title Settings and press the pick button to pull down the Settings menu.

3. Highlight the menu item Layer Control and press the pick button.

4. When the Layer Control dialog box appears, check that the existing layers 0, BOR, and OBJ are present.

5. Type the new layer name **tblock**, but don't press Enter.

6. Move the cursor to the New box and press the pick button.

7. Check that the name TBLOCK appears in the table.

8. Move the cursor to the row containing the new layer name TBLOCK and press the pick button. The row becomes highlighted as in Figure 3.1.

9. Move the cursor to the Current box and press the pick button. This makes TBLOCK the current layer. Anything you draw now will automatically be placed on this layer.

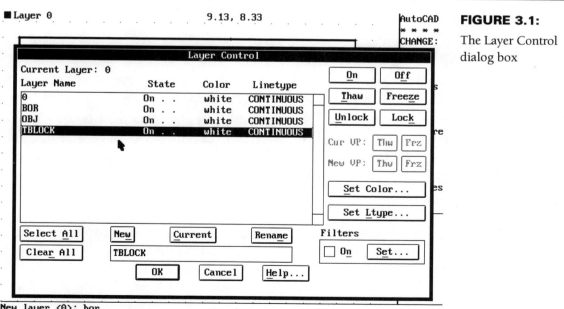

FIGURE 3.1:

The Layer Control dialog box

10. Move the cursor to the OK box and press the pick button to close the Layer Control dialog box.

11. Check the upper-left corner of the drawing screen to make sure TBLOCK is the current layer.

Creating a Title Block

Technical drawings are made up of more than just lines. There is also text explaining the purpose of and giving details about the drawing. With AutoCAD, you can easily add the text you need in a variety of styles and sizes of type. Although you may use only a few type styles routinely, as your expertise with AutoCAD increases, you probably will find other uses for this versatile feature. For example, you can create your own logo and have it appear on your drawings.

Each engineering drawing has a *title block* that identifies the company, drawing title, designer, date, and gives other details. Now that the TBLOCK layer is current, we can begin adding a title block to the template. Let's start with the border.

DRAWING THE TITLE BLOCK BORDER

If we draw the border of our title block in the lower-right corner of the main border, we will be able to use the corner for two of the title block edges. We will have to add only the remaining two—left and top. You have already drawn the main border with a regular line and converted it to a polyline so it could be widened. This time, you will draw the border as a wide polyline. Let's start with the top line of the title block.

1. Type the **Pline** command or its abbrevation **PL** to start a polyline. (Pline is pronounced P-line.)

2. Move the cursor to the right border near coordinate location **10.5,1.5**.

3. Turn on Snap mode.

4. Move the cursor until it has snapped to **10.50,1.50,** then click the left mouse button.

5. Turn off Snap mode.

6. Move the cursor upward and to the left a little. A rubber-band line connects to the cursor.

7. Type **w** (for Width) and press the spacebar to change the line width.

8. Type **0.02** and press the spacebar to define the beginning width.

9. Press the spacebar again to make the ending line width the same as the beginning width.

10. Type the relative polar location **@2.4<180** (no spaces) and press the spacebar to draw the top of the title block border 2.4 inches long to the left.

11. Because the spacing is too coarse, there is no Snap point at the next position. Therefore, we have to use an Osnap option. To continue the polyline, type the Osnap option **per** (for Perpendicular) and press the spacebar to force a perpendicular connection.

The *per* option is called an Osnap (for object snap) and it can be used with other commands such as Line. This is an important method for connecting objects precisely. Notice that the cursor has a target box in addition to the regular crossed lines.

12. Now move the target box down to the bottom line of the main border. The new segment is connected to the end of the previous polyline and to the cursor. Position the target box over the bottom line. The new rubber-band line does not have to appear perpendicular. Because you are using an Osnap option, AutoCAD will automatically make the correct connection.

13. Click the left mouse button to draw the left side of the title block. Notice that a rubber-band line connects to the cursor.

14. Click the second mouse button or press Enter to complete the Pline command.

Enlarging the Title Block with the Zoom Command

In this section, you will use the Zoom command to enlarge the view of the title block. This will make it easier to see what you are doing. Since AutoCAD always keeps track of items in full scale, using the Zoom command will not affect your drawing database.

1. Give the **Zoom** command (or the abbreviation **z**).

2. To put a window around the title block at two opposite corners, move near coordinate position **7.7,1.8** and click the left button.

3. Move to the diagonal corner at **10.7,0.3** and click the left button.

The title block now fills the screen.

DRAWING INTERIOR LINES

To draw the interior lines in the title block, follow these steps:

The First Interior Line

1. Give the **Pline** command (or its abbreviation **PL**) to begin another polyline.

2. Type the coordinates **10.5,1.25** and press Enter. If you have not changed the width setting, it will still be set to the previous value of 0.02.

3. Type the Osnap option **per** (for Perpendicular) and press the spacebar. As before, this will make a perpendicular connection.

4. Position the target box over the left edge of the title block and click the left mouse button to complete the line.

5. Click the second mouse button or press Enter to complete the Pline command.

The Second and Third Interior Lines

You now have one of the three interior lines for the title block. You could draw the other two using the Pline command again, but this time, let's use the Array command instead.

The Array command can make multiple copies of evenly spaced items. The items can be arranged in a one- or two-dimensional rectangular array or in Polar fashion. In Chapters 7 and 9, you will use the Polar array, but for now, you want the rectangular array.

1. Give the **Array** command. The cursor changes to a selection box.

2. Position the selection box over the midpoint of the interior line you just drew, and press the left mouse button. The line becomes spotty to indicate that you have selected it.

3. Click the second mouse button or press Enter to complete the selection. The drawing cursor returns and the selected line returns to normal.

4. Type **r** (for Rectangular array) and press the spacebar.

5. You now must indicate the total number of rows and columns (including the original) for the new array. Type **3** to select three rows and press the spacebar.

6. Now type **1** to select one column and press the spacebar.

7. Next you will need to specify the row spacing. We want the second line to be below the first by 0.25. Therefore, type **–0.25** and press the spacebar. The other two lines are then drawn into the title block.

Dividing the Third Opening

To divide the third opening, follow these steps:

1. Give the **Pline** command (or **PL**).

2. Type the Osnap option **nea** (for Nearest) and press the spacebar.

3. Move the selection box to the top of the third opening and move right to location **9.70,0.97**. Click the left mouse button to start the polyline.

4. Type the Osnap option **per** and press the spacebar.

5. Move the target box down to the next horizontal line. Then move a little to the left. When the coordinate shows about **0.27<240** click the left mouse button to complete the line.

6. Click the second mouse button or press Enter to complete the Pline command. Your drawing should look like Figure 3.2.

Saving the Drawing

To save your drawing, give the **Qsave** command and press Enter.

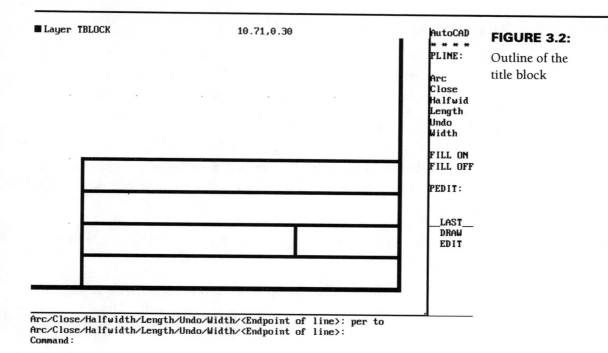

FIGURE 3.2:

Outline of the title block

```
■ Layer TBLOCK                    10.71,0.30
```

```
Arc/Close/Halfwidth/Length/Undo/Width/<Endpoint of line>: per to
Arc/Close/Halfwidth/Length/Undo/Width/<Endpoint of line>:
Command:
```

Using AutoCAD Typefaces

You can add lettering to your AutoCAD drawings easily with the Text and Dtext commands. When you use the Dtext command, each letter appears on the screen as you type it. With Text, the letters will not appear until you finish a complete line.

Although several different typefaces or fonts are available, we will use only Roman Simplex and Roman Complex. Like most of the AutoCAD fonts, these are proportional typefaces; that is, some letters—such as uppercase M and W—are wide, while others—such as lowercase i and l—are narrow. Roman Simplex is drawn with a single line and without serifs and is better suited for smaller lettering. Roman Complex is more attractive because it uses serifs and variable-width lines. It does, of course, take AutoCAD longer to draw Roman Complex letters.

SELECTING THE TYPEFACE

Before starting the lettering of your title block, you need to select the typeface. We will begin with Roman Complex and then switch to Roman Simplex. Typefaces can be selected directly from a dialog box.

Selecting the Typeface from a Dialog Box

You can display AutoCAD's typefaces in a dialog box directly on your video screen. Using the cursor, you can then select one of the typefaces.

1. To display samples of the typefaces, move the cursor to the top line of the screen.

2. When the top line changes to show several menu titles, move the cursor sideways until the menu title Draw is highlighted.

3. Press the pick button on the mouse to pull down the Draw menu.

4. Move the cursor down the menu to highlight Text.

5. Notice that this item shows a right-pointing triangle. This means you can move the cursor to the right to get the Text menu. You can also click the left mouse button to get the Text menu.

6. Move to the Text menu and highlight the menu item Set Style. Press the pick button to get the Select Text Font dialog box as shown in Figure 3.3.

Figure 3.3 also shows the first 20 examples of AutoCAD's typefaces. You can select a typeface by positioning the cursor on the name of the typeface you wish to use and pressing the pick button. Alternatively, you can highlight the corresponding names at the left

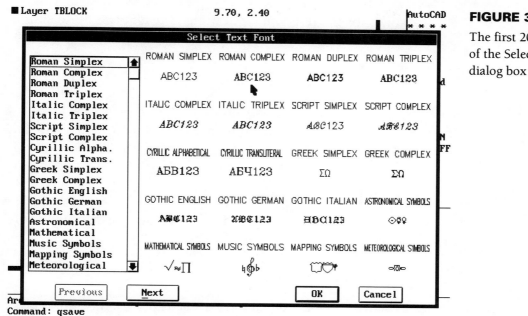

FIGURE 3.3:

The first 20 fonts
of the Select Font
dialog box

side of the dialog box. You can view additional fonts by picking the
Next box and you can return to the first set by picking the Previous box.
Notice that in addition to the usual Roman and Italic letters, there are
Cyrillic, Greek, and Gothic letters, as well as mapping symbols.

7. Move the cursor to the box with Roman Complex type and
click the pick button.

8. Click on the OK box.

9. Look at the bottom line of the screen for the word Romanc
(short for Roman Complex) and the remaining prompts.
The first of these is **Height <0.00>:** allowing you to set the
height. Now type the value **0.14** and press Enter.

10. Press the Enter key five more times to accept the current values for the remaining questions. *Do not* press **^C** to skip this part.

Filling in the Title Block

It's finally time to put some text into your title block. This includes the company name, the drawing name, and a few details about the drawing.

THE COMPANY NAME

To write the company name in the first opening of the title block, follow these steps:

1. Give the **Dtext** command.

2. When you see the **Justify/Style/<Start point>:** prompt type **j** (for Justify) and press Enter.

Several options are presented. Sometimes, you will position the cursor with the mouse and press the pick button to mark the beginning of text. If you do this now, however, the text will spill out beyond the end of the title block. Therefore, you will need to select the Fit option, which will compress the text into the title block.

3. Type **f** (for Fit) and press the spacebar. You now have to mark the left and right boundaries of the opening into which the text will fit.

4. Move to the lower-left corner of the first opening to location **8.18,1.30** and press the pick button.

Before marking the other end of the line, you need to check that Ortho mode is on. Ortho mode automatically aligns your work with the horizontal or vertical axis.

5. Turn on Ortho mode by pressing **^O** or the Ortho function key (**F8** for IBM PC compatibles/**F4** for Sun).

The Ortho function key is a toggle key, enabling you to switch Ortho mode on or off as necessary. When Ortho mode is on, the word Ortho appears on the top line of the screen.

6. Move to the lower-right corner of the opening until the coordinate display shows approximately **2.20<0**. Then press the pick button. (*Do not* press Enter here.)

A box now appears at the beginning of the line to show the text size. The height of the box should be somewhat less than the height of the opening. If it is not, go back to the Font dialog box and reset the height.

7. Move the cursor out of the way.

8. If you are in a drawing class, type your school name and class name. For example **New Mexico Tech, ES 102**. Otherwise, make up a company name such as **Southwest Widget Company**.

Make sure that each letter appears on the screen as you type it. If you type an incorrect letter, press the Backspace key to erase it. Don't worry if the text spills over the end of the title block. You can always read your text on the bottom line of the screen.

9. Press Enter to complete the line.

10. Press Enter again to complete the Dtext command and compress the line of text so it looks like Figure 3.4.

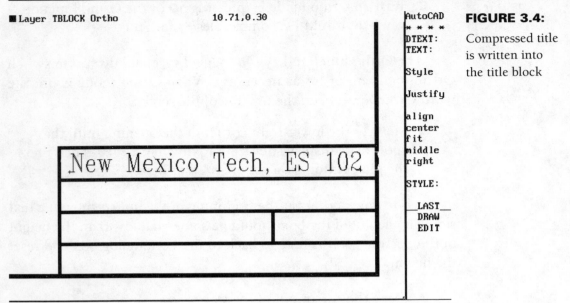

FIGURE 3.4:

Compressed title is written into the title block

```
■ Layer TBLOCK Ortho            10.71,0.30          AutoCAD
                                                    * * * *
                                                    DTEXT:
                                                    TEXT:

                                                    Style

                                                    Justify

                                                    align
                                                    center
                                                    fit
                                                    middle
                                                    right

                                                    STYLE:

                                                    __LAST__
                                                      DRAW
                                                     EDIT
```

New Mexico Tech, ES 102

```
Text: New Mexico Tech, ES 102
Text:
Command:
```

WRITING THE DRAWING TITLE

Each drawing must have a title. To write the title in the second opening, follow these steps:

1. Press the spacebar to repeat the previous Dtext command.

2. At the **Justify/Style/<Start point>:** prompt, type **j** (for Justify) and press Enter.

3. This time, since the text is much shorter than the box, let's center the text. Type **c** (for Center) and press the spacebar. You now have to tell AutoCAD where the center of the text is to be.

You could move the cursor to the center of the opening, near the bottom. Instead, we will ask AutoCAD to locate the precise center.

The easiest guide to the center of the opening is the center of the line across the top of the opening. However, we can take only the X value from there. That is, we would need to separate the X and Y coordinates. This is easy when you use a *point filter.*

4. To give the X value first, type **.x** (decimal point x) and press the spacebar. Now AutoCAD will only take the X coordinate from the next point you choose.

5. Type the Osnap command **mid** (for Midpoint) and press the spacebar. This option precisely selects the midpoint of a line or an arc that you select.

6. Move the target box near the midpoint of the top line of the opening and press the pick button. You can be anywhere near the middle of the line. (Of course, you also can use the second or third line.) You have now specified the horizontal or X location.

7. To show the Y position, move down near the bottom of the second opening so the Y coordinate is about **1.05**. This specifies where the bottom of the letters will be. (This time, the X value is unimportant because you have already specified it). *Do not* type **.y** here.

8. Click the left mouse button.

9. Click the second mouse button to select Rotation angle <0>.

10. Move the cursor out of the way. As before, there should be a box showing the letter height and it should be centered in the opening.

11. Type the title **BORDER** (use all capital letters). Notice the text begins at the center of the opening and moves to the right.

12. Press Enter twice and check that the line of text is centered in the opening.

Let's put the rest of the text in the drawing in Roman Simplex (Romans).

CHANGING TO THE SIMPLEX FONT

1. Move the cursor to the top of the screen to get the menu bar.

2. Highlight the word Draw and press the pick button. This gives not only the Draw menu but also the Text menu. The Set Style entry is automatically highlighted since this was the previous choice.

3. Press the mouse pick button to get the Select Text Font dialog box. If Set Style is *not* highlighted or if you most recently used the Draw menu for something else, pick the Text menu item.

4. Move the cursor to Roman Simplex and click the mouse pick button.

5. Click on the OK box.

6. Set the height by typing **0.13** and pressing Enter.

7. Press Enter five times.

WRITING YOUR NAME

To add your name to the title block, follow these steps:

1. Give the **Dtext** command.

2. Type **j** (for Justify) and press Enter.

3. Type **f** (for Fit) and press the spacebar.

4. Move to the lower-left corner of the third opening and press the pick button to define the left end.

5. Move right, almost to the short divider you just drew, and press the pick button to define the right end.

6. Move the cursor out of the way and check the size of the text box.

7. Type **Dr by:** (for drawn by) and add your name.

8. Press Enter twice to complete the command. Your entry should shrink to fit the opening.

COMPLETING THE TITLE BLOCK

There are still two more openings left to fill. Enter the date on the other half of the third line by following these steps:

1. Press the spacebar to repeat the Dtext command.

2. Follow the previous directions to fit the date into the small space on the right side of the third line.

3. Press the spacebar to repeat the Dtext command again.

4. Move to the lower-left corner of the last opening. Follow the same steps you used to center a line of text in the opening as you did above in "Writing the Drawing Title." Be careful not to center the text on the bottom border line. Use one of the title block lines instead.

5. If you are in a class, write your section number, otherwise, type **Make one, Use CRS** (CRS is the abbreviation for cold-rolled steel.)

6. Press Enter twice to complete the Dtext command. Your title block should look like the one shown in Figure 3.5.

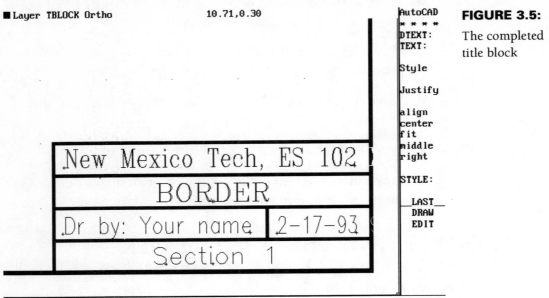

■ Layer TBLOCK Ortho   10.71,0.30

AutoCAD
* * * *
DTEXT:
TEXT:

Style

Justify

align
center
fit
middle
right

STYLE:

__LAST__
DRAW
EDIT

New Mexico Tech, ES 102

BORDER

Dr by: Your name   2-17-93

Section 1

Text: Section 1
Text:
Command:

FIGURE 3.5:

The completed
title block

7. Move the cursor to the top line of the screen to get the menu bar with its menu titles.

8. Move the cursor to highlight the menu title Settings and press the pick button to pull down the Settings menu.

9. Highlight Layer Control and press the pick button.

10. Move the cursor to the OBJ layer and press the pick button to highlight the line.

11. Move the cursor to the Current box and press the pick button.

12. Move the cursor to the OK box and press the pick button to close the Layer Control dialog box.

13. Check the top of the screen to make sure the OBJ layer is current.

Plotting Your Drawing

There are several ways to plot an AutoCAD drawing. If you have a plotter or PostScript printer attached to your computer, you can print a finished drawing by giving the Plot command. If you don't have a plotter or a printer attached to your computer, you can plot directly to a floppy disk. You can then take your floppy disk to another computer that has a plotter or a printer and plot your drawing there. AutoCAD is not needed on the other computer. If you are on a network, you can send the plot file to the system plotter or printer.

When you give the Plot command, the Plot Configuration dialog box appears. You can then specify whether to plot the entire drawing or only a part of it.

There are five options—Display, Extents, Limits, View, or Window. Generally, the option we will use is Limits. Because you have set the drawing limits to 11, 8.5, you will be plotting the entire drawing. On the other hand, if you want to plot a specific part of your drawing, choose Display to plot what is shown on the screen. You can also choose Window and put a window around the specific area you want to plot.

Let's make a plot of your border template using the Limits option.

1. Give the **Plot** command. The Plot dialog box appears.

2. Move the cursor to the Additional Parameters box and click on the Limits radio button. (These buttons are called *radio buttons* because only one can be selected at a time.)

3. Pick the Rotation and Origin box to get the Plot Rotation and Orientation dialog box as in Figure 3.6.

4. Rotate the plot 90 degrees by picking the 90 radio button in the Plot Rotation box.

5. Pick the OK box to complete the rotation selection. The Plot Rotation and Orientation dialog box disappears, exposing the Plot dialog box.

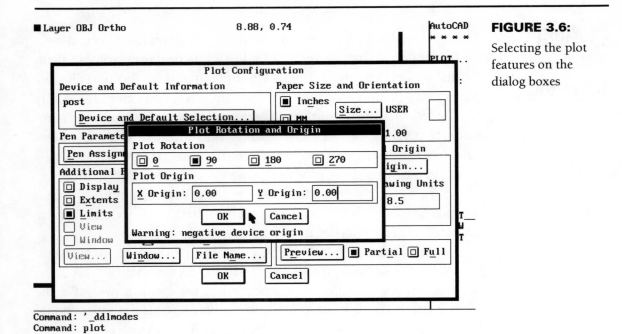

FIGURE 3.6:

Selecting the plot
features on the
dialog boxes

6. On the Plot dialog box, pick the Partial
radio button in the Plot Preview box.

7. Pick the Preview box to get the Preview Effective Plotting
Area dialog box with two rectangles. One represents your
drawing and the other represents the paper.

8. Check that the two rectangles are aligned. If you rotate
the plot when you shouldn't, or don't rotate it when you
should, you will see a small sideways rectangle for your
drawing and a larger rectangle for the paper.

9. Pick the OK box to return to the Plot Configuration dialog
box.

10. Pick the Plot to File button if you don't have a plotter.

11. Pick the OK button to close the Plot dialog box and start
the printing.

12. You will be prompted to position the paper in the printer or plotter. After you have done so, press Enter to begin the plot. If your printer is buffered, you can immediately return to work on your drawing while the printer is printing your drawing.

Now let's save the completed border template and title block.

Saving the Completed Border Template

You can save your completed border template and exit the drawing phase of AutoCAD with one command. Then, each time you start a new drawing, you can begin with a copy of this drawing. And, since the border drawing is saved while still zoomed over the title block, it will appear that way for each new drawing. You can change the drawing title and date easily, and then zoom back out to the full drawing size.

■ Give the **Qsave** command and press Enter to save the latest version of your drawing.

FEATURING

Changing text
**Drawing lines
and circles**
**Correcting
mistakes**
▼

Drawing Lines
and a Circle

n this chapter, you will learn more about some of the AutoCAD commands you've used in previous chapters, and you'll explore some new ones as well. One of AutoCAD's most important features is its ability to select objects for manipulation. By drawing lines and a circle, you will study this very important and useful feature.

Objects which need to be changed can be selected one at a time or, by using a window, several items at once. In addition, you can remove items from the objects you have selected.

Some of the connections in this chapter are made with Grid snap. However, you will not always have a grid point available.

Remember, you must *never* connect items yourself or the database will not be accurate. Therefore, you frequently will need to use one of the Osnap options in order to make precise connections.

In this chapter, you will use the following AutoCAD commands:

- Ddedit (to change text)

- U (to undo the previous command)

- Redo (to reverse the U command)

- Circle (to draw a circle)

- Savetime (to regularly save your drawing)

Let's get started.

Beginning a New Drawing

1. If necessary, start AutoCAD, but *don't* give a drawing name.

2. At the **Command:** prompt, type **new** and press Enter. This tells AutoCAD that you want to start a new drawing. The Create New Drawing dialog box appears.

3. Move the cursor to the box to the right of the Prototype field and click the mouse.

4. Press Backspace four times to delete the default entry **acad**.

5. Type the name **border**, but *do not* press Enter.

6. Move the cursor to the box next to Retain as Default and press the pick button. Make sure there is an X in the box. This tells AutoCAD to use your border drawing as a template for all new drawings.

7. Move the cursor to the blank field to the right of the New Drawing Name field and click the mouse.

8. Type the drawing name **first** and press Enter. This is the name of your next drawing.

Before continuing with the new drawing, verify its name to be sure that you are not editing your border template by mistake.

Verifying the Drawing Name

When your new drawing appears on the screen, it will look exactly like the border drawing you made in the previous chapter. If you zoomed over the title block before you saved the border drawing, the title block will now fill the screen. If not, give the **Zoom** command and put a window around the title block. Then follow these steps:

1. Give the **Status** command.

2. After the text screen appears, look at the end of the first line to check the name of the drawing. If you see the word **FIRST**, continue with step three below. However, if you see the word **BORDER**, leave AutoCAD immediately with the **End** command before you ruin your border template. Then go back to the beginning of this chapter and start again.

3. Press Enter to see the remaining information.

4. To continue, press **F1** to change back to the drawing screen.

5. Your screen should be filled with the zoomed image of the title block. If, on the other hand, the entire drawing is showing, give the **Zoom** command. Place a window around the title block to enlarge it.

Making Changes to Text

Each time you start a new drawing with a copy of your border template, you must change the title and date. This change is rather complicated because AutoCAD treats each line of text as a complete block. Thus, you cannot remove just one or two characters in a line of text by using the AutoCAD Erase command (because the Erase command removes the entire line.) But you did not simply write lines into their title block openings—you centered the title and fitted the date. Therefore, if you erased the originals, you would have to center and fit the new text too.

To help you make changes in existing text, AutoCAD provides an editor. Using the editor, you can delete and add individual characters. Furthermore, if the old text was centered or fitted, the new text will be too, even if the new length is different.

MAKING CHANGES WITH THE DDEDIT COMMAND

You can change the date and title with the Ddedit command.

Changing the Date

1. Give the **Ddedit** command.

2. Move the selection box to the drawing date and press the pick button. Be sure to place the selection box over a number, not on the space between numbers. The Edit Text dialog box appears with the date in the center.

3. Notice that the date is highlighted. Move the cursor to the digit in the date you want to change and press the pick button. Notice that the date is no longer highlighted and that the cursor has become a vertical bar between two characters. To delete the character to the *left* of the cursor, press Backspace. To delete the character to the *right* of the cursor, press Delete. To add a character, just type that character. For example, to change 12-6-92 to 12-8-92, move the cursor to the 6 and press the pick button. Press Backspace to delete the 6, then type **8**. Use the left and right arrows to move the cursor one character at a time. Use the Home and End keys to put the cursor at the beginning and end of the line. When you have made all your changes, press Enter.

4. Make sure the new date shown in the title block is correct and that it is fitted into its opening.

Changing the Title

1. Check the bottom line to make sure that the Ddedit command is still active.

2. To change the drawing title, move the selection box to any character in the title and press the pick button. The Edit Text dialog box appears with the title in the text box.

3. Because the text is highlighted, it will be erased automatically as you begin typing. (If you inadvertently pressed the pick button and the title is not highlighted, pick the Cancel box and pick the Title again.) Type the new title **FIRST DRAWING**.

4. Press Enter to close the dialog box and to change the title.

5. Make sure the new title is correct and centered in the title block.

6. Press Enter to complete the Ddedit command.

Viewing the Entire Drawing

To change the magnification so you can view the entire drawing, follow these steps:

1. Give the **Zoom** (or **z**) command with the **a** (for All) option to display your entire drawing.

2. Check the upper-left corner of the screen to see which layer is current. If it is OBJ, you can skip to the next section.

3. If the current layer is *not* OBJ, you will need to change it. Move the cursor to the top line of the screen to display the menu bar.

4. Move the cursor to highlight the menu title Settings and press the pick button to pull down the Settings menu.

5. Highlight the menu item Layer Control and press the pick button to get the Layer Control dialog box.

6. Move the cursor to the OBJ layer and press the pick button to highlight that line.

7. Move the cursor to the Current box and press the pick button.

8. Move the cursor to the OK box and press the pick button to close the Layer Control dialog box.

9. Again, check the upper-left corner of the drawing screen to make sure that OBJ is the current layer.

Drawing a Line with the Line Command

In the previous chapters, you created a border by putting lines around the drawing. In this section, you will draw more lines to learn some of the additional features of the Line command. You will also use the Ortho command to align your lines automatically with the horizontal and vertical axes.

1. If the grid is off, turn it on.

2. Check the status line. If Snap mode is on, turn it off.

3. If necessary, turn off Ortho mode.

4. Give the **Line** (or **L**) command.

5. Move the cursor upward and to the right. The coordinate readout should change as the cursor moves from one grid point to the next. If the coordinate readout does *not* change as you move the cursor, press **^D** (**F6/F2**).

6. Move the cursor until it is near coordinate position **4.00,3.50**. (As you learned in the previous chapter, it is easier to move near a position with the Snap mode off.)

7. Turn on Snap mode.

8. Make sure the cursor has snapped to the coordinate position. You can verify this by counting the grid points, which should appear at intervals of 0.5 units.

9. To start a line from the cursor position, press the left mouse button.

10. Turn off Snap mode.

11. Move the cursor upward and to the right. A plus symbol marks the start of the line. This symbol will not appear in the database or on the plot. As you move the cursor, you are drawing a line on the screen—one end is attached to the point you selected, the other is fastened to the cursor, as shown in Figure 4.1. As you move the cursor, watch the coordinate display on the top line. Your position should be displayed in Polar coordinates relative to the starting point. If not, press D (**F6/F2**) twice. Move the cursor until the coordinate display shows approximately **4.3<20**. This notation describes a line 4.3 units long oriented at a 20-degree angle.

Notice that this angled line is not smooth. Because lines on the screen are created from sequences of dots that are arranged in horizontal and vertical patterns, only horizontal and vertical lines will be smooth. For that reason, an angled line will have zigzags or steps along its length.

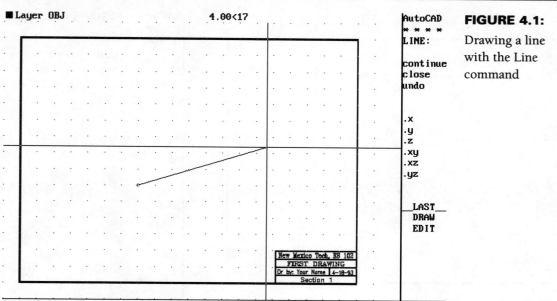

FIGURE 4.1:

Drawing a line
with the Line
command

Now that you're familiar with drawing lines, let's draw a horizontal one. After that, you'll draw a vertical line and, finally, you'll draw several angled lines.

1. Turn on Ortho mode. This forces new lines to be oriented *orthogonally,* that is, either vertically or horizontally (whichever is closer to the cursor). Now, the new line you are drawing will connect with only one line of your cursor rather than at the intersection of both lines. In Figure 4.2, the horizontal cursor line was closer, so the new line was reoriented that way. Notice that the zigzags have disappeared. If your line is oriented vertically, move the cursor more to the right of the first point, as shown in Figure 4.2. The coordinate readout now shows the position of the end of the line rather than of the cursor.

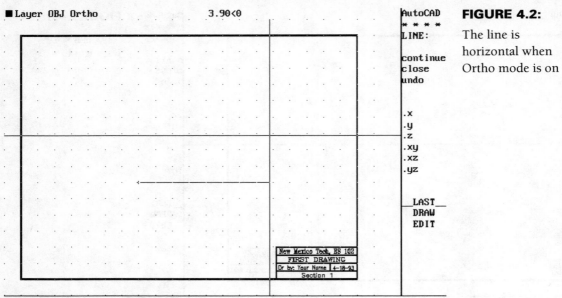

FIGURE 4.2:

The line is horizontal when Ortho mode is on

```
Command:    <Grid on>   <Ortho off> l
LINE From point:  <Snap on>
To point:   <Snap off>   <Ortho on>
```

2. Move the cursor to the right until the coordinate readout shows approximately **6.0<0**. This position is Polar reference to the new line, not to your cursor. It shows that your line has a length of 6.00 units and is oriented at an angle of zero degrees.

3. Turn on Snap mode.

4. When the coordinate readout shows exactly **6.00<0**, press the pick button to establish the first line segment.

DRAWING AN ATTACHED LINE SEGMENT

In the previous section, you drew a line with the Line command. Notice that the bottom line of the screen shows **To point:** rather than the **Command:** prompt. This indicates that the Line command is still active, even though you have drawn a line. (If the **Command:** prompt is displayed, you have inadvertently completed the Line command. Just press the Enter key twice to restart the Line command and connect up to the previous line.) Because the Line command is still active, you can add another line to your first line. Let's do that now.

1. Move the cursor five grid points straight upward from the right end of the line. The coordinate readout is **2.50<90**, indicating a line of 2.50 units at an angle of 90 degrees.

2. Press the pick button to establish the second line segment.

Drawing an Angled Line

Now let's draw four more line segments. But this time, let's make them angled.

1. Turn off Ortho mode. (Remember, while in Ortho mode we can draw only horizontal or vertical lines.)

2. Move the cursor five grid points to the left and three grid points upward to draw a third line. The coordinate display should read approximately **2.9<149**, indicating a line length of 2.9 units oriented at an angle of 149 degrees, as shown in Figure 4.3.

3. Press the pick button to establish the third line.

4. Turn off Snap mode so you can position the cursor between grid points for the next line.

5. Move the cursor downward and to the left until the coordinate position is approximately **4.6<202**.

6. Press the pick button to establish the fourth line.

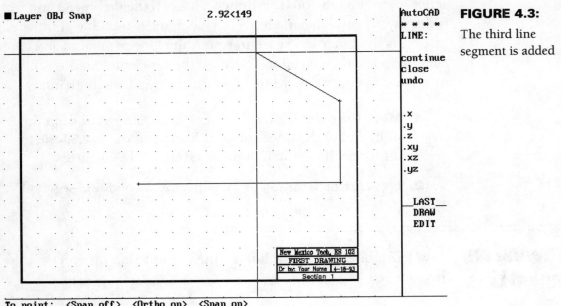

```
To point:  <Snap off>  <Ortho on>  <Snap on>
To point:
To point:  <Ortho off>
```

7. Move the cursor downward and to the left again until the coordinate position shows approximately **4.5<242**. Press the pick button to establish the fifth line.

8. Move the cursor downward and to the right until the coordinate position shows approximately **5.0<350**. Press the pick button to affix the sixth line.

9. Move the cursor upward and to the right. Notice that the **To point:** prompt appears on the bottom line of the screen. AutoCAD is waiting for you to draw another line segment.

You've now drawn six line segments—one horizontal, one vertical, and four angled. Your drawing should look like Figure 4.4.

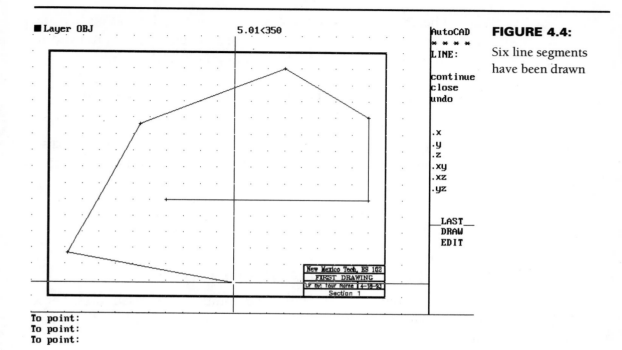

FIGURE 4.4:

Six line segments
have been drawn

Erasing Lines with the U Command

Because AutoCAD keeps track of all the commands you have given, you can easily undo your work, step by step. The U command is used for this purpose. Simply put, the U command undoes the most recent command. (You can give the U command more than once to undo more than one command.)

The U command works on two levels. If you have already completed a command, it can instantly undo everything that was done with that command. On the other hand, if you are still in the middle of a command, the U command (at this point it is considered an *option* rather than a command) can undo parts of it. For example, the U command can erase previously drawn line segments one at a time.

The **To point:** prompt should be displayed, indicating that the Line command is still active. You will now use the U command to erase the two most recently drawn lines. Follow these steps:

1. Check that a rubber-band line connects the cursor to the last line you drew.

2. Type the letter **u** and press Enter. The last line you drew disappears and the rubber-band line now connects the cursor to the previous line.

3. Type **u** again and press Enter. The next line disappears and the rubber-band line moves back one more line.

REDRAWING AN ERASED LINE

Notice that plus signs mark the end points of the erased lines. These marks make it easy to redraw erased lines. They will not be printed with your drawing.

You can remove a line with the U command and then continue to add more lines without ending the Line command. Let's try that.

1. Redraw the second line you erased by moving the cursor to the left plus mark. The coordinate position shows approximately **4.5<242**.

2. Press the pick button to reestablish the fifth line.

COMPLETING THE LINE COMMAND

When you have finished working with a command, you must complete the command before you go to your next task. Here's how to do that:

1. Press **^C**, the second mouse button, the spacebar, or the Enter key to complete the Line command.

2. Check the bottom line of the screen. The **Command:** prompt indicates that the Line command has been completed. Notice that the rubber-band line is no longer attached to your cursor. AutoCAD is now waiting for your next command.

3. Turn off the grid. Notice that the plus marks have disappeared from the screen.

4. Turn the grid back on.

Using U and Redo after a Command Has Been Completed

In the previous exercise, you erased the two most recently drawn line segments one at a time by giving the U command. You were able to erase one line segment at a time because the Line command was still active. However, after the Line command has been completed, the U command works differently.

If you give the U command after completing a command, the *entire* command will be undone and the drawing will be returned to the state it was in *prior* to the last command that you gave. Let's see how this works.

1. Give the **U** command. Now all the lines you created with the last Line command are erased at the same time, rather than individually. If you have given the U command accidentally, don't worry; all is not lost.

2. Give the **Redo** command and press the spacebar. All the lines that were erased by the U command will reappear. Remember, the Redo command completely reverses the effect of the U command, but only if given *immediately* after the U command.

Remember that U and Redo can be applied to any command, not just to the Line command. However, unlike U, Redo cannot be used when a command is current.

Drawing a Circle with the Circle Command

In previous sections, you have seen how to draw straight lines by using the Line command and marking the two ends of the line with the mouse pick button. To draw a circle, the process is similar: give the Circle command and then mark two or three points. There are several other ways to draw circles, but let's start with AutoCAD's default method: marking the center and the radius.

1. If Ortho mode is on, turn it off.

2. If Snap mode is on, turn it off.

3. Be sure that the **Command:** prompt is displayed, indicating that you have completed the most recent command. If not, type **^C**.

4. Now, type the **Circle** (or **c**) command and press the spacebar.

5. To specify the circle center, type the coordinates **7,4** (no spaces) and press Enter. A plus symbol marks the center. The radius of the circle is the distance from the center to the cursor position.

6. Establish the circle size by moving the cursor three grid points to the right and three upward from the center. The further you move outward from the center, the larger the size of the circle. The edge or perimeter of the circle goes through your cursor position. Your drawing should now look like the one in Figure 4.5.

7. When the cursor is close to the grid point and the coordinate readout shows **2.12<45**, turn on Snap mode.

8. Press the pick button to fix the circle size. Notice that the **Command:** prompt is displayed, indicating that the Circle command has been completed.

9. Turn off Snap mode.

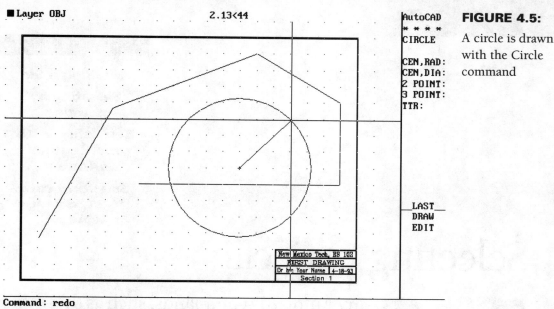

FIGURE 4.5:

A circle is drawn with the Circle command

```
Command: redo
Command: c CIRCLE 3P/2P/TTR/<Center point>: 7,4
Diameter/<Radius>:
```

Saving Your Work Automatically

1. Give the **Qsave** command and press Enter.

2. Give the system variable **savetime** and press Enter. The value **<120>** means that your drawing will automatically be saved every 120 minutes.

3. Type **15** and press Enter. From now on, your work will be automatically saved every 15 minutes—no matter what drawing you are working on.

   If you want to take a break, you can leave your drawing on the screen since you will need it again in the next chapter. If, however, you want to quit for a longer time, give the **End** command.

5 CHAPTER

FEATURING

Recalling a file
Selecting by pointing
Selecting with the Regular window
Selecting with the Crossing window
▼

Selecting Objects

Many AutoCAD commands, such as those that move, copy, or erase, require you to select the objects with which you want to work. In previous chapters, you selected items for the Change, Layer, Pedit, and Chtext commands. The selection process is the same for all these commands.

When AutoCAD wants you to select an item, the cursor changes from crossed lines to a small box (the *objection selection target* or simply *target*.) You position the box over the item, then press the pick button. The box must touch the item itself rather than the space it encloses. For example, to select a circle, you must put the section box on the *perimeter* of the circle, not the center. If you need to select many items, it would be rather tedious to select each one individually.

Therefore, AutoCAD allows you to select several items at the same time by placing a window around them or a fence through them.

There are several ways to select items in AutoCAD. In this chapter, you will learn how to use each one. You will then be able to choose the method best suited to your task. We will start exploring item selection with the AutoCAD List and Move commands, but the selection technique is the same for other commands as well.

In this chapter, you will learn the following AutoCAD commands:

- Endp Osnap option (to reference the end of a line or arc)

- List (to learn about how an object is stored)

- Previous option (to choose the previously selected object)

- Last option (to select the last item drawn)

- Window option (to select a group of items)

- Remove option (to remove an object from a selection set)

- Add option (to select an object)

- Erase (to erase an object)

- Crossing option (to select objects with the Crossing window)

- Polygon window option (to choose items)

- Crossing polygon window option (to choose items)

- Fence option (to choose items using connected lines)

AutoCAD Selection Methods

Let's begin with the simplest method of selection—simply pointing with the cursor. You will start by selecting two lines and a circle.

To learn about selecting items, you'll use the drawing you made in Chapter 4. If your drawing does not look like the one in Figure 4.5, please go back to Chapter 4 and complete the drawing before continuing any further.

1. If your drawing from the previous chapter is still on the screen, skip to Step 2. If AutoCAD is not running, you can start it up and retrieve the drawing at the same time by typing **acad first** and pressing Enter.

2. Check the top line to verify that the current layer is OBJ.

3. Make sure Snap and Ortho modes are off.

4. Move the cursor into the drawing area if it is not already there.

5. You need to draw another line—one that will close the polygon—by connecting the first and last lines you previously drew. This time, let's start the Line command from a pull-down menu. Move the cursor to the top line to display the menu bar.

6. Move the cursor along the menu bar to highlight Draw. Then click the left mouse button to pull down the Draw menu.

7. Move the cursor to highlight Line and click the left mouse button to get the Line menu.

8. Click on **1 Segment** to start the Line command.

9. Press the third mouse button or hold the shift key and press the second mouse button to get the Osnap menu.

10. Move down the menu to highlight the Endpoint option and press the left button. A combination target box appears with crossed cursor lines.

11. Move the box to the lower-left end of the left line near location **1.1,1.9** and click the left mouse button. You don't have to be precise when you use Osnaps—just make sure the target box touches the line near the end to which you want to

attach the new line. The new line should connect the left line with the cursor.

12. Type the **endp** Osnap option and press the space bar.

13. Move the selection box to the left end of the line through the circle. When the coordinates show approximately **3.3<30**, click the left mouse button. (If the coordinates are not Polar, type **^D** twice.) The new line now completes the polygon.

Selecting by Pointing

In this section, you will study the selection method using the List command.

1. Give the **List** command and press the spacebar. The cursor changes to the selection box. AutoCAD now wants you to select the object about which you want information. The bottom line of your screen displays the **Select objects:** prompt.

2. Position the selection box over the line that crosses the circle. Choose a point well away from the points where the line and the circle intersect (coordinate location **7.0,3.5**, for example.) If you put the selection box at the intersection of two lines, AutoCAD will not know which line you mean and may select the wrong one.

3. Press the pick button to select the horizontal line. Notice that, as usual, the line you selected becomes spotty as shown in Figure 5.1. The other objects on the screen do not change appearance because you have not selected them.

The **Select objects:** prompt is displayed again. Also notice that the following message appears on the next-to-last line: **1 found**. This means that AutoCAD accepted the item you selected.

4. To see how important this message is, move the selection box upward a little so that it is not touching any line and press the pick button twice. Notice that the next-to-last line now reads: **0 found**, to show that no items were located at the point you chose.

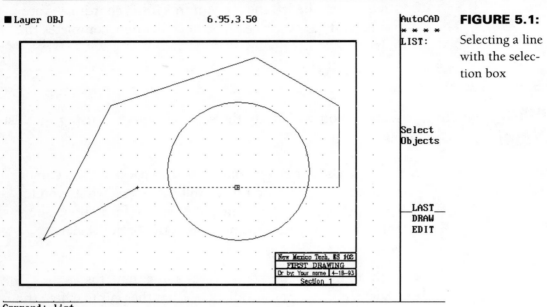

| ■ Layer OBJ | 6.95,3.50 |

AutoCAD
* * * *
LIST:

Select
Objects

___LAST___
DRAW
EDIT

New Mexico Tech, ES 102
FIRST DRAWING
Dr by: Your name | 4-18-93
Section 1

```
Command: list
Select objects: 1 found
Select objects:
```

FIGURE 5.1:

Selecting a line with the selection box

5. Now add another item to the selection set by positioning the selection box over the *edge* or perimeter of the circle.

6. Press the pick button. The circle also becomes spotty and the words **1 found** appear on the next-to-last line again, telling you that AutoCAD has found another object.

The two objects you selected—a line and a circle—should both be spotty, indicating that they are part of the selection set. Next you must tell AutoCAD you have finished selecting the items for this set. *Do not skip this step.* AutoCAD cannot continue with the current command until you signal that you have completed the selection process.

7. To complete the selection process, press the second mouse button or press Enter. A text screen, similar to the one in Figure 5.2, appears with a description of the line and the circle. Notice that the first line of text shows the type of object (LINE or CIRCLE) and its layer (OBJ). Other important information, such as the location of the end points of the line and the center and radius of the circle, is also given.

```
          LINE      Layer: OBJ
                    Space: Model space
     from point, X=    4.00  Y=    3.50  Z=    0.00
       to point, X=   10.00  Y=    3.50  Z=    0.00
   Length =    6.00,  Angle in XY Plane =    0
          Delta X =    6.00, Delta Y =    0.00, Delta Z =    0.00

          CIRCLE    Layer: OBJ
                    Space: Model space
   center point, X=    7.00  Y=    4.00  Z=    0.00
     radius       2.12
circumference     13.33
          area    14.14


Command:
```

FIGURE 5.2:

The List command describes items in the database

8. Press **F1** to return to the drawing screen.

9. Make sure the **Command:** prompt is displayed on the bottom line of your screen.

Selecting Previously Selected Items

You may sometimes want to perform a sequence of operations on the same group of items. In order to do this, AutoCAD allows you to use the Previous (or P) option to re-select items you have previously selected. For example, you might want to start with the List command to check the database for some objects. Then you might move them and, finally, make copies of them. Let's try it.

1. Give the **Move** command (or the abbreviation **m**) and press the spacebar.

2. At the **Select objects:** prompt, type **p** (for Previous) and press the spacebar. The line and circle you selected previously are again marked as selected. The Previous command works for any command that requires selection.

Selecting Previously Drawn Items

Because you are still adding items to the selection set, the line and circle should be spotty. Let's add another item to your selection set. This time, we'll use the Last option—a variant of the Previous option. With the Last option, you can select the most recently *drawn* item rather than the most recently *selected* item. Let's see how this works by selecting the line you just drew.

1. Type **L** (for Last) and press Enter. The line you just drew becomes spotty.

2. To complete the selection process, press the second mouse button, or Enter. The cursor changes back to crossed lines, but the objects are still marked.

3. At this point, you would ordinarily continue the Move command. However, since we are only working on the selection process, type **^C** to interrupt this command. The selected objects should return to normal and the **Command:** prompt should be displayed.

Congratulations. You've just learned three ways to select items. Let's learn a few more.

Selecting with a Regular Window

You can select an entire group of objects by surrounding them with a window. There are two types of windows—Regular and Crossing. The Regular window selects all items that are entirely within the window border. Objects that cross the window border is not selected. The Crossing window selects objects that are either completely or partially within the window border. Let's start with the Regular window and save the Crossing window for later.

1. Give the **List** command and press the spacebar. As usual, the selection box and the **Select objects:** prompt appear.

2. Type **w** (for Window) and press Enter. The cursor changes back from a small box to crossed lines and the **First corner:** prompt appears on the bottom line of the screen.

3. Position the cursor at the upper-right corner of the border, then move down and a little to the left to position **10.25,7.75**. Press the pick button to mark the first corner of the window. The crossed lines of the cursor disappear and the **Other corner:** prompt appears.

4. The second corner *must* be the one diagonally opposite the first corner. Move the cursor down and to the left. You'll see a box begin to grow on the screen. One corner of the box is fixed at the first point you selected. The diagonally opposite corner automatically follows your cursor.

5. Move the cursor until the box completely encloses all but the two far-left lines as shown in Figure 5.3. Make sure the window does not include the title block or the border. The second coordinate position is near **1.7,1.7**. The locations of the window corners do not have to be precise. On the other hand, if the window does not enclose all the desired objects because you have selected the wrong starting point, press **^C** to cancel the command and begin again at step 2.

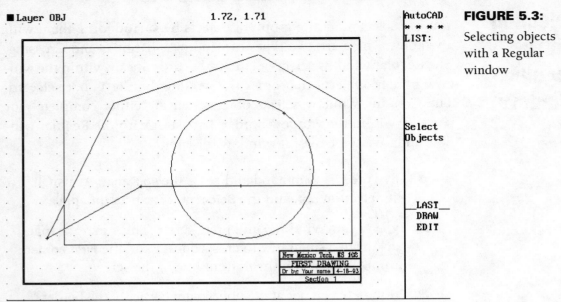

AutoCAD
* * * *
LIST:

FIGURE 5.3:

Selecting objects
with a Regular
window

Select
Objects

LAST
DRAW
EDIT

New Mexico Tech, ES 102
FIRST DRAWING
Dr by: Your name | 4-18-93
Section 1

```
Command: list
Select objects: w
First corner: Other corner:
```

6. When the lower-left corner is correctly positioned, press
the pick button to establish the window size. The selected
four lines and the circle become spotty and, as shown in
Figure 5.4, the window disappears. The bottom of the
screen now shows:

5 found
Select objects:

This means that AutoCAD has located five objects completely
surrounded by the window and that it is waiting for you to select additional items. You can do this by pointing to them as you have done
previously, or by using another window. You also can remove some
of the selected objects. Let's see how.

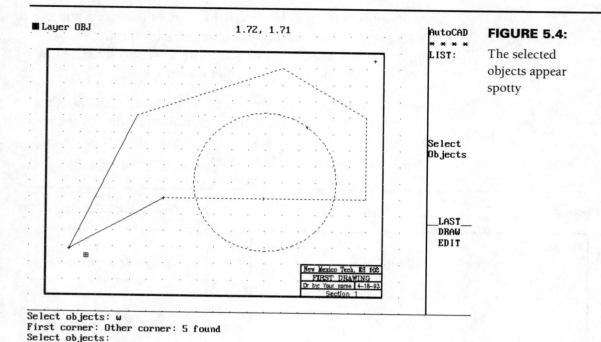

FIGURE 5.4:

The selected objects appear spotty

```
Select objects: w
First corner: Other corner: 5 found
Select objects:
```

Removing Objects from the Selection Set

Occasionally, you may not want to select *all* the items in the window. When this happens, you'll find it easier to use the Regular window to select all the items and then remove selected items from the window with the Remove option. You also can use the Remove option if you have selected an object by mistake. Let's explore this command by continuing with the previous selection.

The circle and four lines on the drawing screen should still be selected and the **Select objects:** prompt displayed. If not, return to the previous section and select these items.

1. Type **r** (for Remove) and press Enter. AutoCAD displays the **Remove objects:** prompt. You will now remove two items.

2. Position the selection box over the edge of the circle and press the pick button. The circle returns to normal, showing that it has been removed from the selection set. The bottom line now shows: **1 found, 1 removed**.

3. Now position the selection box over the horizontal line that crosses the circle and press the pick button again. As shown in Figure 5.5, this line also returns to normal and AutoCAD responds with **1 found, 1 removed**.

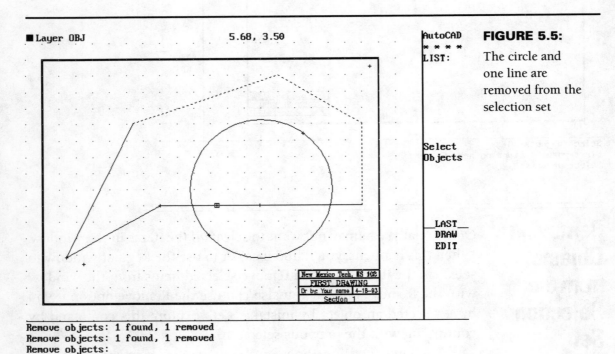

FIGURE 5.5:

The circle and one line are removed from the selection set

If you wish, you can use a window to remove items from the selection set.

Adding Objects to the Selection Set

The Add option is the exact opposite of the Remove option. It is used to add more items to the selection set after you have used the Remove option. Let's add another line to our set of selected objects.

- Type **a** (for Add) and press Enter. The **Select objects:** prompt returns, indicating that AutoCAD has changed back to Selection mode.

REMOVING THE MOST RECENTLY ADDED OBJECT

You can remove the most recently added object or group of objects with the Undo command. With Undo, you can also remove the next most recently added item.

1. Select the circle again to make it spotty.

2. Type **u** (for Undo) and press Enter to unselect the circle.

SELECTING WITH A FENCE

Another useful way to select a collection of items is with the Fence option, which lets you draw a sequence of connected lines. Any object crossed by the fence is selected. Let's use this technique to select the remaining unselected items.

1. Type **f** (for Fence) and press Enter.

2. Move the cursor to the left of the left-most angled line near location **1.0,2.5** and press the pick button.

3. Move the cursor upward and to the right, crossing the second angled line, the circle, and the horizontal line. Stop at location **8.3,3.8** and press the pick button. A spotted line (fence) now connects the two points.

4. Press the second mouse button to complete the fence.

5. Make sure that the three lines and circle are now selected and the words **4 found** appear at the bottom of the screen.

6. Press **^C** to interrupt the command.

Now let's take a look at how to select objects with the Crossing window.

Selecting with a Crossing Window

Sometimes you may want to use a window, but it might be inconvenient or impossible to draw one around all the items you want to select. As you saw in the previous section, the Regular window requires that all the parts of the selected items be *entirely* within the window boundary.

On the other hand, a Crossing window allows you to include even objects that cross the window's edge in your selection set. The technique used to draw the Crossing window is the same as for the Regular window. Let's use a Crossing window to select the circle and all but two of the lines.

1. Give the **List** command and press the spacebar. The cursor changes to the selection box and the **Select objects:** prompt appears.

2. Now type **c** (for Crossing) and press Enter. The cursor changes back to the crossed lines and the **First corner:** prompt should appear on the bottom line of your screen.

3. Move the cursor to the plus mark near the upper-right corner of the border. Stop near coordinate location

10.25,7.75 and press the pick button to establish one corner of the window. The crossed lines of the cursor disappear.

4. Move the cursor downward and to the left and notice that the window grows larger. Stop at the approximate coordinate position **2.0,4.0**. The window should cross or enclose all objects except the line through the circle and the last line you drew as shown in Figure 5.6.

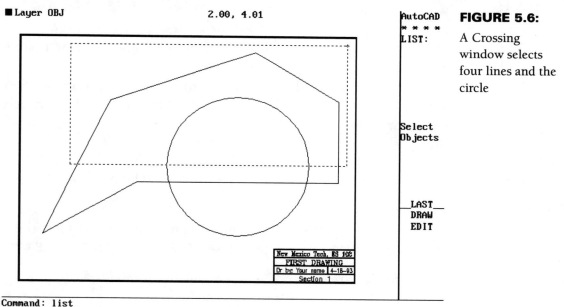

FIGURE 5.6:

A Crossing window selects four lines and the circle

```
Command: list
Select objects: c
First corner: Other corner:
```

The crossing window has dashed lines to distinguish it from the regular window.

5. Press the pick button to select the items that are within or crossed by the window. The circle and four lines, even those that penetrate the window boundary, become spotty. The cursor has returned to a small box.

6. Press **^C** to terminate the command.

SELECTING WITH A POLYGON

Sometimes, instead of using a Regular or Crossing window (which are both rectangles with vertical or horizontal sides), it may be easier to select items by surrounding them with a polygon consisting of three or more sides. As with the windows, there is both a Regular polygon and a Crossing polygon. You choose the Regular polygon with the Wp (Window polygon) option.

Pick a sequence of points so that all the items to be selected are wholly within the polygon. After you have picked more than two points, AutoCAD will complete the corresponding polygon. Lines, including one from the most recently drawn point to the first point, connect all the points you've selected.

On the other hand, if you choose the Crossing polygon window with the Cp (Crossing polygon) option, all items either entirely within or crossing the polygon will be selected. Let's use the Wp option to erase several items from your drawing.

1. Give the **Erase** command (or the abbreviation **e**) with the **wp** option.

2. Move the cursor the to following four points and press the pick button at each point: **0.8,1.5**; **3.0,7.7**; **10.2,7.7**; **10.3,5.4**.

3. Make sure your polygon window has four sides—you drew three, AutoCAD drew the fourth.

4. Press the second mouse button to complete the selection.

5. Check that all items except the circle and the horizontal and vertical lines have been selected.

6. Select the vertical line by covering it with the selection box and pressing the pick button.

7. Check again to be sure that, with the exception of the circle and the horizontal line, all the items have been selected.

8. Press the second mouse button to complete the Erase command.

Undoing the Previous Command

You have previously used the U option with the Line command to erase the most recently drawn line or circle. The U command can be used to undo *any* previous command. Let's use Undo to undo the most recent Erase command.

1. Type **u** (for Undo) and press Enter. The erased lines are instantly restored.

2. To erase the lines again, type **redo** and press Enter. In this manner, you can switch back and forth between the last two commands by alternately giving the U and Redo commands.

If you want to undo more than one command, use Undo. Then you can back up several commands at once. However, Redo will only restore the most recent command.

CENTERING THE CIRCLE

You can move the circle and line to the center of the drawing with the **.x** command by following these steps:

1. Give the **Move** command (or its abbreviation **m**).

2. Select the circle and line.

3. Press the second mouse button to complete the selection.

4. Type the **cen** Osnap option.

5. Pick the edge of the circle.

6. Give the **.x** command.

7. Type the **mid** Osnap option.

8. Pick the top line of your border.

9. Type **mid** again.

10. Pick the left line of your border.

Your circle and line are now centered.

Congratulations. You've learned several ways to select objects with AutoCAD. If you want to quit for a while, give the End command. Otherwise, let's move on to Chapter 6.

FEATURING

Copying objects
Rotating objects
Moving objects
Trimming objects
Extending objects
▼

Trimming and Extending

ow that you're familiar with the various methods of selecting items, let's add a few more lines to your drawing. You will then selectively remove parts of your drawing with the Break and Trim commands.

In this chapter, you will also increase your understanding of the Osnap options. In previous chapters, you have made precise connections using Grid snap as well as the Per (perpendicular), Nea (nearest), Endp (endpoint), and Mid (midpoint) Osnaps. When marking break points and making connections, you must always use Grid snap or an Osnap to ensure precision. However, when picking objects for a selection set, you do not have to be as precise.

In this chapter, you will use the Cen, Qua, and Int Osnaps. Cen (for center) finds the center of a circle or arc when you select the perimeter. Qua (for quadrant) selects exactly the top, bottom, right, or left edge of a circle (respectively, north, south, east, or west). Int (for intersection) finds the intersection of two items.

First, you will add another line to the drawing. The line will appear zigzagged, or stepped. Later, you will use the Change command to straighten it. You will then duplicate the two lines with the Copy command, turn them with the Rotate command, and move them with the Move command. In the end, you will have a drawing of a circle with four lines—two horizontal and two vertical. You will then remove parts of the drawing with the Break and Trim commands and extend other parts with the Extend command.

In this chapter, you will learn the following AutoCAD commands and options:

- Change (to alter an object)

- Copy (to duplicate an object)

- Center Osnap option (to select the center of a circle)

- Quadrant Osnap option (to select one quadrant of a circle)

- Rotate (to turn an object)

- Move (to move an object)

- Break (to remove part of an object)

- Trim (another way to remove part of an object)

- Extend (to lengthen a line)

- Int Osnap option (to select an intersection)

Using the Change Command

If necessary, start AutoCAD and retrieve the drawing named FIRST. With the Ortho mode off, we begin by drawing a second line across the circle. This one will be deliberately slanted, but we'll make it horizontal later with the Change command. Of course, if we had turned the Ortho mode on to start with, the line would have been made horizontal automatically. However, in order to learn a little more about the Change command, we'll do it this way.

1. If Ortho mode is on, turn it off.

2. If Snap mode is on, turn it off.

3. If the grid is on, turn it off.

4. Move the cursor and look at the coordinate readout on the top line of the screen. If the coordinates do not change with cursor movement, press the **^D** (**F6/F2**) to turn on the coordinate display.

5. Give the **Line** command (or the abbreviation **L**) and press the spacebar.

6. Type the coordinate position **4,4.74** (no spaces) and press the spacebar to mark the beginning of another line.

7. Move the cursor to the right and upward a little. Stop when the coordinate readout shows approximately **3.0<5**. (Remember, this is a Polar reference and shows a line 3.0 units long at an angle of 5 degrees. If the coordinate display is not Polar, press **^D** twice.) Notice that the new line has steps or zigzags (as do all lines that are not horizontal or vertical).

8. Press the pick button to establish this line. Notice that the **To point:** prompt is displayed, indicating that the Line command is still active.

9. Press the second mouse button or the Enter key to complete the Line command. Notice now that the **Command:** prompt has returned. Compare your drawing to Figure 6.1.

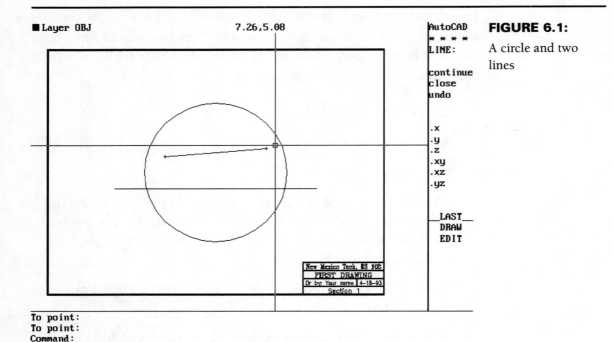

AutoCAD
* * * *
LINE:

continue
close
undo

.x
.y
.z
.xy
.xz
.yz

___LAST___
DRAW
EDIT

New Mexico Tech, ES 102
FIRST DRAWING
Dr by: Your name | 4-18-93
Section 1

To point:
To point:
Command:

FIGURE 6.1:

A circle and two lines

MAKING LINES HORIZONTAL WITH THE CHANGE COMMAND

Since the Ortho mode was off, the line you just drew is not horizontal. What if you decide that you want to move the right end and change it to a horizontal line? In this section, you will learn how to change the location of the right end point of a line so that it will align with the coordinate system.

1. Turn on Ortho mode and make sure the word Ortho appears on the status line.

2. Give the **Change** command and press the spacebar. The cursor changes to a selection box.

In Chapter 2, you used the Change command to change the border from one layer to another. This time, you will use it to move a point. AutoCAD stores a line in the database as the two end points. Because we want to change the angle of the upper line, we will move the point at one end with the Change command.

3. Put the selection box over the upper line and press the left mouse button. (Alternatively, you can type **L** (for Last), since this is the last thing you drew.) The zigzag line becomes spotty to show that it has been selected.

4. Press the second mouse button or the Enter key to complete the selection step. The cursor changes back to crossed lines. AutoCAD responds with the **Properties/<Change point>:** prompt.

5. You have previously used the Property option to change the layer of an object. However, this time you will use it to change the location of a point. Since the Change-point option is the default, all you have to do is move the cursor inside the circle (near location **7.0,4.7**) and click the pick button. The right end of the new line moves downward until it becomes horizontal.

6. Turn off Ortho mode.

Notice that the left end of this line did not change. The Change-point option of the Change command moves only one end of a selected line. The end nearest the cursor moves as close to the cursor as possible. However, because Ortho mode was on, the line could move only as far as the vertical line of the cursor.

In the next section, you will add two more lines to the circle by copying the two you've already drawn. This is easier than drawing two new lines with the Line command as you already did for the first two lines. But first, we will take a look at how to make precise connections with the Osnap options.

Making Precise Connections with the Osnap Options

When the Snap mode is on, AutoCAD can precisely position a line by snapping the cursor to the nearest grid point. But with the Osnap option, AutoCAD can position or snap the cursor to a particular part of an object—much more precisely than you can—for example, to the end of a line or to the center of a circle. If you need to review how Osnap works, re-read Chapter 3.

There are four ways to select an Osnap option in AutoCAD. You can pick it from the Osnap screen menu, pick it from the Osnap cursor menu, pick it from the Object Snap menu of the Assist pull-down menu, or type the option from the keyboard. The second and fourth methods are the easiest to use. However, since the screen menu is useful for learning the Osnap abbreviations, let's try it first.

USING THE OSNAP SCREEN MENU

1. Give the **Line** (or **L**) command.

2. Check the upper-right corner of the screen for the word AutoCAD with a row of four asterisks just below it.

3. Move the cursor to highlight the row of four stars and press the pick button. The Osnap menu appears as in Figure 6.2.

4. You can choose an Osnap option by highlighting it and pressing the pick button. Pay special attention to the abbreviations AutoCAD uses in this menu. For example, the first three letters of the Midpoint option are capitalized. This means that you can select that option by typing only **mid**. You can also select the Endpoint option by typing the first three letters. In this case, however, it is safer to type the first *four* letters to avoid confusion with the End command. (If you type **End** at the **Command:** prompt, AutoCAD will save your drawing and quit working.)

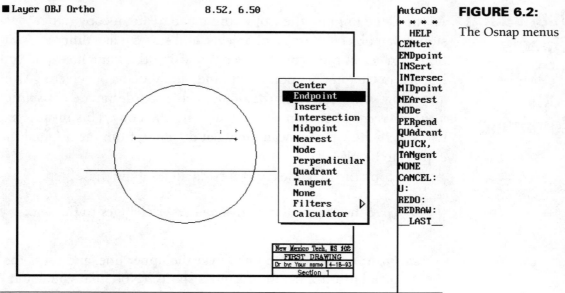

FIGURE 6.2:

The Osnap menus

```
Select objects:
Properties/<Change point>:
Command: 1 LINE From point:
```

USING THE OSNAP CURSOR MENU

Let's take a moment to review how to use the Osnap cursor menu.

1. Make sure the Line command is still active.

2. Move the mouse to location **8.5,6.5**.

3. Click the third mouse button, or press the Shift key at the same time as you click the second mouse button. The Osnap Cursor menu appears as in Figure 6.2.

4. Choose the Endpoint Osnap option by highlighting it and pressing the pick button.

5. Press **^C** to cancel the Line command.

Duplicating Objects with the Copy Command

As the name implies, the Copy command creates a copy (a new version) of an object or group of objects, and stores it at a different location. You select the items to be copied using the same methods you learned in Chapter 5—pointing to individual items or selecting with a window. After selecting the items, you must designate a *displacement,* or *vector,* between the original and the copy. This means you will specify how far away and in what direction from the original the copy is to be placed.

To copy the two lines in your drawing, follow these steps:

1. Give the **Copy** command. The cursor changes to the selection box.

2. Position the selection box over the upper line, and press the pick button. The line becomes spotty. (Note that you could have typed the **L** option for Last item drawn.)

3. Now position the selection box over the lower line and press the pick button again. The second line becomes spotty too.

4. Click the second mouse button or press Enter to complete the selection process. The **<Base point or displacement>/ Multiple:** prompt appears, reminding you that you still need to give the displacement.

ESTABLISHING THE DISPLACEMENT

You can establish displacement in one of two ways: by typing the relative displacement (either Cartesian or Polar), or by selecting two points with the cursor. The marked items will then move the distance between the two points and in the corresponding direction. We'll start with the second method.

The pair of original lines is centered on the circle. We now want a copy of the two lines to be centered over the top of the circle. In this case, then, the displacement is equal to the radius in the vertical direction. Therefore, the two points we need are the center and the top of the circle.

1. Since we need to locate the precise center of the circle, we will use the Osnap option. Type **cen** (for Center) and press the spacebar. A target box, appears around the crossed lines of the cursor.

2. Move the cursor so the target box covers the top edge of the circle and click the left mouse button. This establishes the first point of the displacement to be the center of the circle. The **Second point of displacement:** prompt appears on the bottom line.

3. We want to select the top edge of the circle for the second point and again, we will use an Osnap option for precision. Type **qua** (for Quadrant) and press the spacebar. As before, a larger selection box appears at the crossed cursor. The Quadrant Osnap precisely locates the closest quadrant (top, bottom, right, or left edge—whichever is closest to the cursor).

4. The selection box should still be at the top edge of the circle. Notice that images of the two marked lines appear around your cursor. Spotty images remain at the original locations.

5. Press the pick button to establish the two new lines as shown in Figure 6.3.

Rotating an Object

We will now rotate the upper lines from a horizontal to a vertical position.

1. Give the **Rotate** command and press the spacebar.

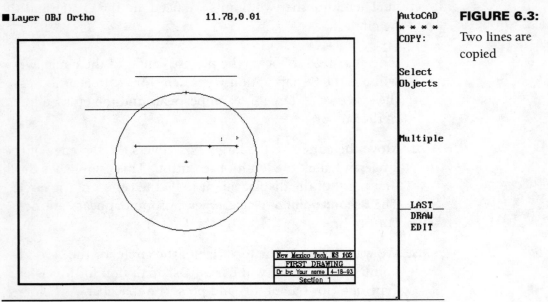

AutoCAD
* * * *
COPY:

Select
Objects

Multiple

__LAST__
DRAW
EDIT

FIGURE 6.3:

Two lines are
copied

New Mexico Tech, ES 102
FIRST DRAWING
Dr by: Your name | 4-18-93
Section 1

```
<Base point or displacement>/Multiple: cen of Second point of displacement: qua
of
Command:
```

2. At the **Select objects:** prompt, move the selection box over the new upper line and press the pick button.

3. Move the selection box over the lower new line and press the pick button.

4. Press the second mouse button to complete the selection step.

5. AutoCAD now displays the **Base point:** prompt. The base point will be the point about which the lines will rotate. Since we want this to be the top of the circle, we will use the Quadrant Osnap option. We can select it from the cursor menu.

6. Press the third mouse button or hold Shift and press the second mouse button.

7. Move the cursor down the menu to highlight Quadrant and press the pick button.

8. Position the cursor at the top edge of the circle and press the pick button. Move the cursor to see the lines rotate.

9. At the **<Rotation angle>/Reference:** prompt, type the value **90** and press Enter. Notice that the two new lines are now turned 90 degrees from their original position.

Moving Objects within a Drawing

We will now move the two new lines down until they are centered on the circle. The Move command is similar to the Copy command, except that after the copy is made, the original is erased.

1. Give the **Move** (or **m**) command and press the spacebar.

2. Select the two vertical lines again by typing **p** (for Previous) and pressing the spacebar. The Previous option selects the items you selected for the previous command (in this example, the Rotate command).

3. When both vertical lines are spotty, click the second mouse button to complete the selection process. We are going to move the two lines over the center of the circle. Therefore, the displacement is just the opposite of the one we used in the previous Copy command. We will use the top edge of the circle first and then the center of the circle. Using the Osnap options will ensure precision.

4. At the **Base point or displacement:** prompt, type the **qua** (for Quadrant) Osnap option and press the spacebar.

5. Move the selection box to the top edge of the circle and press the pick button.

6. For the second point, type the **cen** (for Center) Osnap option and press Enter.

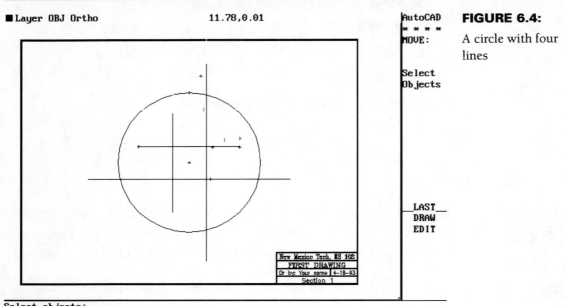

```
■ Layer OBJ Ortho               11.78,0.01                    AutoCAD
                                                              * * * *
                                                              MOVE:

                                                              Select
                                                              Objects




                                                              _LAST_
                                                              DRAW
                                                              EDIT
```

```
Select objects:
Base point or displacement: qua of Second point of displacement: cen of
Command:
```

7. With the selection box still at the top edge of the circle, press the pick button. Your drawing should now look like the one shown in Figure 6.4.

Before continuing, save a copy of your current work to a disk. Give the **Qsave** command and press Enter.

If you are a student, make a plot of your drawing at this point and give it to the instructor.

You will now remove parts of the lines and the circle with the Break and Trim commands. In Chapter 4, you used the Erase command to remove lines from the drawing screen. However, that command can remove only complete objects such as lines or circles. To remove parts of a line or a circle, you will use the Break or Trim command.

The Break Command

The Break command can be used to remove a section of any entity. If a center portion of a line or arc is removed, two separate pieces are left. You can also use the Break command to shorten a line or an arc by removing a piece from one end. (Note that removing a piece from a circle converts it into an arc.)

When using the Break command, you will select only one object—the item to be broken. There are two ways to do this: two-point and three-point. With the two-point method, you remove a part of an object by selecting two exact end points. You then remove the part between the two points. This is easily done on a line or arc. However, when the Break command is used on a circle, the piece is removed from the first to the second point in a *counterclockwise direction*.

Be particularly careful when breaking an object at the intersection of two lines. You cannot simply select the intersection point, or AutoCAD will not know which of the two lines to break. In this situation, you will use the three-point method. To use the three-point method, first, select the object to be broken, then type **f** (for First). You will then mark the part to be removed by selecting two points.

Your drawing screen should look like the one shown in Figure 6.4. To shorten the upper end of the right vertical line, follow these steps:

1. Give the **Break** command and press Enter. AutoCAD responds with the **Select object:** prompt. To remove the upper end of the right vertical line you must precisely mark two points—the upper end of the line, and the intersection of the line with the circle. We'll use an Osnap option for precision.

2. Type the **endp** (for Endpoint) Osnap option and press the spacebar. This time, the selection box is doubled, one box inside the other. This is how Osnap locates the nearer end of a line or arc.

3. Move the selection box near the upper end of the right vertical line. The selection box doesn't have to be exactly at the
end of the line. (If the line end is off the screen, don't worry,
the Endp Osnap will find it.)

4. Press the left mouse button to mark the first point. The
entire line becomes spotty.

5. Type the **int** (for Intersection) Osnap option and press the
spacebar.

6. Move the cursor down the line until it meets the circle.
When the target box is over both the line and the circle,
click the left mouse button. This marks the second point
and trims the line exactly back to the circle. Note that you
could not pick the lower point first because there are two
entities there.

Now let's trim the remaining three lines back to the circle with
the Trim command.

Using the Trim Command

The Trim command, like the Break command, can remove a part of a
line, arc, or circle. Its operation, however, is much more complicated
because you must define both the line you want to trim and the *trim
boundary*. On the other hand, the Trim command is more powerful
than the Break command because you can trim several items at once,
using several different boundaries.

With the Break command, you directly select the places the line
will be broken, but with the Trim command you must select items in
two steps. First, you select the *boundary* or line to trim to. Then, you
select the lines that will be trimmed. When you use the Trim command, you do not use Osnap options. You only have to pick objects,
not the places to be broken.

TRIMMING LINES

Let's begin by trimming the three remaining ends that stick out of the circle.

1. If the **Command:** prompt is not displayed, type **^C** to cancel the current command.

2. Type **trim** and press the spacebar. AutoCAD responds with

   > **Select cutting edge(s)**…
   > **Select objects:**

   The cursor changes to a small selection box. At this point, you must select the boundary you want to trim to, *not* the object to be trimmed.

3. Since you are going to trim the three pieces that stick out beyond the circle, the circle itself will be the trim boundary. Move the selection box to the edge of the circle, well away from the lines, and press the pick button. The entire circle becomes spotty, marking it as the trim boundary. AutoCAD responds with **1 found**, just as it does when you are selecting items for the List and Erase commands. Then AutoCAD repeats the **Select objects:** prompt so you can mark another boundary.

4. Because this is the only boundary we need, click the second mouse button or press Enter to complete the boundary-selection phase. Now you can select the part of each line you want to trim back to the spotted boundary.

5. Remember, you must mark the part to be trimmed, not the part that will remain. Move the selection box over the right end of the lower horizontal line as shown in Figure 6.5. The selection box does not have to be exactly at the end— just be sure you are outside the circle. Press the pick button. Notice that this line is neatly trimmed back to the circle. There is a mark on the screen, showing the position

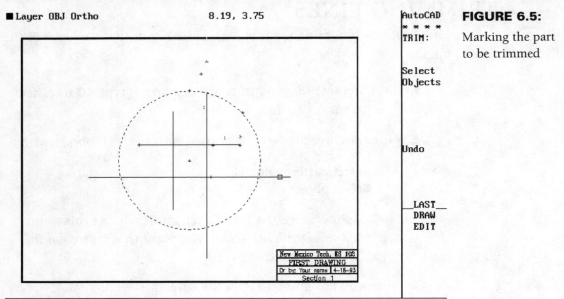

AutoCAD
* * * *
TRIM:

Select
Objects

Undo

LAST___
DRAW
EDIT

FIGURE 6.5:

Marking the part
to be trimmed

```
Select objects: 1 found
Select objects:
<Select object to trim>/Undo:
```

of the selection box when you trimmed the line. The circle remains spotty, indicating that it is still a trim boundary.

6. Move the selection box to the part of the line that sticks out from the bottom of the circle. Press the pick button to trim that part back to the circle.

7. Trim the remaining piece back to the circle in the same fashion. The circle stays spotty because the Trim command is still active.

8. After trimming the three lines, try to trim those parts of the lines that are within the circle. Move the selection box to the right vertical line inside the circle and press the pick button. Nothing happens. The Trim command can erase an object only on one side of the trim boundary. Of course, if you want, you can remove the remainder with the Erase command.

9. Now click the second mouse button or press Enter to complete the Trim command. The spotty circle returns to normal and the **Command:** prompt reappears.

10. Turn the grid on and then back off to redraw the screen without the blips that marked the cursor position during trimming. Alternatively, you can type **r** (for Redraw) and press Enter.

The Trim command requires two stages of object selection. To designate the trim boundary, you can use any selection method, including windows and fences. However, you must pick the objects to be trimmed, one at a time.

Using the Extend Command

You've just learned how to trim the parts of the long lines that stuck out of the circle. Now you will use the Extend command to lengthen the short lines so they meet the circle. As with the Trim command, you must first select the boundary, then select the lines to be extended. We'll start by extending the upper horizontal line to meet the circle.

1. Give the **Extend** command and press the spacebar. The cursor changes to a selection box.

2. To select the boundary, move the selection box to the edge of the circle, well away from the lines, and press the left mouse button. The circle becomes spotty, marking it as the boundary.

3. Press the second mouse button to complete the boundary selection. You will now select the lines to be extended.

4. Move the selection box to the left end of the upper horizontal line, near location **4.2,4.74**. The selection box does not

have to be positioned exactly. It only needs to be close to the end you want to extend.

5. Click the left mouse button to extend the left end of the line to the circle.

6. Move to the other end of the same line and press the left mouse button to extend this end.

7. Using the same technique, extend both ends of the left vertical line.

8. When all lines meet the circle, complete the Extend command by clicking the second mouse button or Enter.

Breaking the Circle

In this section, let's remove a few parts of the circle, converting it into several independent arcs. We'll start by using the three-point Break command to remove the top edge.

1. Give the **Break** command and press the spacebar. The cursor changes to a selection box.

2. Because we want to remove a section that is bounded on each end by the intersection of lines with the circle, we must use the three-point method. Therefore, move the selection box to the top edge of the circle, to the region marked 1 in Figure 6.6. Press the pick button. The circle becomes spotty.

3. Type **f** (for First) and press the spacebar to choose the three-point method. You can now mark the two points to be broken.

4. To mark the first point exactly, type the **int** (for Intersection) Osnap option and press the spacebar. Again, the cursor changes to a target box.

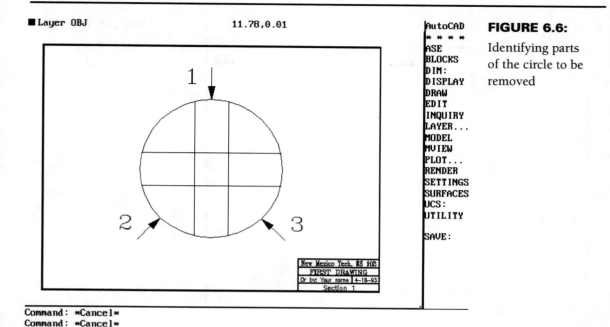

5. Move the cursor until it covers both the circle and the upper end of the right vertical line (approximately **6.0,6.3**) and press the left mouse button.

6. Type the **int** Osnap option again and press the spacebar.

7. Move the cursor left until it covers both the circle and the upper end of the left vertical line (approximately **5.0,6.3**) and click the left mouse button. The top edge of the circle, between the two vertical lines, is erased as shown in Figure 6.7.

Notice that you selected the two break points moving counter-clockwise (from right to left). If you had selected them in the reverse order (clockwise), the part that was erased would have remained and the part that remained would have been erased.

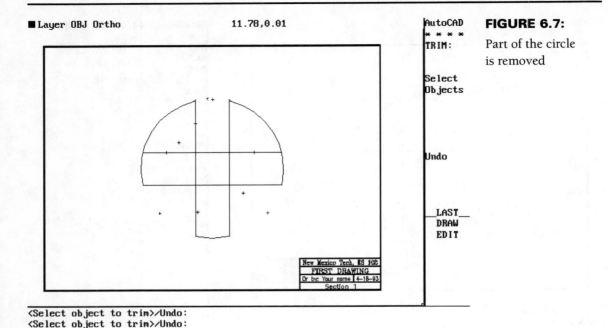

AutoCAD
* * * *
TRIM:

Select
Objects

Undo

LAST
DRAW
EDIT

FIGURE 6.7:

Part of the circle
is removed

New Mexico Tech, ES 102
FIRST DRAWING
Dr by: Your name | 4-18-93
Section 1

```
<Select object to trim>/Undo:
<Select object to trim>/Undo:
Command:
```

Trimming the Circle

To remove the lower-left and lower-right parts of the circle with the Trim command, follow these steps:

1. Give the **Trim** command and press the spacebar. The cursor changes to a selection box.

2. You will need to mark all four lines. You could do this by positioning the selection box over each one and pressing the pick button. This time, however, we'll use a Crossing window instead. Type **c** (for Crossing window) and press the spacebar.

3. Move the cursor to location **4.5,5.0** and click the left mouse button to start the Crossing window.

4. Move the cursor down and right to location **6.4,3.5** and press the left mouse button to complete the selection. Make sure that all four lines have been selected as trim boundaries.

5. Click the second mouse button to complete the selection of the trim boundary.

6. Move the selection box to the lower-left edge of the circle, to the region marked 2 in Figure 6.6.

7. Press the pick button to erase this segment.

8. Using the same technique, erase the section marked 3 in Figure 6.6.

9. Press the second mouse button. Your drawing should now look like Figure 6.7.

PLOTTING THE DRAWING

If you are a student, plot your completed drawing and turn it in to the instructor. When you are done, use the End command to exit the drawing editor and to save the latest version of your drawing to a disk.

FEATURING

Stretching objects
Dynamic zoom
Mirror images
Polar array
▼

Drawing a Pulley

n this chapter, you will create a drawing of an object resembling a drive belt on pulleys. You will use the Stretch command to make it longer, and the Zoom command to magnify it. Then, you will remove parts of the circles with the Trim command. Finally, you will use the Polar Array and Mirror commands to add detail and complexity to your drawing.

Here are the new commands and options you'll be using in this chapter:

- Tan Osnap option (to make a line tangent to a circle)

■ Stretch command (to stretch connected objects)

■ Regen command (to redraw the screen)

■ Polar Array command (to draw radial copies of an object)

■ Arc command (to draw a part of a circle)

■ Mirror command (to make a mirror image)

Beginning a New Drawing with the Border Template

1. If it isn't already running, start AutoCAD.

2. When the drawing screen appears, you should see the zoomed title block from your border drawing. If not, you did not set the default prototype drawing at the beginning of Chapter 4. Please go back and do that now.

3. Type **new** and press Enter to get the Create New Drawing dialog box.

4. Type the drawing name **pulley**.

5. Change the drawing title to **PULLEY** with Ddedit.

6. Change the date with Ddedit.

Drawing Two Connected Circles

In this section, you will begin by drawing two circles. You will then draw lines tangent to the two circles. After several more changes, the finished drawing will look like two pulleys connected by a drive belt as shown in Figure 7.1.

1. Give the **z** (for Zoom) command with the **a** (for All) option to see all of your drawing.

2. Check that the current layer is OBJ. Change to this layer if it is not.

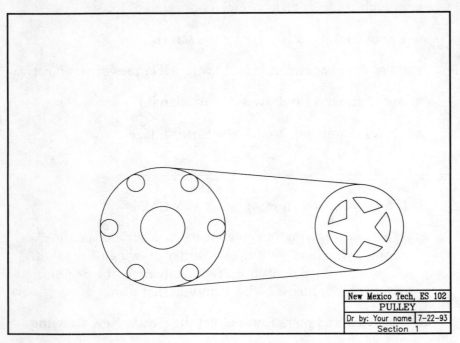

FIGURE 7.1:

Completed pulley drawing

3. If necessary, turn off the grid.

4. If necessary, turn off Ortho mode.

5. Give the **c** (for Circle) command and press the spacebar.

6. Establish the circle center by typing the coordinate **4,3** (no spaces) and press the spacebar. This is an absolute reference.

7. Type the radius **@1,1** (no spaces) and press the spacebar. This is a relative reference to the circle center. It makes the radius the square root of 2 (approximately 1.414).

8. Restart the Circle command by clicking the second mouse button or by pressing Enter.

9. Establish the second circle center by typing **@3,3** (no spaces) and press the spacebar. This is a relative reference that puts the second circle 3 units over and 3 units up from the first circle.

10. Type the radius **1** and press the spacebar. Your screen should look like Figure 7.2.

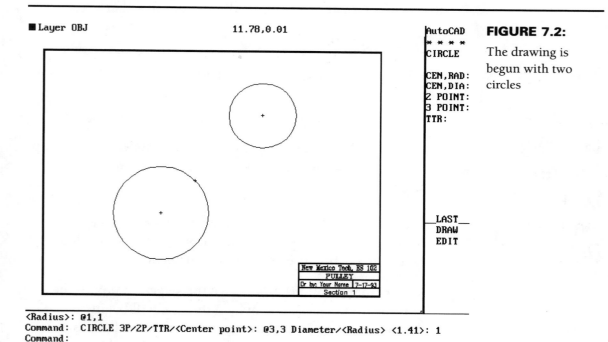

FIGURE 7.2:

The drawing is begun with two circles

Turning On Tangent Osnap Mode

You have already learned that when you are drawing an object, you can make AutoCAD locate a position precisely with the Osnap options. You have used the Center Osnap to find the center of a circle and you also have used the Quadrant, Midpoint, Perpendicular, Endpoint, and Intersection options. Up to now, you used an Osnap option to define a particular location only while a command such as Line was active. In addition, you had to specify an Osnap option each time you wanted to use it. It is possible, however, to turn on an Osnap option *before* starting a command, thereby making that option the default method of point selection. This will eliminate the need to select the Osnap option every time you want to use it.

In the next section, you will use the Tangent Osnap four times in a row. Therefore, let's make it the default.

1. Give the **Osnap** command and press the spacebar.

2. Type **tan** and press Enter.

The Tangent Osnap is now the default.

Drawing Tangent Lines with the Tangent Option

You will now draw two lines tangent to the two circles. The Tan option of the Osnap command forces a line to be tangent to the circle (or the arc) you select.

1. Give the **L** (for Line) command and press the spacebar. Note that the target box appears around the crossed lines of the cursor because an Osnap mode is on.

2. At the **From point:** prompt, move the selection box to the top edge of the left circle, where the line will begin, as shown in Figure 7.3. When the coordinate position is approximately **3.2,4.1**, press the pick button. You do not have to position the cursor too precisely for the Tan Osnap option to work. There is no change in your drawing as yet, because AutoCAD does not yet know where the other end of the line will be. The **To point:** prompt is asking you for that information.

3. To complete the line, move the target to the top edge of the right circle (near position **6.4,6.8**) and press the pick button. A line appears that is tangent to both circles.

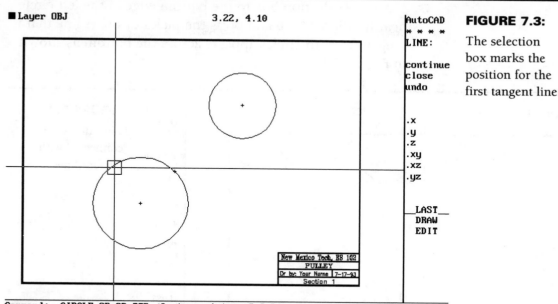

AutoCAD
* * * *
LINE:

continue
close
undo

.x
.y
.z
.xy
.xz
.yz

LAST
DRAW
EDIT

New Mexico Tech, ES 102
PULLEY
Dr by: Your Name | 7-17-93
Section 1

FIGURE 7.3:

The selection box marks the position for the first tangent line

```
Command:  CIRCLE 3P/2P/TTR/<Center point>: @3,3 Diameter/<Radius> <1.41>: 1
Command: osnap Object snap modes: tan
Command: 1 LINE From point:
```

4. Move the cursor up and to the left.

5. Click the second mouse button or the Enter key to complete the Line command.

Now using the procedure outlined above, let's draw a second line along the bottom of the circles.

6. Click the second mouse button or press Enter to start the Line command again.

7. At the **From point:** prompt, move the selection box to the bottom edge of the right circle near location **7.6,5.2** and press the pick button.

8. Move the selection box to the bottom edge of the left circle near location **4.7,1.8** and press the pick button. A line that is tangent to both circles appears across the bottom as shown in Figure 7.4.

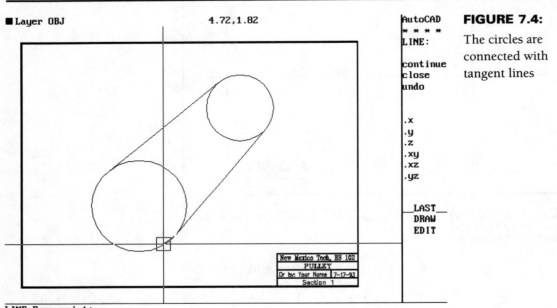

Layer OBJ   4.72,1.82   AutoCAD

```
* * * *
LINE:

continue
close
undo

.x
.y
.z
.xy
.xz
.yz


LAST
DRAW
EDIT
```

New Mexico Tech, ES 102
PULLEY
Dr by: Your Name | 7-17-93
Section 1

FIGURE 7.4:

The circles are connected with tangent lines

LINE From point:
To point:
To point:

9. Click the second mouse button or press Enter to complete the Line command.

Congratulations. You have completed the first part of the drawing. In the sections that follow, you will move objects in the drawing. But first, we need to turn off the Tangent Osnap mode.

TURNING OFF TANGENT OSNAP MODE

1. Give the **Osnap** command and press the spacebar.

2. Type **off** and press Enter.

Rotating the Drawing

The pulley assembly you just drew is inclined upward at a 45-degree angle. Suppose that after drawing it, you realize you really want it in a horizontal position. You can easily make this change with the Rotate command.

The Rotate command enables you to turn selected parts or the entire drawing. Furthermore, you can rotate the object you select by any angle you wish. For example, in Chapter 6 you used the Rotate command to turn two lines 90 degrees. Here's how:

1. Give the **Rotate** command and press the spacebar. The cursor changes to a selection box. AutoCAD asks you to select the objects to be rotated. Since you want to rotate both circles and both lines, you must select all four objects. You can select the objects to be rotated by moving the selection box to each one and pressing the pick button. However, it is more convenient to simply select a group of items with the Window option. Let's do that.

2. Type **c** (for Crossing) and press the spacebar. The selection box changes to crossed lines.

3. The crossing window does not need to surround all the items you want to select—it only has to cross them. Move the cursor near the center of the lower-left circle, near coordinate position **4.0,3.0**, and press the pick button.

4. Now move the cursor near the center of the upper-right circle, near location **7.0,6.0**. Note that the window (made up of dashed lines which indicate a crossing window) grows as the cursor is moved.

5. When the selection window crosses the two circles and the two lines, press the pick button. The four items become spotty to show that they have been selected.

6. Check the next-to-last line of the screen to see that AutoCAD acknowledges finding four items.

7. Press the second mouse button to complete the selection step. The **Base point:** prompt appears on the bottom line of your screen. AutoCAD needs to know the point around which to rotate the objects.

8. This time, we will rotate the object around the center of the lower-left circle. Click the third mouse button, or hold the Shift key while you press the second mouse button to get the Osnap Cursor menu.

9. Highlight the Center Osnap and press the pick button.

10. Move the target box to the rim of the lower-left circle, well away from the tangent lines, and press the pick button. Now as you move the cursor, an image of your object, centered on the left circle, rotates onto the screen.

11. In Chapter 6, you rotated two lines in the positive, or counterclockwise, direction. This time, type the number **-45** and press Enter to rotate the object 45 degrees in a minus (clockwise) direction. Your drawing should look like that shown in Figure 7.5. Alternatively, you could have moved the cursor until the object rotated into the desired position and then have pressed the pick button. In that case, however, it would not have been as precisely located.

Elongating an Object with the Stretch Command

You have already seen how to move objects by using the Move command. If, however, the moved items are connected to other items, the connections will be broken. The Stretch command enables you to move some items that are connected to other items, yet still preserve the connections.

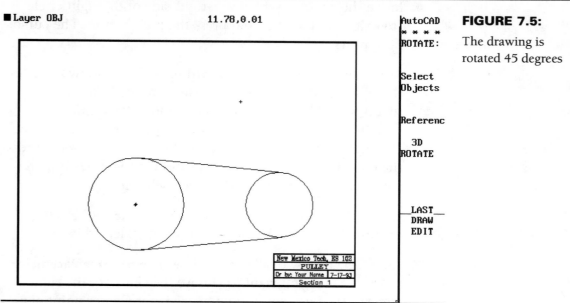

11.78,0.01

AutoCAD
* * * *
ROTATE:

Select
Objects

Referenc

3D
ROTATE

LAST
DRAW
EDIT

FIGURE 7.5:

The drawing is
rotated 45 degrees

New Mexico Tech, ES 102
PULLEY
Dr by: Your Name | 7-17-93
Section 1

```
Base point: _center of
<Rotation angle>/Reference: -45
Command:
```

Let's try an example. In this section, you are going to move the right circle a little farther to the right, away from the left circle. We want to position the center of the right circle on a grid point.

1. Check the top line of the screen to make sure that Snap mode is off.

2. Type the **Stretch** command and press the spacebar. The cursor changes to the familiar selection box. AutoCAD asks you to select the objects to stretch. You want to select the right circle and the two tangent lines connecting the circles. To do so, you must use a Crossing window since those items entirely within the window are moved without change, while those that are crossed by the window will stretch to maintain the connections at each end.

3. Type the option **c** (for Crossing window) and press the spacebar. The cursor changes back to crossed lines.

4. Move the cursor to the lower-right side of the right circle (near location **9.5,1.8**) and press the pick button. The cursor disappears.

5. Move the cursor left and upward until the window includes the right circle and cuts across the two lines. You can see that it would be impossible to use a Regular window for this process. Be careful that the window does not touch the left circle or title block or they will be selected as well. Press the pick button. The right circle and the two lines become spotty to show that they have been selected.

6. Click the second mouse button to complete the selection process. You are now ready to move the selected items.

7. AutoCAD is now displaying the **Base point or displacement:** prompt. Since you want to choose the center of the right circle as the base point, type the **cen** (for Center point of a circle) Osnap option, and press the spacebar. The cursor shows a target box around the crossed lines.

8. Move the target box to the right edge of the right circle, well away from the lines, and press the pick button.

9. Move the cursor to the right. Notice that the right circle moves too. Notice also how the two tangent lines have "stretched" to remain connected to both circles.

10. Type the relative length **@0.2,0** (no spaces) and press the spacebar. This moves the right part of the pulley 0.2 units to the right.

The Stretch command can also be used to move parts of your drawing closer together. Let's continue to the next section, where you will enlarge the view of the drawing.

Enlarging the View of an Object with the Zoom Command

In this section, you will enlarge the view of the left circle with the Zoom command. The circle will appear larger, although its size in the database will not change. This command enables you to work with objects on a more convenient scale.

In Chapter 4, using the List command, you learned that a circle is stored in the database simply as the center and the radius. AutoCAD, however, draws a circle on the screen as a polygon—in other words, as a series of straight lines. The number of lines is a compromise between speed and smoothness, and depends on the display size of the circle. Usually, there are enough lines to make the circle appear round. But when you enlarge the view of a circle with the Zoom command, the number of lines does not change immediately and the enlarged view of the circle will sometimes appear to have flat sides.

To make the circle look rounder on the screen, you can use the **regen** (for Regenerate) command. Then AutoCAD will then redraw the circle using more lines. Again, using the Regen command does not change any of the information in the database or in the plotted drawing.

Let's enlarge and regenerate the left circle of your drawing.

1. Give the **Zoom** (or **z**) command but *do not* type the **w** option, since it is already the default.

2. Move the cursor to the upper-left side of the left circle, to location **1.9,4.6**, and press the pick button.

3. Move the cursor to the lower-right side of the same circle to enclose it in the window.

4. When the coordinate readout is **6.2,1.4**, press the pick button. The image within the window enlarges to fill the screen as shown in Figure 7.6.

5. Give the **Regen** command to make the enlarged circle appear rounder.

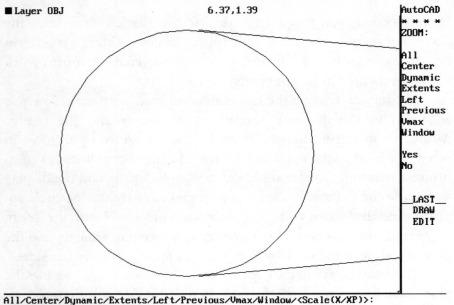

AutoCAD
* * * *
ZOOM:

All
Center
Dynamic
Extents
Left
Previous
Vmax
Window

Yes
No

LAST__
DRAW
EDIT

FIGURE 7.6:

An enlarged view
of the left circle
shows flat sides

All/Center/Dynamic/Extents/Left/Previous/Vmax/Window/<Scale(X/XP)>:
Other corner:
Command:

6. Before continuing, give the **Qsave** command and press
Enter to save a copy of your current work to disk and accept the default file name.

Drawing a Concentric Circle

Drawing a concentric circle is easy—you simply use the Circle command and the Center Osnap option. Let's draw a smaller concentric
circle to represent a shaft for this pulley drawing.

1. Give the **c** (for Circle) command.

2. To make the new circle concentric with the left circle, type
the **cen** (for Center) Osnap option and press the spacebar.

3. Move the target cursor to the edge of the left circle and
press the pick button.

4. Move the cursor to the center and then to the right and watch the new circle grow larger. You can mark the radius at any point by pressing the pick button. However, because a grid point is not available, we will specify the diameter from the keyboard.

5. Give the **d** (for Diameter) option and press Enter.

6. Type the value **1** and press Enter to draw a circle with a diameter of 1.

Drawing Tangent Circles

In this section, you will draw a small circle inside and tangent to the large circle. You will then use the polar Array command to make a total of six small circles. Previously, you drew circles by marking the center and then one edge, or by giving the diameter. This time, you will draw a small circle by designating two points as the diameter. One of the points will be located on the perimeter of the larger circle.

1. Give the **c** (for Circle) command. (Or, you can just press the spacebar to repeat the previous circle command.)

2. Select the two-point option by typing **2p** and pressing the spacebar.

3. Type the **qua** (for Quadrant) Osnap option and press the spacebar. A selection box is added to the cursor.

4. Move the target cursor to the left edge of the large circle and press the pick button. This locks the left edge of the new circle to the left edge of the larger circle.

5. Move the cursor to the right to see the circle grow.

6. You can define the right edge of the circle by moving the cursor to the right and pressing the pick button. This time, however, we will give the value from the keyboard. Type **@0.4<0** and press Enter. (You can omit the leading zero.) Your drawing should look like Figure 7.7.

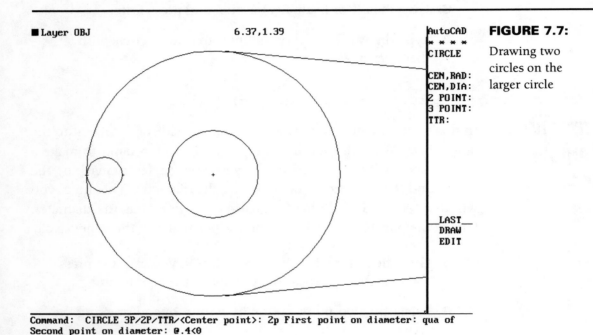

FIGURE 7.7:

Drawing two circles on the larger circle

```
Command:  CIRCLE 3P/2P/TTR/<Center point>: 2p First point on diameter: qua of
Second point on diameter: @.4<0
Command:
```

Making Multiple Copies with the Array Command

In previous chapters, you used the Copy command to duplicate objects. You also used the Array command to make multiple copies of regularly spaced objects. In addition, you used the Rectangular option of Array to multiply one line in the title block to three lines. The Array command also can make copies in a circular or polar fashion. In the sections that follow, you will use the Array command with the Polar option to make six circles and a five-pointed star.

MAKING A POLAR PATTERN

We are going to make a pattern of six circles around the inside of the left circle.

1. Give the **Array** command with the **L** (for Last item drawn) option. The small circle becomes spotty as it is selected.

2. Press the second mouse button to complete the selection step.

3. At the **Rectangular or Polar array (R/P)<R>:** prompt, type **p** (for Polar) and press Enter.

4. AutoCAD then wants to know where you want the center of the polar array. We want to select the center of the large circle. Therefore, type the **cen** Osnap option and press the spacebar so that AutoCAD can precisely find the center.

5. Move the target cursor to the rim of the larger circle, well away from the small circle and the tangent lines, and press the pick button.

6. Next, AutoCAD needs to know the number of items, including the original, in the new array. Type the value **6** and press Enter.

7. At the **Angle to fill (+=ccw,-=cw)<360>:** prompt, press enter to accept the default value of 360 degrees. AutoCAD will now draw the copies equally spaced around the circle. The prompt you just saw, however, allows you to select less than a full circle by specifying the angle and the direction.

8. Press Enter again to accept rotation during copying. There will now be six small circles equally spaced around the larger circle, as shown in Figure 7.8.

In the next section, you will see how Array can be used to decorate your drawing by adding interesting detail.

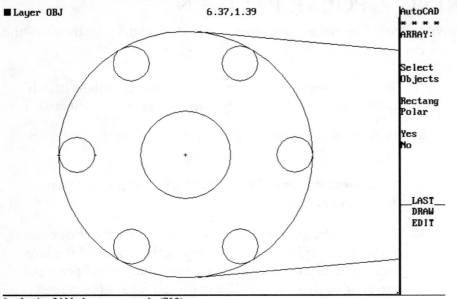

AutoCAD
* * * *
ARRAY:

Select
Objects

Rectang
Polar

Yes
No

___LAST___
DRAW
EDIT

FIGURE 7.8:

Six small circles produced by the Array command

```
Angle to fill (+=ccw, -=cw) <360>:
Rotate objects as they are copied? <Y>
Command:
```

Drawing an Arc

In the remainder of this chapter, you will decorate the right circle with a five-pointed star. You will start with a line and an arc, form a wedge, then use Array to make the star. But first, you want to see an enlarged view of the right circle. You can do that with the Dynamic option of the Zoom command.

1. Give the **z** (for Zoom) command with the **d** (for Dynamic Zoom) option.

The screen changes to show the entire drawing area that you previously defined as shown in Figure 7.9. The two connected circles are shown along with two windows, one dotted and one solid. The dotted window marks the limits of the previous view, this time the left circle. The other window—with the X in the middle—moves with your mouse. It will define the next view.

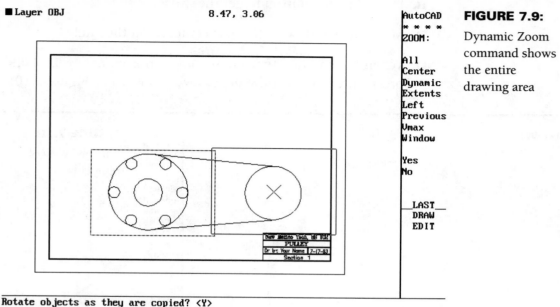

```
Rotate objects as they are copied? <Y>
Command: z ZOOM
All/Center/Dynamic/Extents/Left/Previous/Vmax/Window/<Scale(X/XP)>: d
```

2. Move your mouse and watch the window with the X move accordingly. When there is an X in the cursor window, it moves without changing size.

3. Press the pick button and notice that now there is a right-pointing arrow in the cursor window.

4. Move the mouse and see that the cursor window changes size when there is a right-pointing arrow. Only the left edge is fixed.

5. Press the pick button to get the X back in the cursor box.

6. Move the selection window so the X is centered on the right circle.

7. If necessary, press the pick button so you can change the window size. You want a window that just surrounds the right circle.

8. Press the pick button to get the X back.

9. Move the window so the X is centered on the circle.

10. When the coordinate readout shows approximately **8.5,3.0**, press Enter to select the next view, as shown in Figure 7.10.

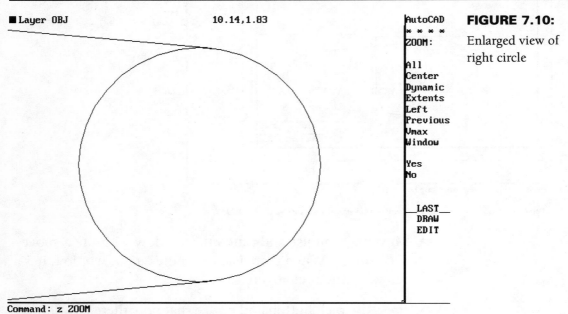

FIGURE 7.10:

Enlarged view of right circle

```
Command: z ZOOM
All/Center/Dynamic/Extents/Left/Previous/Vmax/Window/<Scale(X/XP)>: d
Command:
```

Before we begin the arc, let's draw a *temporary construction line*. You'll use this line as an aid in drawing the arc. We will remove it later.

1. Give the **L** (for Line) command.

2. Give the **cen** Osnap option and press the spacebar.

3. Move the target box to the right edge of the circle, well away from the tangent lines, near location **9.45,3.0**, and press the pick button to start a line at the center of the circle. The other end is fastened to the cursor.

4. Move the cursor upward a little so that you can distinguish the new line from the cursor.

5. Type the relative length **@0.7,0** (no spaces) and press the space bar. This draws a line 0.7 units long.

6. Press the second mouse button to complete the Line command.

Now let's draw the first part of the arc using the Arc command. You will establish three parts of the arc by choosing from six options. We will select the center, the starting point, and the included angle.

1. Give the **Arc** command (or the abbreviation **a**).

2. Type the **c** (for center point) Arc option (*do not* type cen, which is an Osnap option) and press Enter to designate the center of the arc first.

3. Now type the **cen** Osnap option and press Enter. (Alternatively, you could have used the Endp option and picked the left end of the construction line.)

4. Move the target box to the right edge of the circle and press the pick button. This causes the center of the arc to coincide with the center of the circle.

5. Give the **endp** Osnap option and press Enter so you can lock onto the right end of your construction line.

6. Move the target box to the right end of the construction line and press the pick button.

7. Check the status line to make sure the Ortho mode is off.

8. Move the cursor upward a little and watch the arc begin to grow.

9. Type **a** (for Angle) and press Enter so you can enter the angle size from the keyboard.

10. Type **30** (for 30 degrees, the angle of the arc), and press Enter. The arc is now in place. The circle with the construction line and the arc is shown in Figure 7.11.

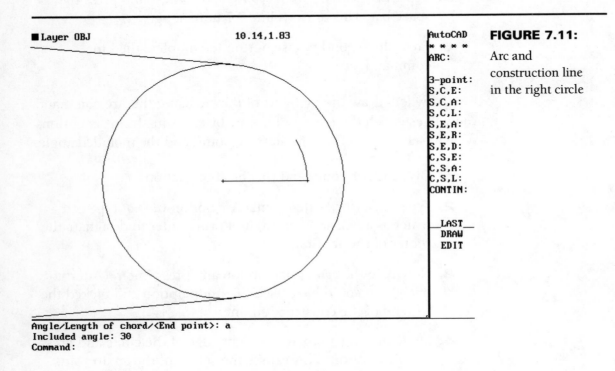

FIGURE 7.11:

Arc and construction line in the right circle

Drawing a Wedge

1. Give the **L** (for Line) command.

2. Type the **endp** Osnap option and press the spacebar.

3. Move the target cursor to the upper end of the arc, near **9.05,3.36**, and press the pick button.

4. Move the cursor to see that one end of the new line is fastened to the upper part of the arc.

5. Give the Osnap option **mid** (for Midpoint) and press Enter to lock onto the middle of a line.

6. Move the cursor to the middle of the construction line near location **0.5<221**, as shown in Figure 7.12, and press the pick button.

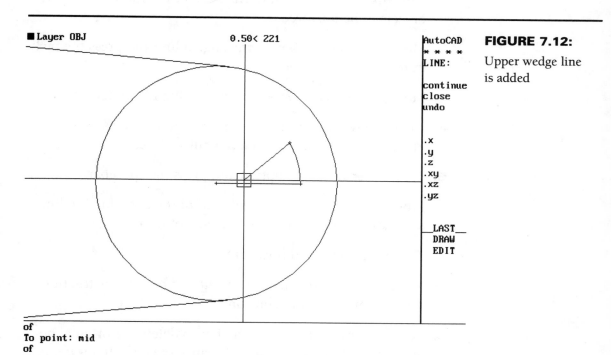

■Layer OBJ   0.50< 221

FIGURE 7.12:

Upper wedge line is added

of
To point: mid
of

7. Click the second mouse button or press Enter to complete the Line command. You now have the upper edge of the wedge.

REPLICATING OBJECTS WITH THE MIRROR COMMAND

We are going to draw the lower edge of the wedge with the Mirror command. This command creates a mirror image of the object being copied by reversing the direction of objects with respect to a mirror or reflection line. To specify the reflection line, you designate two points on that line. We will use the temporary construction line as the mirror line.

1. Give the **Mirror** command. AutoCAD asks you to select the objects to be mirrored.

2. Move the selection box to the angled line and press the pick button.

3. Move to the arc and select it by pressing the pick button.

4. Click the second mouse button to complete the selection. You are next asked to define the mirror line.

5. Type the **endp** Osnap option and press the spacebar.

6. Move the target box to the left end of the construction line at location **8.5,3.0** and press the pick button.

7. Type **endp** again and press Enter.

8. Move the target box near the right end of the construction line and press the pick button.

9. AutoCAD wants to know whether to delete the original objects that are being mirrored. Because the default answer is *no*, just click the second mouse button or press Enter. The angled line and the arc are now mirrored below the construction line.

Erasing the Construction Line

To erase the temporary construction line follow these steps.

1. Type **erase** or **e** and press the spacebar.

2. Move the selection box to location **8.6, 3.0** and press the pick button.

3. Press the second mouse button to erase the construction line.

Replacing Two Arcs with One

On your screen, the arcs you just created with the Mirror command look like a single arc. They are, however, two separate arcs placed end-to-end. This unnecessarily complicates the database. Therefore, before replicating the wedge, we will replace the two arcs with a single one.

1. Give the **e** (for Erase) command and press the spacebar.

2. Move the selection box over the upper part of the arc and press the pick button. Since there are two end-to-end arcs, notice that only the upper end becomes spotty.

3. Move the selection box over the lower part of the arc and press the pick button. Now both parts of the arc are spotty.

4. Press the second mouse button to erase the two arcs.

5. Type **a** (for Arc) and press the spacebar.

6. Type the Arc option **c** (for Center) and press the spacebar, so you can give the center first.

7. Type the Osnap option **cen** (for Center) and press the spacebar.

8. Move the selection box to the right edge of the circle and press the pick button.

9. Type the **endp** Osnap option and press the spacebar.

10. Move the target box to the lower-right end of the lower line, near location **9.05,2.66**, and press the pick button.

11. Move the cursor upward to see the arc grow.

12. Type **endp** again and press the spacebar.

13. Move the target box to the upper-right end of the upper line to coordinate **0.70<29**. Press the pick button to complete the arc. Notice that you chose the arc points in a counterclockwise order.

14. Give the **List** command and select the new arc to see that it is now one entity.

15. Press **F1** to return to the drawing screen.

The Default W and C Options for Window Selection

As you have seen, you can select items for commands such as Erase, Move, and Rotate by using one of two windows—regular (with the W option) or crossing (with the C option).

By using AutoCAD's defaults, however, it is possible to select either a crossing or regular window *without* having to use the C or W option. To get a regular window, for example, simply click your mouse for the first pick point of the window and move to the *right* to pick the second corner. The regular window is automatically selected. On the other hand, to automatically get a crossing window, move to the *left* to pick the second corner. As an added check, the regular window is drawn with a continuous line, while the crossing window is drawn with a dashed line. If you find that trying to remember which way to move to activate the default is a bother, you can still give the W or C options as before.

Replicating the Wedge with the Array Command

Now, let's use the Array command to replicate the wedge around the circle, creating a total of five wedges.

1. Give the **Array** command and press the spacebar.

2. To enclose the wedge with a selection window, move the cursor to the lower-left corner of the wedge to location **8.7,2.6** and press the pick button. Remember, the W option is unnecessary if the second point is to the right of the first.

3. Move the cursor to the upper-right corner of the wedge to location **9.3,3.4**.

4. When the window encloses the wedge as shown in Figure 7.13, press the pick button.

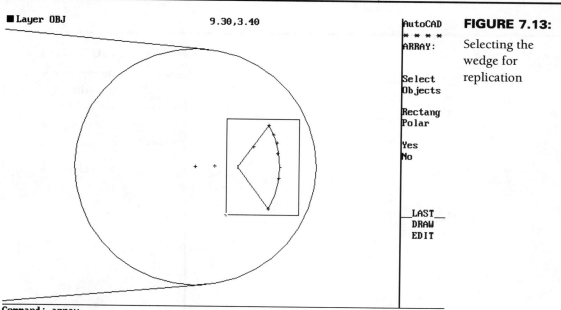

FIGURE 7.13:

Selecting the wedge for replication

5. Press the second mouse button to complete the selection step.

6. Type **p** (for Polar array) and press Enter. Notice that P is the default this time since you chose it last time.

7. At the **Center point of array:** prompt, type the Osnap option **cen** (for Center) and press Enter.

8. Move the target box to the edge of the large circle and press the pick button.

9. At the **Number of items:** prompt, type the value **5** and press Enter to specify a total of five copies of the wedge.

10. As before, press Enter twice more to accept defaults (shown in angle brackets) for the **Angle to fill (+=ccw,-=cw)<360>:** and **Rotate objects as they are copied? <Y>** prompts. You will now have a five-pointed star on your circle as shown in Figure 7.14.

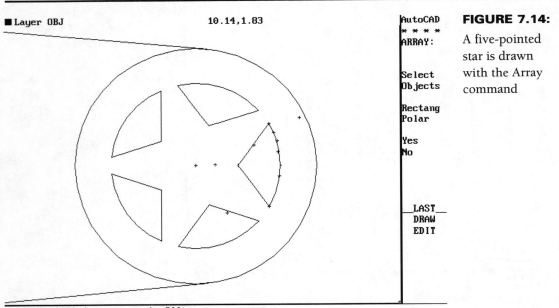

■ Layer OBJ   10.14,1.83

AutoCAD
* * * *
ARRAY:

Select
Objects

Rectang
Polar

Yes
No

LAST
DRAW
EDIT

```
Angle to fill (+=ccw, -=cw) <360>:
Rotate objects as they are copied? <Y>
Command:
```

FIGURE 7.14:

A five-pointed star is drawn with the Array command

11. Give the **z** (for Zoom) command with the **a** (for All) option. The screen changes to show the entire drawing.

12. Plot your drawing as you did previously. If you are a student, turn in the drawing to the instructor.

13. Give the **End** command and press Enter to save the drawing and leave AutoCAD.

8 CHAPTER

FEATURING

Drawing wide lines

Drawing a square

Separating a square with Explode

Rounding corners with Fillet

Drawing hidden lines

▼

Drawing Three Views of a Bracket

n previous chapters, you learned how to draw lines and circles. You saw how to use AutoCAD's grid-snap and object-snap features to position objects precisely in your drawing. You also learned how to select portions of your drawing and how to make changes to them.

In this chapter, you will apply your knowledge to creating a three-view drawing of the bracket shown in Figure 8.1. The three views show the front, top, and right side of an object. The top view is aligned above the front view and the right view is placed on the right side of the front view. You will draw the object lines and hidden lines

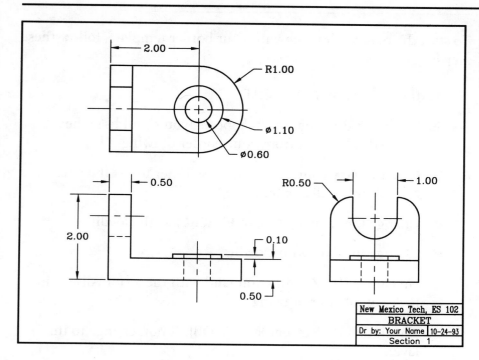

New Mexico Tech, ES 102
BRACKET
Dr by: Your Name | 10-24-93
Section 1

FIGURE 8.1:

Front, right, and top views of the bracket

in this chapter. In Chapter 10, you will add the center lines and dimensions. Refer to Figure 8.1 to help you visualize the three views of the bracket as you draw them.

The bracket will be drawn with continuous lines for the boundaries on the OBJ layer and dashed lines for the hidden parts drawn on the HID layer. New AutoCAD commands used in this chapter are:

- Polygon (to draw a square polyline)

- Explode (to separate the lines of a polyline)

- Donut (to draw a circle)

- Fillet (to round corners)

- Ltscale (to change the scale of dashed lines)

Starting the Bracket Drawing with the Border Template

To start the bracket drawing with your border template, follow these steps:

1. If necessary, start AutoCAD.

2. When the drawing screen appears, you should see the zoomed title block from your border drawing.

3. Give the **New** command and press Enter to get the Create New Drawing dialog box.

4. Change the drawing title to **BRACKET** with Ddedit.

5. Change the date with Ddedit.

6. Give the **z** (for Zoom) command with the **a** (for All) option to see all of your drawing.

7. Check that the current layer is OBJ. If not, change to this layer.

8. If necessary, turn on the grid.

Loading the Hidden and Center Line Types

Engineering drawings use lines of varying thickness and style for different purposes. So far, the lines you have drawn all represent visible edges—edges we could see if we looked at the object we are drawing. Visible edges are represented by wide, continuous lines called *object lines*. There are also a great number of other line types used in engineering drawings. For example, thin dashed lines (called *hidden lines*) represent "hidden edges"—edges that are not visible because they are on the back side or in the middle of an object. Lines made of alternating dashes and dots indicate the center lines of circles and arcs; thick lines with an alternating dash and two dots pattern signify a section plane. AutoCAD can produce all of these line types easily, as well as set line widths.

In this chapter, you will be drawing hidden lines that will represent the circular openings cut into the bracket. The hidden-line type is built into AutoCAD and you can specify that all lines drawn on a particular layer be shown with a particular line type.

In previous chapters, you created several layers—BOR for the border, TBLOCK for the title block, and OBJ for object lines. Now you will create two more layers: HID for hidden lines, and CEN for center lines (we'll be drawing center lines in Chapter 10). Then you will change to the appropriate line type for these layers. However, before you can draw hidden and center lines, you must load the corresponding line types into your drawing. Let's do that now.

1. Give the **Linetype** command and press Enter. AutoCAD responds with the **?/Create/Load/Set:** prompt.

2. Type **L** (for Load) and press Enter.

3. Type **hidden,center** (no spaces) and press Enter.

4. Press Enter again to load the hidden and center line types from the default file.

5. Press Enter a third time to complete the command.

CREATING THE HIDDEN AND CENTER LAYERS

Now that the hidden and center line types are loaded, you can create the corresponding layers and set their line types accordingly.

1. Move the cursor to the top line of the screen to get the menu bar with its menu titles.

2. Move the cursor to highlight the menu title Settings and press the pick button to pull down the Settings menu.

3. Highlight the menu item Layer Control and press the pick button.

4. When the Layer Control dialog box appears, check that the existing layers 0, BOR, OBJ, and TBLOCK are present.

5. Type the new layer names **hid,cen** (no spaces) but *don't* press Enter.

6. Move the cursor to the New box and press the pick button.

7. Check that the names HID and CEN now appear in the table.

SETTING THE LINE TYPE FOR THE HIDDEN AND CENTER LAYERS

1. Check that the Layer dialog box is still present.

2. Move the cursor to the row containing the new layer named HID and press the pick button. The row becomes highlighted.

3. Pick the Set Ltype box get the Select Linetype dialog box as shown in Figure 8.2.

4. Move the cursor to the pattern for hidden lines and press the pick button.

5. Make sure the word Hidden appears in the Linetype box at the bottom of the dialog box.

6. Pick the OK box of the Select Linetype dialog box.

7. Pick the row for layer HID so it is no longer highlighted.

8. Move the cursor to the row containing the new layer named CEN and press the pick button. The row becomes highlighted.

9. Pick the Set Ltype box get the Select Linetype dialog box.

10. Move the cursor to the pattern for center lines and press the pick button.

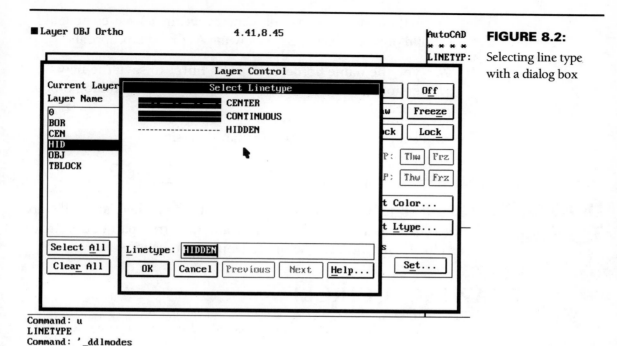

11. Check that the word Center appears in the Linetype box at the bottom of the dialog box.

12. Pick the OK box of the Select Linetype dialog box.

13. Check that the line types for layers HID and CEN are correct.

14. Move the cursor to the OK box and press the pick button to close the Layer Control dialog box.

UPDATING YOUR BORDER DRAWING TEMPLATE

1. Check that Ortho, Snap, and Grid modes are off.

2. Now that you have established the new layers HID and CEN, and set their line types, update your Border drawing by saving the current version. Then you will not have to set up these layers for later drawings. Give the **Saveas** command and press Enter. The Save Drawing As dialog box appears.

3. Type the name **border** and press Enter to save the new version of the border. An AutoCAD Message dialog box appears.

4. Pick the Yes box to save the latest version.

Drawing the Top View

You will begin by drawing the top view of the bracket. You will start with a circle, add the perimeter lines, and then trim part of the circle. The circles will be drawn with the Donut command.

DRAWING A CIRCLE

1. Check that the current layer is OBJ. If it is not, change to OBJ.

2. Give the **c** (for Circle) command.

3. Type the location of the circle center as **4.5,6** (no spaces) and press Enter.

4. Type the number **1** and press the spacebar to create a circle with a radius of 1.

DRAWING THE REST OF THE PERIMETER

Complete the perimeter of the top view by following these steps:

1. Give the **L** (for Line) command.

2. Type the **qua** Osnap option and press the spacebar.

3. Move the target box to the top of the circle and press the pick button.

4. To draw the top edge, type the relative polar distance **@2<180** (no spaces) and press the spacebar to draw the first line.

5. The line for the left edge is next. It goes straight down from the left end of the previous line. Instead of giving the length of this line, you will specify that the bottom is even with the bottom of the circle. To do this, give the **.y** filter and press the spacebar. Previously, you used the .X filter to give the X value before the Y value.

6. Type the **qua** Osnap option and press the spacebar.

7. Move the target cursor to the bottom of the circle and press the pick button. Now the bottom end of the new line will have the same Y value as the bottom of the circle. Now you must give the X value.

The X value of the bottom end of the line is the same as the top. Therefore, you could give the endp Osnap option and pick the left end of the top line. Because, however, the line is to be vertical, it is easier to turn on Ortho mode and move the cursor so the new line goes straight down. Your Y value is not important because you have already specified it with .Y.

8. Turn on Ortho mode.

9. Press the pick button to draw the second line (the left end of the top view).

10. To draw the bottom line, type **qua** again and press the spacebar.

11. Move the target box to the bottom of the circle and press the pick button to complete the perimeter.

12. Click the second mouse button to complete the Line command.

13. Turn off Ortho mode.

14. Compare your screen to Figure 8.3.

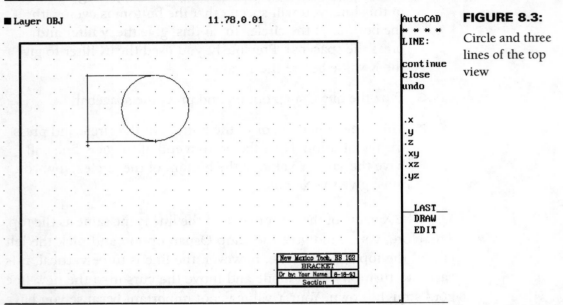

AutoCAD
* * * *
LINE:

continue
close
undo

.x
.y
.z
.xy
.xz
.yz

__LAST__
DRAW
EDIT

New Mexico Tech, ES 102
BRACKET
Dr by: Your Name | 8-18-93
Section 1

FIGURE 8.3:

Circle and three lines of the top view

```
To point: qua of
To point:
Command:  <Ortho off>
```

TRIMMING THE LEFT EDGE OF THE CIRCLE

You now have a full circle—which is more than you need. To trim the left half of the circle, follow these steps:

1. Give the **Trim** command.

2. Move the selection box to the upper horizontal line and press the pick button.

3. Move the selection box to the lower horizontal line and press the pick button.

4. Click the second mouse button to complete the selection step.

5. Move the cursor to the left side of the circle and press the pick button. The left half of the circle is removed.

6. Press the second mouse button to complete the Trim command. You now have a completed perimeter.

DRAWING TWO CONCENTRIC CIRCLES OF THE BOSS

Look at Figure 8.1. The top view shows two concentric circles that correspond to a raised area in the other two views. This raised area is known as a *boss*.

Let's draw the two concentric circles of the boss next. Then you will widen these circles. However, because a circle cannot be widened, while polylines and arcs can, you will draw the circles as arcs. Using the Donut command will make this easy to accomplish.

Normally, with the Donut command you draw two concentric circles that are connected, yet have different diameters. However, we want our two circles to be separate. Therefore, you will need to give the Donut command twice. Each time you will use the same outside and inside diameter. This will draw two semicircular arcs that will appear as a circle. To draw the circles, follow these steps:

1. Give the **Donut** command and press the spacebar.

2. Type **1.1** and press the spacebar for the inside diameter.

3. Type **1.1** and press the spacebar again for the outside diameter.

4. To locate the center, type the **cen** Osnap option and press the spacebar.

5. Move the target cursor to the right edge of the arc and click the left mouse button to draw a polyline circle.

6. Click the second mouse button to complete the Donut command.

7. Click the second mouse button again to restart the Donut command.

8. Repeat the steps above to draw a smaller donut with a **0.6** diameter.

9. Click the second mouse button to complete the Donut command.

COPYING THE VERTICAL LINE

We still need three more lines to finish the top view. The vertical line can be copied from the left edge. Follow these steps:

1. Give the **Copy** command to create the vertical line.

2. Move the selection box over the left edge and press the pick button.

3. Press the second mouse button to complete the selection step.

4. Type the displacement **0.5,0** and press Enter twice to copy the left end line.

5. Turn on the grid.

Because you did not give a second coordinate, the first value is taken as a displacement.

DRAWING THE SHORT HORIZONTAL LINES

We will now use the Pline command to draw the short horizontal lines. Later in this chapter you will widen the narrow object lines to make them as wide as the ones in Figure 8.1. However, at this point, we will draw the short horizontal lines as wide polylines.

1. Give the **PL** command.

2. Move the cursor to the upper-left corner of the top view.

3. Turn on Snap mode and check that the cursor has snapped to the corner.

4. Move down one grid point to location **2.50,6.50** and press the pick button to start the upper horizontal line.

5. Type **w** (for Width) and press the spacebar.

6. Type **0.02** and press Enter twice to set the beginning and ending width of the polyline.

7. Move one grid point to the right and press the pick button. The new line should be noticeably wider than the other lines.

8. Click the second mouse button to complete the Pline command.

9. Click the second mouse button to restart the Pline command.

10. Move down two grid points to location **3.00,5.50** and press the pick button to start the lower horizontal line.

11. Move left one grid point and press the pick button to draw the second horizontal line. Make sure that it also is wide.

12. Click the second mouse button to complete the Pline command.

Drawing the Front View

We will now draw the bracket's L-shaped front view. To make this part of the bracket, you will draw six line segments.

DRAWING THE PERIMETER OF THE FRONT VIEW

1. Turn off Snap mode.

2. Give the **L** (for Line) command.

3. We will start at the upper-left corner of the front view. The left edge of this view must align with the left edge of the top view. Because they both have the same X value, we will use the .X filter. Type **.x** and press the spacebar.

4. Type the **endp** Osnap option and press the spacebar.

5. Move the target cursor to the lower-left corner of the *top* view and press the left mouse button.

6. Move straight down two grid points and turn on Snap mode.

7. When the cursor has locked on the grid point **2.5,4.0**, press the pick button to start a new line.

8. Turn off Snap mode.

9. Type the relative direction **@2<-90** (no spaces) and press Enter to draw the left edge of the front view.

10. We will draw the bottom line next. The right end of this line must align with the right end of the top view, which is the right quadrant of the arc. Therefore, we can use the .X filter here too.

11. Type **.x** and press the spacebar.

12. Type the **qua** Osnap option and press the spacebar.

13. Turn on Ortho mode.

14. Move the selection cursor to the right edge of the large arc in the top view and press the pick button.

15. Move the cursor down so the new bottom line is horizontal and press the pick button. Check that the right end of the bottom line aligns with the right end of the top view.

16. Type the relative direction **@0.5<90** (no spaces) and press Enter to draw the right edge.

17. Type the relative distance **@2.5<180** and press Enter. Also check that the vertical cursor aligns in the top view with the second vertical line you drew.

18. Type **@1.5<90** and press Enter to fix the fifth line segment.

19. Type **c** (for Close) and press Enter to complete the outline of the front view.

20. Turn off Ortho mode.

DRAWING THE BOSS IN THE FRONT VIEW

The .X filter will help with drawing the boss, but you must first enlarge the view of the central region of the drawing.

1. Give the **z** (for Zoom) command.

2. Put the corners at locations **2.3,1.8** and **9.8,7.2**.

3. Give the **PL** command.

4. To align the left edge of the boss with the left edge of the circle in the top view, type **.x** and press the spacebar.

5. Give the Osnap option **qua** and press the spacebar.

6. Move the cursor to the top view and stop at the left edge of the outer circle. The coordinate position is approximately **3.95,6.0**. Press the pick button to locate the X value.

7. Give the **mid** (for Midpoint) Osnap option and press the spacebar.

8. Move down to the top line of the front view and press the pick button. You have specified the X value from the top view and the Y value from the front view. Move the cursor up a little and notice that a line grows from the top line of the front view.

9. Type the relative distance **@0.1<90** (no spaces) and press the spacebar to draw the short vertical line.

10. Type **@1.1<0** (no spaces) and press the spacebar to draw the horizontal part.

11. Type the **per** (for Perpendicular) Osnap option and press the spacebar.

12. Move down a little to the top edge of the view and press the pick button to complete the boss.

13. Press the second mouse button to complete the Line command.

14. Give the **Qsave** command to safeguard your work.

15. Double-check your drawing against Figure 8.4.

Drawing the Right View

In this section, you will draw the right view of the bracket. You will start with a square outline. You will then add semicircular arcs and use the Fillet command to round the upper-left and upper-right corners so that your drawing will finally look like Figure 8.1.

DRAWING THE SQUARE OUTLINE OF THE RIGHT VIEW

Because the gross outline is a two-by-two square, we can start with the AutoCAD Polygon command.

1. Give the **Polygon** command with the **4** (for four-sided) option to create a square.

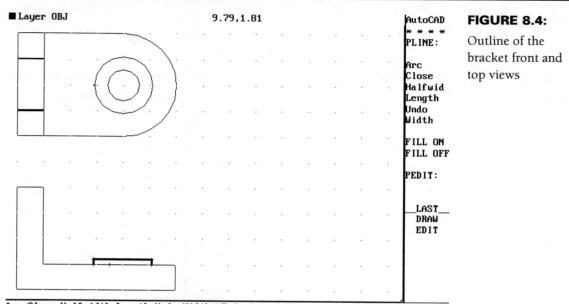

```
■ Layer OBJ                    9.79,1.81                          AutoCAD
                                                                 * * * *
                                                                 PLINE:

                                                                 Arc
                                                                 Close
                                                                 Halfwid
                                                                 Length
                                                                 Undo
                                                                 Width

                                                                 FILL ON
                                                                 FILL OFF

                                                                 PEDIT:


                                                                 _LAST_
                                                                 DRAW
                                                                 EDIT
```

```
Arc/Close/Halfwidth/Length/Undo/Width/<Endpoint of line>:
Command: saveas
Command:
```

2. At the **Edge/<Center of polygon>:** prompt, type the option **e** (for Edge) and press the spacebar.

3. Move the cursor to the lower-right corner of the front view. Then move to the right four grid points.

4. Turn on Snap mode.

5. Lock onto coordinate position **7.50,2.00**. The horizontal line of the cursor aligns with the bottom part of the front view.

6. Be sure that Snap mode is on and press the pick button to fix the first corner of the square. (You can also use the .Y filter to align the next point with the bottom edge of the front view).

7. Move the cursor four grid points to the right to location **9.50,2.00**. Watch the square grow larger as you move the cursor. Press the pick button to draw a square with two-inch sides.

8. Turn off Snap mode.

9. Double-check your drawing against Figure 8.5.

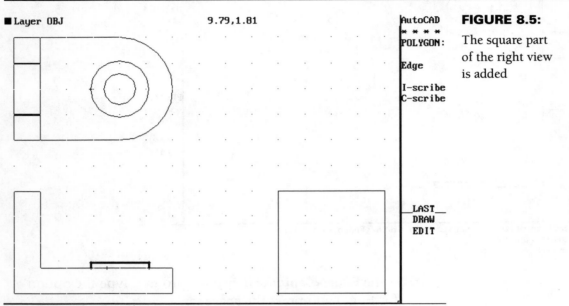

AutoCAD
* * * *
POLYGON:

Edge

I-scribe
C-scribe

LAST
DRAW
EDIT

FIGURE 8.5:
The square part
of the right view
is added

```
Edge/<Center of polygon>: e
First endpoint of edge:  <Snap on> Second endpoint of edge:
Command:  <Snap off>
```

USING THE EXPLODE COMMAND

You have just drawn a square for the outline of the right view. In this section, you will need to remove parts of the square so you can draw three arcs. Unfortunately, since the square is a polyline (one entity rather than four separate lines), you cannot simply erase a part of the square without erasing the whole thing.

First, you will have to separate the square into its constituent parts. The AutoCAD Explode command is used for this purpose. The command name is misleading—the components do not move apart or explode in the usual sense of the word. As a matter of fact, after you give the Explode command, there is no apparent change. Instead,

Explode changes the four lines from one entity, a polyline, to four separate entities, or lines.

Let's see how it works. First, you will check the square with the List command to make sure it is one entity. You will then explode the square and erase one edge. Later, you'll add more parts.

1. Give the **z** (for Zoom) command to enlarge the right view.

2. Put corners at **7.1,1.85** and **9.7,4.3**.

3. Give the **List** command.

4. Move the selection box to any edge of the square and press the pick button. The entire square becomes spotty to show that it is all one entity.

5. Click the second mouse button to see that the square is stored in the database as a closed polyline.

6. Press Enter and **F1** to return to the drawing screen.

7. Give the **Explode** command.

8. Move the selection box to one line of the square and press the pick button.

9. Click the second mouse button. No change is apparent, but you have just exploded the square in the right view. This means that you have converted the polyline into four separate lines.

10. Give the **List** command.

11. Select the bottom line of the square and notice that it is the only one that becomes spotty.

12. Click the second mouse button to see how that line is now stored in the database.

13. Press **F1** to return to the drawing screen.

ADDING THREE LINES TO THE TOP OF THE RIGHT VIEW

To add three lines to the top of the right view, follow these steps:

1. Now that the bottom line of the square is a separate entity, you can copy it. Give the **Copy** command. (In this case, *do not* abbreviate to **c**, which stands for Circle.)

2. Select the bottom line of the square.

3. Complete selection with the second mouse button.

4. Type the displacement **0,0.5** (no spaces) and press Enter twice.

5. Draw the short left line near the top of the front view next, as shown in Figure 8.6. Give the **L** command.

6. Turn on Snap mode.

7. Move to the upper-left corner of the right view. Then move one grid position right to coordinate position **8.00,4.00** and press the pick button.

8. Move down one grid point and press the pick button to establish the line.

9. Click the second mouse button to complete the Line command.

10. Draw the second short line next. Restart the Line command by clicking the second mouse button.

11. Move to the upper-right corner, then move one grid point to the left. When the coordinate location is **9.0,4.0**, press the pick button to start the line.

12. Move down one grid point and press the pick button to draw the line.

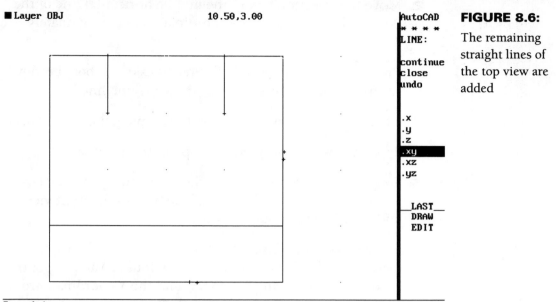

The remaining
straight lines of
the top view are
added

13. Press the second mouse button to complete the Line command.

14. Turn off Snap mode.

15. Compare your drawing to Figure 8.6.

16. Return to the previous view by giving the **z** (for Zoom) command with the **p** (for Previous) option.

DRAWING THE BOSS IN RIGHT VIEW

Because of its circular symmetry, the boss has the same shape in both the front and right view. Therefore, we can copy it from one view to the other.

1. Give the **Copy** command.

2. Move the selection box to the middle horizontal line of the boss in the *front* view. The coordinates are approximately **4.5,2.6**.

3. Press the pick button and all three lines of the boss become spotty because they are part of the same polyline.

4. Click the second mouse button to complete the selection.

5. Type the Osnap option **mid** and press the spacebar.

6. To select the beginning of the displacement, move the target box to the horizontal line of the boss in the front view and press the pick button.

7. Since there is no object at the new position in the right view to use for a snap location, we will use a filter to get the X coordinate from the front view and the Y coordinate from the right view. Type **.y** and press the spacebar.

8. Type the **mid** Osnap option and press the spacebar.

9. To select the Y value of the ending displacement, put the selection cursor on the horizontal line of the boss in the front view and press the pick button. (This is the same point you just used.)

10. To select the X value of the end of the displacement, type the **mid** Osnap option and press the spacebar.

11. Move to the right view, put the target cursor near the middle of the bottom line, and press the pick button. A copy of the boss should now appear in the right view, as shown in Figure 8.7.

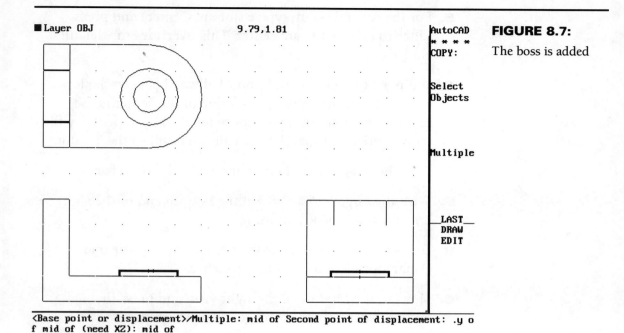

Layer OBJ   9.79,1.81   AutoCAD
                                                * * * *
                                                COPY:

                                                Select
                                                Objects

                                                Multiple

                                                LAST
                                                DRAW
                                                EDIT

```
<Base point or displacement>/Multiple: mid of Second point of displacement: .y o
f mid of (need XZ): mid of
Command:
```

FIGURE 8.7:

The boss is added

ADDING A SEMICIRCULAR ARC TO THE RIGHT VIEW

In this section, you will draw a semicircular arc between the two short lines of the right view.

1. Give the **a** (for Arc) command.

2. Type the **endp** Osnap option and press the spacebar.

3. Move the target cursor to the lower end of the left short line. The coordinate position is **8.0,3.5**.

4. Press the pick button to establish the starting position of the arc.

5. For the second point, type **c** (for arc Center) and press Enter to choose the arc center. This overrides the default choice of end point.

6. You need to pick the grid point halfway between the lower ends of the short lines. The Y value of the center is the same as the first point you chose for the arc. Type the **.y** filter and press the spacebar so you can point to the Y value.

7. Type the **endp** Osnap option and press the spacebar.

8. With the target cursor still at the bottom end of the short line, press the pick button.

9. To specify the X value for the arc center, type the **mid** Osnap option and press the spacebar.

10. Move to the top line of the right view and press the pick button. Notice that the image of an arc appears.

11. Type **endp** and press the spacebar.

12. Move the selection box to the lower end of the other short line. Press the pick button for the third point to complete the semicircular arc.

ADDING TWO ARCS WITH THE FILLET COMMAND

In this section, you will round the upper-left and upper-right corners of the bracket. You could draw arcs in these corners, then trim out the extra lines. Instead, we will use the Fillet command. In drafting, fillets are added to sharp edges to round them. The Fillet command draws arcs between lines or circles or other arcs. Initially, the fillet radius is zero—that is, the command makes a sharp corner. You run the Fillet command once to set the radius, then you use it to smooth the corners.

1. Give the **Fillet** command with the **r** (for Radius) option.

2. Type the value **0.5** and press Enter to set a radius of one-half.

3. Press the spacebar to repeat the Fillet command. You want to select the left and top lines near the upper-left corner.

4. Move the selection cursor to the upper-left corner. Then move down a little. (You can move down as far as one-third the height of the bracket.) Press the pick button to select the top end of the left line.

5. Move the selection cursor back to the upper-left corner. Then move a little to the right. Press the pick button to select the left end of the top line. AutoCAD trims both lines back one-half inch and draws an arc.

6. Press the spacebar to repeat the Fillet command so you can round the upper-right corner.

7. Move the selection cursor to the upper-right corner. Then move down a little. Press the pick button to select the top end of the right line.

8. Move the selection cursor back to the upper-right corner. Then move a little to the left. Press the pick button to select the right end of the top line. AutoCAD trims both lines back one-half inch and draws another arc.

9. The fillet radius will stay at 0.5 for this drawing unless you reset it. Let's reset it to zero. Give the **Fillet** command with the **r** (for Radius) option.

10. Type the value **0** (zero) and press Enter.

11. Give the **e** (for Erase) command.

12. Move the cursor to the top line in the right view and press the pick button.

13. Press the second mouse button to erase the top line.

14. Make sure that your screen looks like Figure 8.8.

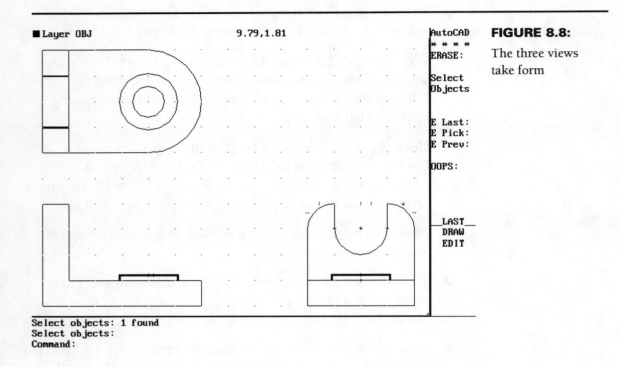

AutoCAD
* * * *
ERASE:

Select
Objects

E Last:
E Pick:
E Prev:

OOPS:

LAST
DRAW
EDIT

Select objects: 1 found
Select objects:
Command:

FIGURE 8.8:

The three views take form

Drawing Hidden Lines

In this section, you will draw hidden lines that must have the dashed lines characteristic of hidden lines. Therefore, you will now have to change to the new layer named HID which you set for hidden lines. If you don't change to the HID layer, all your lines will be continuous instead of broken. We'll change to the HID layer by first using the Change Layer dialog box.

CHANGING LAYERS WITH A DIALOG BOX

To change to the HID layer, follow these steps:

1. Move the cursor to the top line of the screen.

2. When the menu bar appears, move left or right to highlight the Settings menu.

3. Press the pick button to pull down the Settings menu.

4. Move the cursor down the menu to highlight the item Layer Control.

5. Press the pick button to get the Layer Control dialog box.

6. To change the current layer to HID, move the cursor to the word HID and press the pick button to highlight it.

7. Click on the Current box.

8. Move the cursor to the OK box and press the pick button to close the dialog box.

9. Look at the upper-left corner of the screen to see that Layer HID is current.

DRAWING TWO VERTICAL HIDDEN LINES IN THE FRONT VIEW

Now that Layer HID is current, you can draw hidden lines with the Line command and they will automatically be drawn dashed. Let's begin with the lower part of the front view (see Figure 8.1). The two vertical dashed lines correspond to the hole in the top view and therefore must be aligned with it. In other words, they must have the same X coordinate.

1. Give the **L** (for Line) command with the **.x** filter.

2. Type the **qua** Osnap option and press the spacebar.

3. Move the target cursor to the top view, at the left edge of the hole. This is the smaller circle. The coordinate is **4.20,6**. Press the pick button. This defines the X coordinate.

4. Type the **mid** Osnap option and press the spacebar.

5. For the Y coordinate, move straight down to the front view and stop when you reach the top of the boss.

6. Press the pick button to locate the top of the left dashed line.

7. Type the **per** (for Perpendicular) Osnap option and press the spacebar.

8. Move straight down to the bottom line of the front view and press the pick button to draw the line.

9. Press the second mouse button to complete the Line command. Be sure the line is connected to the boss.

10. Press the second mouse button to restart the Line command.

11. Draw the right hidden line in the front view in the same manner. Go back to step 2 and continue through as before, except for step 3. There, you want to select the right edge of the hole, near location **4.8,6.0**.

12. Press the second mouse button to complete the Line command.

DRAWING A HORIZONTAL HIDDEN LINE IN THE FRONT VIEW

The horizontal hidden line in the front view corresponds to the bottom of the slot in the right view. Therefore, you can align this hidden line with the slot bottom using the .Y filter.

1. Press the spacebar to repeat the Line command.

2. Type the **.y** filter and press the spacebar.

3. Type the **qua** Osnap option and press the spacebar.

4. Move the target cursor to the right view, to the bottom of the slot (at coordinate **8.5,3**) and press the pick button. This defines the Y coordinate.

5. Type the **mid** Osnap option and press the spacebar.

6. For the X coordinate, move to the left edge of the front view and press the pick button to locate the left end of the horizontal dashed line.

7. Type the **per** Osnap option and press the spacebar.

8. Move right one grid point to the right vertical edge and press the pick button to draw the horizontal hidden line.

9. Press the second mouse button to complete the Line command.

DRAWING THE VERTICAL HIDDEN LINES IN THE RIGHT VIEW

Because of the circular symmetry, the vertical hidden lines in the right view of the bracket are identical to those in the front view, including the separation. Therefore, you can simply copy the lines from the front view to the right view.

1. Give the **Copy** command.

2. Move the selection cursor to the left vertical hidden line in the front view and press the pick button.

3. Move the selection cursor to the right vertical hidden line in the front view and press the pick button.

4. Click the second mouse button to complete the selection.

5. Type the **mid** Osnap option and press the spacebar.

6. To select the beginning of the displacement, move the selection cursor to the horizontal line of the boss in the front view (coordinate **4.5,2.6**) and press the pick button.

7. Type **mid** again and press the spacebar.

8. Move the selection cursor to the horizontal line of the boss in the right view and press the pick button. A copy of the two hidden lines now appears in the right view.

CHANGING THE SCALE OF THE LINE TYPE

The five lines you have drawn in the previous sections are broken lines, but because they are so short, there is only one opening in each line. You can make hidden lines show more openings by changing the scale of the line type. Let's do that now.

1. Give the **Ltscale** (for Line Type Scale) command. You can see that the default is 1.0000.

2. First, just to see what happens, let's change to a larger scale by giving the value **2.0** and pressing the spacebar.

3. All five hidden lines immediately change. Because you have selected a scale that is too large, the lines now appear to be continuous.

4. Press the spacebar to restart the Ltscale command.

5. Type **0.6** and press the spacebar to change the scale to a smaller value. With this smaller scale, each line now has two openings as shown in Figure 8.1.

Widening the Object Lines of the Bracket

You have drawn the boss and two other lines with wide polylines. In the following section, you will widen the object lines in all three views by converting them to polylines. To do this, you will use the Pedit command. The Pedit command can widen only polylines or lines that can be converted into polylines. Circles, for example, cannot be widened. You drew the two circles in the top view with the Donut command because it creates two connected arcs that are polylines.

CHANGING TO LAYER OBJ

1. Give the **Layer** command with the **s** (for Set) option.

2. Type the layer name **obj** and press Enter.

3. Press Enter again to complete the Layer command. Check that the current layer identified in the upper-left corner of the screen is OBJ.

CHANGING LINES TO POLYLINES

Let's convert the object lines to polylines and widen them. We'll begin with the front view first.

1. Give the **Pedit** command to start the polyline editor.

2. At the **Select polyline:** prompt, move the selection box to the lower line of the front view and press the pick button. The lower line becomes spotty.

3. AutoCAD now informs you that the object you selected is *not* a polyline (you know that already) and asks you whether you want to convert it to a polyline. Press the second mouse button to accept the default value of Y (for Yes). The line you marked is converted to a polyline.

4. Type **w** (for Width) and press Enter.

5. Type the width **0.02** and press Enter. Notice that the bottom line becomes wider to match the width of the boss.

6. Type the **j** (for Join) option and press Enter to combine the perimeter into one polyline. The Join option can do three things at once: convert additional lines to polylines, connect them to the first polyline, and widen them.

7. To select the other five lines of the front perimeter to be converted, move the selection box to the left edge of the front view and press the pick button. This line becomes spotty to show that it has been selected.

8. Continuing clockwise, move to the short top edge and press the pick button.

9. Move to each remaining line of the perimeter and press the pick button.

10. When the remaining five lines of the perimeter are spotted as shown in Figure 8.9, press the second mouse button to complete the selection. All the object lines around the front view become wide, matching the width you gave for the bottom line.

11. Press the second mouse button to complete the Pedit command.

Converting Right-View Object Lines

Using the same procedure as above, we will now convert the object lines of the right view to polylines.

1. Press the second mouse button to restart the Pedit command.

2. Move the selection box to the bottom line of the right view. Press the pick button to select this line.

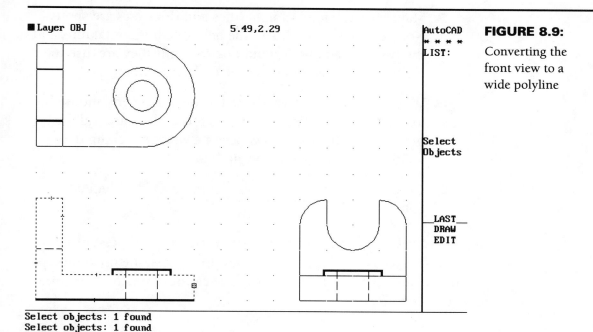

FIGURE 8.9:

Converting the front view to a wide polyline

```
Layer OBJ                    5.49,2.29                          AutoCAD
                                                                * * * *
                                                                LIST:



                                                                Select
                                                                Objects



                                                                LAST
                                                                DRAW
                                                                EDIT

Select objects: 1 found
Select objects: 1 found
Select objects:
```

3. Again, you are informed that the object you have selected is *not* a polyline. Press the second mouse button to accept the default value of Y to convert this line to a polyline.

4. Type **w** (for Width) and press Enter to change the polyline width.

5. As before, give the width **0.02** and press Enter. Notice that the bottom line of the right view becomes wider.

6. Type **j** (for Join) and press Enter to make the other lines around this view become part of the polyline.

7. Put a Crossing window around the upper part of the right view using the corners **9.6,4.3** and **7.3,2.8**. Notice that since the second point is to the left of the first, it is not necessary to use the C option.

8. Make sure the four straight lines and three arcs are spotty. None of the interior lines (the boss, the horizontal line, and the two hidden lines) should be spotty. If they are, use the R (for Remove) option and select them again.

9. When the perimeter is selected, press the second mouse button to complete this step. All the object lines around the perimeter of the right view become wide, matching the width you gave for the bottom line.

10. Click the second mouse button to complete the Pedit command.

Now let's convert the interior horizontal (representing the upper surface of the bracket) to a polyline. This line must be separately changed since a closed polyline cannot *branch* or be joined to another line.

1. Press the second mouse button to restart the Pedit command.

2. Move the selection box under the boss to the horizontal line just above the bottom line of the right view (coordinate **8.5,2.5**). Press the pick button to select this line.

3. AutoCAD informs you that the object you have selected is not a polyline. Press the second mouse button to accept the default value of Y to convert this line to a polyline.

4. Type **w** (for Width) and press Enter to set the polyline width.

5. Give the width **0.02** and press Enter. Note that this line becomes wider.

6. Press Enter to complete the Pedit command.

Converting Object Lines in the Top View

We will now convert the top view to polylines.

1. Click the second mouse button to repeat the Pedit command.

2. Move the selection box to the bottom line of the top view. Press the pick button to select this line.

3. Click the second mouse button or press Enter to convert this line to a polyline.

4. Type **w** (for Width) and press Enter to set the polyline width.

5. Give the width **0.02** and press Enter. Note that the bottom line becomes wider.

6. Type **j** (for Join) and press Enter so you can make the other lines around this view become part of the polyline. There are two lines and an arc of the perimeter to be joined to the bottom edge.

7. Move the selection cursor to the left edge of the top view and press the pick button.

8. Move the selection cursor to the top edge of the top view and press the pick button.

9. Move the selection cursor to the arc at the right edge of the top view and press the pick button.

10. When both straight lines and the arc are selected, click the second mouse button to complete the selection. The other two lines and the arc in the top view become wide, matching the width you gave for the bottom line.

11. Click the second mouse button or press Enter to complete the Pedit command.

Now let's change the interior vertical line to a polyline. Again, you will have to run the polyline editor for this operation.

1. Click the second mouse button to restart the Pedit command.

2. Move the selection box to the vertical line near the left edge **3.0,6.0**. Press the pick button to select this line.

3. Click the second mouse button to convert this line to a polyline.

4. Type **w** (for Width) and press the spacebar.

5. Give the width **0.02** and press Enter. Note that this line becomes wider.

6. Press Enter to complete the Pedit command.

Widening the Circles

You will now increase the line width of the two circles. This would not be possible if you had drawn them with the Circle command instead of the Donut command. Because circles drawn by the Donut command are already polylines, they do not have to be converted.

1. To check that your "circles" are really polylines, give the **List** command.

2. Move the selection cursor to the outer circle and press the pick button.

3. Press the second mouse button.

4. Check the first line on the text screen to see that the object is identified as a polyline.

5. Press Enter and **F1** to return to the drawing screen.

6. Give the **Pedit** command.

7. Move the selection cursor to the edge of the outer circle and press the pick button.

8. Type **w** (for Width) and press Enter.

9. Give the width **0.02** and press Enter. Note that this circle becomes wider.

10. Press the second mouse button to complete the Pedit command.

11. Press the second mouse button to restart the Pedit command.

12. Move the selection cursor to the edge of the inner circle and press the pick button.

13. Type **w** and press Enter.

14. Give the width **0.02** and press Enter. Note that this circle becomes wider.

15. Press Enter to complete the Pedit command.

You have now widened the object lines and arcs of the three views of the bracket. You may have noticed that some of the polylines appear to be wider than others, even though you gave the same width for all polylines. The reason for this is that the line width has a value between two and three scan lines on the video screen. Therefore, these lines are drawn sometimes with two scan lines and sometimes with three. If you use a dot-matrix printer, you may experience a similar problem. However, if you use a regular plotter or a laser printer, you should have no problems.

Plotting the Bracket

Before plotting the drawing, zoom to show the entire drawing.

1. Give the **z** (for Zoom) command with the **a** (for All) option.

2. Save the latest version of the drawing by giving the **Qsave** command and pressing Enter.

3. Check that your drawing looks like Figure 8.10.

4. Plot your Bracket drawing with the L radio button. If you are a student, turn in the drawing to your instructor.

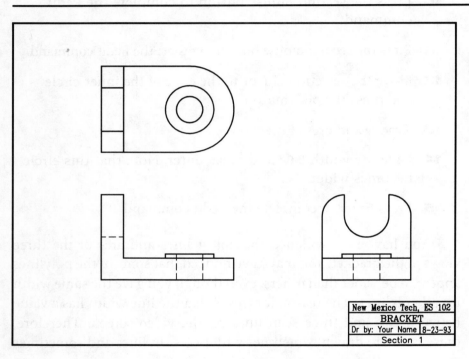

FIGURE 8.10:

Front, right, and top views of the bracket

9 CHAPTER

Drawing the Flange

FEATURING

Transparent Zoom

Saving a View

Drawing a sectional view

Hatching the sectioned opening

Making multiple copies

▼

n the previous chapter, you drew three views of a bracket. In this chapter, you will draw the top and front views of a flange. Only two views are needed for this object because of circular symmetry.

This drawing will also utilize another feature of mechanical drawing—the *sectional view*. With this technique, we draw a view that is obtained by slicing through the object with a *cutting plane*. Therefore, hidden lines are not needed. Part of the object on one side of the cutting plane is removed to expose the cut surface. The sectioned area, representing the material cut by the plane, is surrounded by regular object lines and cross-hatched with thin parallel lines. Because different styles of hatch patterns show different types of material, Auto-CAD provides a wide variety of hatch patterns.

The cutting plane in the view adjacent to the section view is marked with a *cutting-plane line*. This is a wide line formed with long dashes alternated with two short dashes. The cutting-plane line is created with the AutoCAD phantom line type. Arrowheads are placed at the ends of the cutting-plane line to show the direction of the cut-away view.

In this chapter, you will learn the following new commands:

- 'Zoom (to zoom while another command is running)

- View (to save and restore a view)

- Bhatch (to fill an area with a hatching pattern)

Starting the Flange Drawing with the Border Template

As usual, you will start the drawing with the border template.

1. If necessary, start AutoCAD.

2. When the drawing screen appears, you should see the zoomed title block from your border drawing.

3. Type **new** and press Enter to get the Create New Drawing dialog box.

4. Type the drawing name **flange** and press Enter.

5. Change the drawing title to FLANGE with Ddedit.

6. Change the date.

7. Give the **z** (for Zoom) command with the **a** (for All) option to see all of your drawing.

8. Check that the current layer is OBJ. If not, change to this layer now.

9. Turn on the grid.

Drawing the Top View

In this section, you will draw the top view of the flange shown in Figure 9.1. First you will draw three circles—one large, one medium, and one small. The large and medium circles are concentric, while the smaller one is tangent to the rim of the larger one. Parts of the large and small circles will be removed to create a bolt slot. You will then replicate the slot around the rim of the larger circle with the Array command.

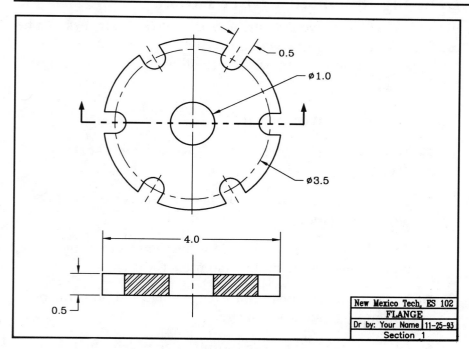

FIGURE 9.1:

Complete view of the flange

DRAWING THE THREE CIRCLES

We will begin by drawing the largest of the three circles.

1. Give the **c** (for Circle) command.

2. Type the coordinate position **4.5, 5.5** (no spaces) and press Enter to establish the circle center. You could also have moved the cursor to this position, turned on Snap mode, and pressed the pick button.

3. Type the option **d** (for Diameter) and press the spacebar to switch to diameter.

4. Type the value **4** and press the spacebar to draw the large circle.

Drawing the Small Center Circle

In Chapter 8, you converted lines and arcs to wide polylines. But because circles cannot be converted to polylines, you had to draw two circles with the Donut command. We will use the Donut command for the small circle.

1. Give the **Donut** command.

2. Type the value **1** and press the spacebar to set the inside diameter.

3. Type the value **1** again and press the spacebar to set the outside diameter.

4. To make the center of the donut the same as the large circle, type the **cen** Osnap option and press the spacebar.

5. Move the target cursor to the large circle and press the pick button to draw the small circle.

6. Click the second mouse button to complete the Donut command.

Drawing the Circle for the Bolt Slot

You will now draw a small circle which you will later convert into the bolt slots as shown in Figure 9.1. But first, let's enlarge the view.

1. Give the **z** (for Zoom) command.

2. To enlarge the view, put the window corners at **2, 3** and **7, 8**. Since the window option is the default, it is not necessary to type the W option.

3. Give the **c** (for Circle) command with the **2p** (for two-point circle) option. Using this method, you will specify the circle size by giving two points on the diameter rather than the default center and radius or diameter.

4. Type the **qua** Osnap option and press the spacebar.

5. Move the target box to the right edge of the large circle to location **6.5, 5.5**. Press the pick button to establish the first point of the circle.

6. Type the relative distance **@0.5<180** (no spaces) and press the spacebar to draw the small circle. Compare your drawing to Figure 9.2.

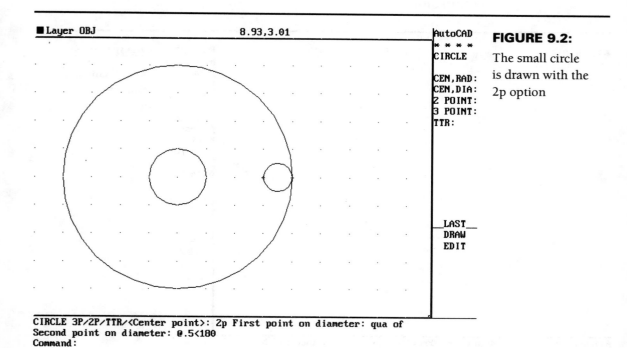

FIGURE 9.2:

The small circle is drawn with the 2p option

CONVERTING A CIRCLE TO AN ARC

In this section, you will draw parallel lines tangent to the small circle. You will trim parts of the small and large circles to create a notch. Finally, you will remove most of the large circle. But first, let's enlarge the view a second time.

1. Give the **z** (for Zoom) command.

2. Put the window corners at **5.8,5.1** and **6.7,5.9**.

The doubly enlarged small circle shows flat sides as in Figure 9.3. As you remember, AutoCAD draws circles with straight lines and, to save time, uses only the minimum number to make the circles look reasonably round. However, when plotting, AutoCAD always uses enough lines to make your circles look completely round. If you want to make this circle look round now, give the **regen** (for Regenerate) command.

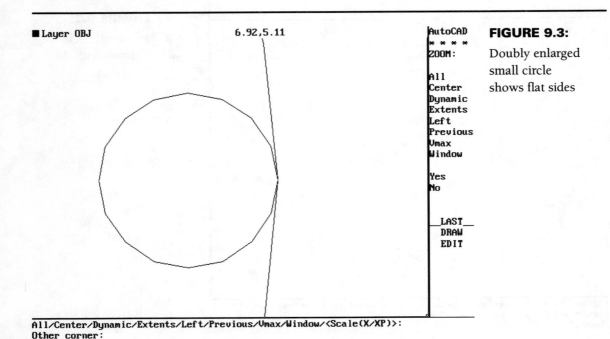

■ Layer OBJ   6.92,5.11

AutoCAD
* * * *
ZOOM:

All
Center
Dynamic
Extents
Left
Previous
Vmax
Window

Yes
No

LAST
DRAW
EDIT

FIGURE 9.3:

Doubly enlarged small circle shows flat sides

All/Center/Dynamic/Extents/Left/Previous/Vmax/Window/<Scale(X/XP)>:
Other corner:
Command:

Connecting Two Circles

First you will add two short horizontal lines and then convert the small circle to an arc.

1. Give the **L** (for Line) command.

2. Type the **qua** Osnap option and press the spacebar.

3. Move the target cursor near the top edge of the small circle and press the pick button.

4. If necessary, turn on Ortho mode.

5. Move the cursor to the right, stopping short of the large circle.

6. Press the pick button to establish the right end of this line.

7. Click the second mouse button to complete the Line command.

8. Click the second mouse button again to restart the Line command.

9. Type the **qua** Osnap option again and press the spacebar.

10. Move the cursor to the bottom edge of the small circle and press the pick button.

11. Move the cursor to the right, stopping short of the large circle. Press the pick button to establish the right end of the second line.

12. Press the second mouse button to complete the Line command. Your screen should look like Figure 9.4.

13. Turn off Ortho mode.

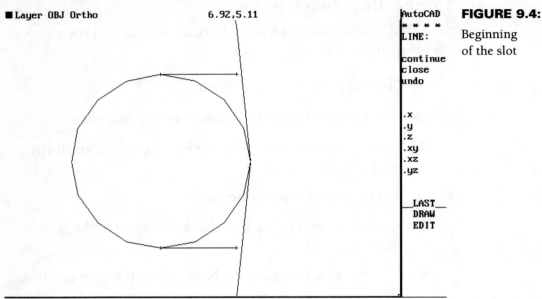

```
AutoCAD
* * * *
LINE:

continue
close
undo


.x
.y
.z
.xy
.xz
.yz


__LAST__
 DRAW
 EDIT
```

```
To point:
To point:
Command:
```

FIGURE 9.4:

Beginning
of the slot

Extending Lines with the Extend Command

In this section you will extend the two short lines until they meet the
large circle, making a precise connection. If you tried to make this connection manually, it would not be accurate.

1. Give the **Extend** command.

2. Move the selection box to the edge of the large circle, well
   away from the small circle, and press the pick button.
   The large circle becomes spotty, showing that it is marked
   as an extension boundary.

3. Click the second mouse button to complete selection of the
   extension boundary.

4. Move the selection box to the right end of the short line at the top of the small circle and press the pick button. The upper line extends until it connects to the large circle.

5. Move the selection box to the right end of the short line at the bottom of the small circle and press the pick button. The lower line extends until it connects to the large circle.

6. Click the second mouse button to complete the Extend command.

Opening the Slot by Trimming the Circles

In this section, you will trim a part of the small and large circles to make a bolt slot.

1. Give the **Trim** command.

2. Move the selection box to the upper line that connects the small circle to the large circle. Press the pick button to mark this line as a trim boundary.

3. Move the selection box to the lower line that connects the small circle to the large circle. Press the pick button to mark this line as a trim boundary.

4. Click the second mouse button to complete the selection of the trim boundary. Now you must select the lines to be trimmed.

5. Move the target box near the right edge of the small circle, well away from the large circle. Press the pick button to remove the right half of the circle.

6. Move the target box to the right edge of the large circle and position it between the two short lines. Press the pick button to remove a small part of the large circle.

7. Click the second mouse button to complete the Trim command. The opening now looks like a bolt slot.

8. Compare your drawing to Figure 9.5.

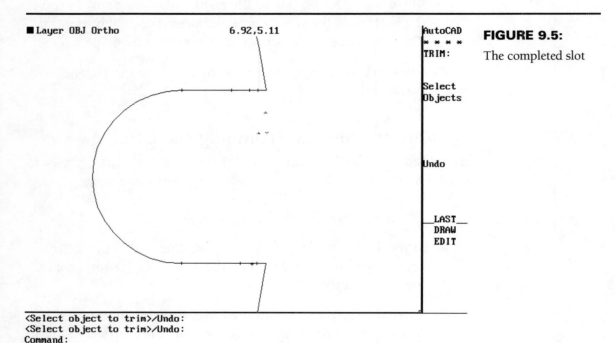

■ Layer OBJ Ortho   6.92,5.11

AutoCAD
* * * *
TRIM:

Select
Objects

Undo

LAST
DRAW
EDIT

<Select object to trim>/Undo:
<Select object to trim>/Undo:
Command:

FIGURE 9.5:

The completed slot

REPLICATING THE CIRCLE OPENING

In the following sections, you will replicate the bolt slot to create five copies. We will remove all but one-sixth of the large circle. Then we will replicate the remaining part with the Array command and the polar option.

Saving the Current View

Before we go on, let's use the View command to save the current view (the current zoom ration and position). You will then be able to return to the saved view anytime you want.

1. Give the **View** command with the **s** (for Save) option.

2. Type the view name **slot** and press the spacebar.

Drawing a Temporary Construction Line

Drawing a temporary construction line from the center of the large circle to the diameter will make our task easier.

1. Give the **z** (for Zoom) command with the **p** (for Previous) option. This returns you to the previous view.

2. Give the **L** (for Line) command and press the spacebar.

3. Type the **cen** (for Center) Osnap option and press Enter.

4. Move the target box to the edge of the large circle and press the pick button to start a construction line from the center of the large circle.

5. It will be easier to locate the other end of the line if you return to the previous view (which you can do by starting the command with an apostrophe). This is called a *transparent* command. Type the command **'view** (don't forget the apostrophe) and press the spacebar.

6. Type **r** (for Restore) and press Enter.

7. Type the name **slot** and press Enter to return to the previous view.

8. Now you can continue with the Line command. Type the **endp** Osnap option and press the spacebar so you can connect the line to the lower-right opening of the slot.

9. Move the target cursor to the intersection of the large circle and the lower short line that extends from the small circle as shown in Figure 9.6. The coordinate is approximately **2.0<353**.

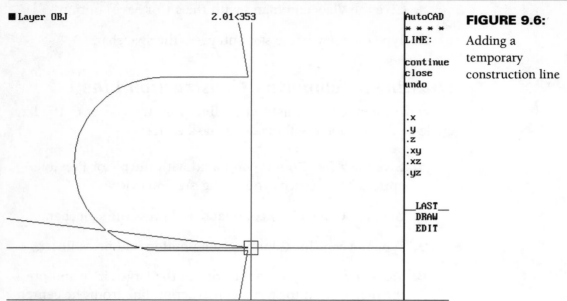

AutoCAD
* * * *
LINE:

continue
close
undo

.x
.y
.z
.xy
.xz
.yz

LAST
DRAW
EDIT

FIGURE 9.6:

Adding a temporary construction line

```
>> View name to restore: slot
Resuming LINE command.
To point: endp of
```

10. Press the pick button to create a temporary construction line. Be sure that the right end of the line connects to the right end of the lower short line from the small circle.

11. Click the second mouse button or press Enter to complete the Line command.

12. Give the **z** (for Zoom) command with the **p** (for Previous) option to return to the complete view of the large circle.

Rotating the Temporary Construction Line

We now need to trim away all but 60 degrees of the large circle (which is now actually an arc). To do this, you will rotate the construction line by 60 degrees. You then will be able to use the rotated construction line as a trim boundary.

1. Give the **Rotate** command.

2. Move the selection box to the new construction line and press the pick button. The line becomes spotty. (You can also type **L** for Last item drawn.)

3. Click the second mouse button to complete the selection.

4. The **Base point:** prompt asks for the center of rotation. Type the **cen** (for Center) Osnap option and press the spacebar.

5. Move the selection box to the edge of either circle and press the pick button. This designates the center of the circles as the center of the rotation.

6. Type the angle **60** and press Enter to rotate the construction line 60 degrees.

Trimming the Circle

Now we are ready to remove most of the large circle.

1. Give the **Trim** command.

2. Move the target box to the new construction line and press the pick button (or type **L** for Last).

3. Move the target box to the lower short line connecting the small circle to the large circle. The coordinate is **6.35,5.25**. Press the pick button.

4. Click the second mouse button to complete boundary-selection.

5. Move the cursor to the left edge of the large circle. Press the pick button to erase most of the large circle.

6. Click the second mouse button again to complete the Trim command.

Erasing the Temporary Construction Line

Now that we don't need it anymore, we will erase the temporary construction line.

■ Give the **e** (for Erase) command and remove the construction line. Your screen should look like Figure 9.7.

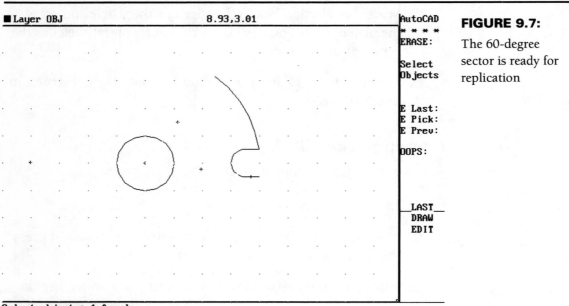

FIGURE 9.7:

The 60-degree sector is ready for replication

```
Select objects: 1 found
Select objects:
Command:
```

Replicating the 60-Degree Sector

The next step is to replicate the bolt hole around the flange. We will choose four items—the remaining 60° arc of the large circle, the left half of the small circle, and the two short horizontal connecting lines. You could select each item individually. However, it's easier to select them with a window.

1. Give the **Array** command.

2. Put the corners of your window at **5.4,7.3** and **6.7, 5.0**.

3. Press the second mouse button to complete the selection.

4. Type **p** (for Polar array) and press Enter.

5. At the **Center point of array:** prompt, type the **cen** Osnap option and press the spacebar.

6. Move the target cursor to the arc of the large circle and press the pick button. This will replicate the arc around the center of the large circle.

7. For the number of items to create, answer **6** and press Enter.

8. Press Enter twice to accept the defaults of 360° rotation and rotation during copying.

You now have a full circle with six bolt holes as shown in Figure 9.8. Before moving on to the next section, save a copy of your

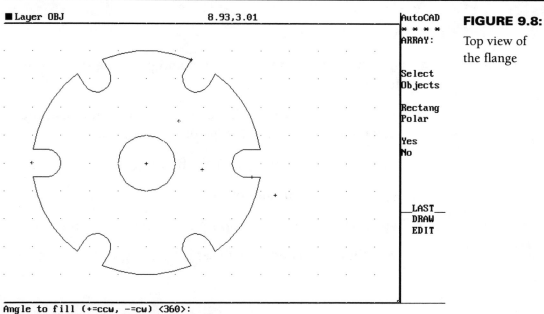

```
■ Layer OBJ                    8.93,3.01              AutoCAD
                                                      * * * *
                                                      ARRAY:

                                                      Select
                                                      Objects

                                                      Rectang
                                                      Polar

                                                      Yes
                                                      No



                                                      __LAST__
                                                        DRAW
                                                        EDIT

Angle to fill (+=ccw, -=cw) <360>:
Rotate objects as they are copied? <Y>
Command:
```

FIGURE 9.8:

Top view of the flange

current work to disk. Follow these steps:

1. Give the **z** (for Zoom) command with the **a** (for All) option.

2. Give the **Qsave** command and press Enter to accept the current file name of FLANGE.

Drawing the Front View

Let's draw the front view next. Since this will be a sectional view, there will be interior lines representing the center hole and the slots. There also will be cross-hatching for the part of the diameter that is cut by the section plane.

OUTLINING THE FRONT VIEW

In this section, you will draw the object lines of the front view as polylines so they can be the correct width.

1. Turn on Ortho mode.

2. Turn on Snap mode.

3. Give the **PL** (for Pline) command and press the spacebar to start a polyline.

4. Move to location **2.5,1.5**. Check that the vertical line of the cursor aligns with the left edge of the top view.

5. Press the pick button to start the first line.

6. Type **w** (for Width) and press Enter.

7. Type **0.02** and press Enter to set the beginning width.

8. Press Enter a second time to set the ending width to the beginning width.

9. Move the cursor right until the vertical cursor aligns with the right edge of the top view. The coordinate readout should show **4.00<0**. Press the pick button to establish the first line.

10. Move upward one grid point and press the pick button. Notice that the first line is wider than a regular line.

11. Move left until the vertical cursor aligns with the starting point and press the pick button.

12. Type **c** (for Close) and press Enter to complete the outline.

13. Turn off Snap mode.

14. Turn off Ortho mode.

ADDING THE INTERIOR LINES

You now need to add four interior lines, which will represent the limits of the cut surfaces. These lines correspond to the left and right edges of the small arcs and the center hole in the top view.

Drawing the First Interior Line

To draw the first interior line, follow these steps:

1. Press the spacebar to repeat the Pline command.

2. Type the **.x** filter and press the spacebar.

3. Type the **qua** Osnap option and press the spacebar.

4. Move the cursor to the center of the top view. Then move left to the right edge of the left slot. The coordinate readout shows approximately **3.0,5.5**.

5. Press the pick button to give the X coordinate.

6. Type the **mid** Osnap option and press the spacebar.

7. Move the cursor down to the middle of the upper line of the front view. When the coordinate readout shows approximately **4.5,2.0**, press the pick button to start the pline.

8. Type the **per** (for Perpendicular) Osnap option and press the spacebar.

9. Move down to the lower line of the front view and press the pick button to complete the polyline.

10. Press the second mouse button to complete the Pline command.

Drawing the Remaining Interior Lines

You can draw the remaining three interior lines with the Copy command and the Multiple option.

1. Because you will need the Qua Osnap option four times in this section, turn it on by giving the **Osnap** command and pressing the spacebar.

2. Type **qua** and press the spacebar.

3. Give the **Copy** command with the **L** (for Last) option. The line you just drew becomes spotty.

4. Press Enter to complete the selection step.

5. Type **m** (for Multiple) and press the spacebar. This allows you to make more than one copy easily.

6. Check that the cursor has a target box in addition to the crossed lines. This indicates that an Osnap mode is on.

7. Because the four interior lines represent the edges of the arcs and the circle, we will use the corresponding edges in the top view for placement of the new lines in the front view.

8. Move the cursor to the center of the top view. Then move to the right edge of the left slot (approximately position **3.0,5.5**).

9. Press the pick button to mark the base point.

10. Move to the left edge of the circle in the center of the top view (approximately position **1.00<0**).

11. Press the pick button to draw the second interior line.

12. Because you picked the Multiple option of the Copy command, you can continue making copies. Move right to the right edge of the small circle (approximately position **2.00<0**).

13. Press the pick button to draw the third interior line.

14. To draw the fourth line, move right to the left edge of the right slot (approximately position **3.00<0**).

15. Press the pick button to draw the fourth interior line.

16. Click the second mouse button to complete the Copy command.

17. To turn off Tan Osnap, give the **Osnap** command and press Enter.

18. Type **off** and press Enter.

19. Check that the front view shows four interior lines as shown in Figure 9.9.

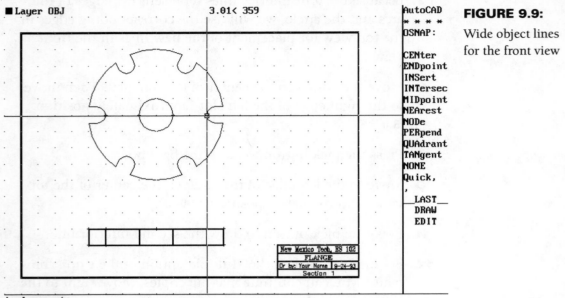

■ Layer OBJ   3.01< 359

AutoCAD
* * * *
OSNAP:

CENter
ENDpoint
INSert
INTersec
MIDpoint
NEArest
NODe
PERpend
QUAdrant
TANgent
NONE
Quick,
,
 LAST
 DRAW
 EDIT

New Mexico Tech, ES 102
FLANGE
Dr by: Your Name | 9-24-93
Section 1

isplacement:
Command: osnap Object snap modes: off
Command:

FIGURE 9.9:

Wide object lines
for the front view

CREATING THE HATCH
LAYER WITH A DIALOG BOX

In Chapters 3 and 8, you created new layers with the Layer dialog box. Now you will use the dialog box to create another new layer and make it current.

1. Move the cursor to the top line of the screen.

2. When the menu bar appears, highlight the Settings menu.

3. Press the pick button to pull down the Settings menu.

4. Move the cursor to highlight Layer Control.

5. Press the pick button to get the Layer dialog box.

6. Type the layer name **hat** but *do not* press Enter.

7. Pick the New box.

8. Check that the name HAT appears in the table.

9. Move the cursor to the HAT layer and press the pick button to highlight that line.

10. Move the cursor to the Current box and press the pick button.

11. Move the cursor to the OK box and press the pick button to close the Layer Control dialog box.

12. Check the upper-left corner of the screen to see that Layer HAT is current.

HOW TO ADD SECTION LINES WITH A HATCH PATTERN

In this section, you will fill in two boxes on your construction layer with the steel hatch pattern.

1. Give the **Bhatch** (for boundary hatch) command and press Enter. The Boundary Hatch dialog box appears as in Figure 9.10.

2. Pick the Hatch Options box to get the Hatch Options dialog box.

3. Check that the Stored Hatch Patterns radio button is selected. If not, select it.

4. Pick the Pattern box to get the Choose Hatch Pattern dialog box as in Figure 9.11. Notice that twelve patterns are displayed.

5. Pick the Next box at the bottom of the dialog box. You now see twelve more patterns.

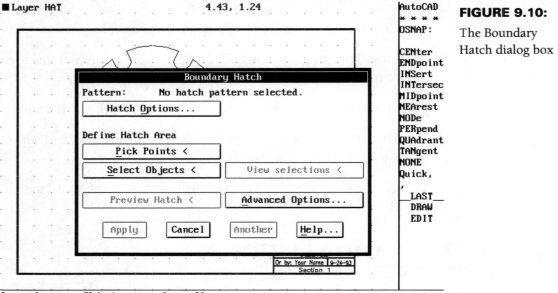

The Boundary Hatch dialog box

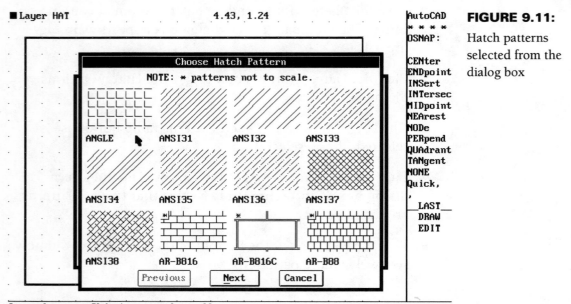

Hatch patterns selected from the dialog box

6. Pick the Next box three more times until the Steel pattern appears.

7. Pick the Steel pattern. The Hatch Options dialog box appears again. Make sure the word STEEL appears next to the pattern box.

8. Pick the OK box. The Boundary Hatch dialog box reappears.

9. Move the cursor to the Pick Points box and press the left mouse button. The dialog box disappears.

10. Move the cursor to the middle of the left area to be hatched (location **3.5,1.7**), and press the pick button. The perimeter changes to show selection.

11. Move the cursor to the middle of the right area to be hatched (location **5.5,1.7**), and press the pick button.

12. Press the second mouse button to complete selection and the Boundary Hatch dialog box reappears.

13. Pick the Apply box and the pattern will be drawn. (If you want to see how a pattern will look, select the Preview Hatch box instead.)

14. Make Layer OBJ current by giving the **Layer** command with the **s** (for Set) option.

Widening the Top View Lines

We now have to widen the outer circle with its six bolt slots. Let's begin with the bottom arc of the top view.

1. To enlarge the top view, give the **z** (for Zoom) command with the **d** (for Dynamic) option.

2. Move the X in the cursor box over the top view.

3. Press the pick button to change the X to an arrow.

4. Move the cursor to change the box size until it matches the size to the top view.

5. Press the pick button to get back the X.

6. Center the X on the circle in the top view and press Enter. The top view now fills the screen.

7. Give the **Pedit** command.

8. At the **Select polyline:** prompt, move the selection box to the arc at the bottom of the top view (location **4.5, 3.5**) and press the pick button. The bottom arc becomes spotty.

9. AutoCAD informs you that the object you have selected is not a polyline and then asks whether you want to convert it to a polyline. Click the second mouse button to accept the default value of Y for yes.

10. Type the option **w** (for Width) and press the spacebar so you can change the polyline width.

11. Type the value **0.02** and press Enter. Check that this bottom line becomes wider.

12. Type **j** (for Join) and press the spacebar so you can convert the remainder of the perimeter to a polyline.

13. We will use a regular window to enclose the perimeter.

14. Put a window around the entire top view, using the corners **2.0, 3.4** and **7.0, 7.6**. The entire perimeter of the top view and the inner circle become spotty to show that they are selected.

15. To remove the inner circle from the selection set, give the **r** option and press the spacebar.

16. Move the selection box to the circle inside the top view and press the pick button. Check that it changes from spotty back to normal.

17. Click the second mouse button to complete the selection step. The entire perimeter, including the bolt slots, is converted to a wide polyline.

18. Press the second mouse button to complete the command.

There is only one object line that is not drawn with a wide line— the inner circle at the center of the top view. Let's widen this line now. Since we drew the circle with the Donut command, which made it a polyline, widening the line will be quite easy.

1. Press the spacebar to repeat the Pedit command.

2. At the **Select polyline:** prompt, move the selection box to the perimeter of the inner circle and press the pick button.

3. Type **w** (for Width) and press the spacebar to change the polyline width.

4. Give the value **0.02** and press the spacebar. Note that the circle becomes wider.

5. Press Enter to complete the Pedit command.

6. Turn off the grid.

Completing the Drawing

1. Give the **z** (for Zoom) command with the **a** (for All) option to see all of the drawing. It should look like Figure 9.12.

2. Plot your FLANGE drawing, and if you are a student, turn it in to your instructor.

3. Give the **End** command to leave AutoCAD or, if you wish, you can move on to the next chapter.

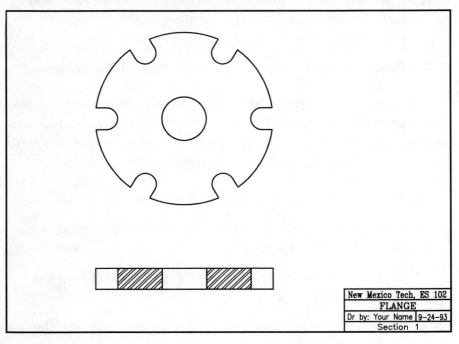

FIGURE 9.12:

Top and front views of flange with hatch pattern

10 CHAPTER

Dimensioning the Bracket

FEATURING

Making text disappear

Dimensioning with the one-point method

Dimensioning with the two-point method

▼

n previous chapters, you have created several scale drawings (also called *shape descriptions*). Someday, your AutoCAD drawings might be sent directly to a machine that will actually produce the items you've drawn. However, whether a machine makes your objects directly or a person interprets your drawings, you will need to include specific information about the object's actual dimensions.

In this chapter, you will use several different methods to add dimensions and centerlines to the bracket drawing you made in Chapter 8. You will be working with the following Dimension subcommands:

- Hor (for a horizontal dimension)

- Ver (for a vertical dimension)

- Dimcen (to set the centerline style)

- Rad (to dimension a radius)

- Dia (to dimension a diameter)

In addition, you will learn these new AutoCAD commands:

- Qtext (to temporarily change a line of text to a box)

- Style (to change fonts and character height)

- Dim (to add dimensions to a drawing)

Before starting, let's go over some of the principles and terminology of dimensioning.

Principles of Dimensioning in AutoCAD

The *dimension* for each part of a drawing is the linear distance between two points. The *dimension line* shows the orientation and extent of the dimension. For an engineering drawing, a dimension line is thin, with arrowheads at each end, drawn on both sides of the number or numeric dimension which appears in the center of the broken dimension line. On an architectural drawing, however, dimension lines are continuous and the numeric dimensions are placed above the line. In addition, circles or shapes other than arrows might mark the ends of architectural dimension lines. AutoCAD uses engineering conventions as its default settings. You can change these defaults, however, so that AutoCAD will follow architectural conventions.

A dimension line normally does not touch the object to which it refers. Rather, an *extension line*—a thin line extending from the object—meets the dimension line at a right angle. Sometimes a line called a *leader* is used instead of a dimension line. The leader is a thin line that connects the dimension (or a short note) to the object to which it refers.

A *centerline* is a thin line, drawn with alternating long and short dashes, that marks the center of circular symmetry. It is often convenient to use a centerline as an extension line for dimensioning.

Avoiding redundancy is an important principle in dimensioning machine drawings, although you must include enough information to describe the object completely. For example, if you give the overall dimensions for a rectangular item, you should not give a sequence of dimensions along a direction that adds up to the overall length—you must omit one of the dimensions in the sequence. Where there is circular symmetry, the overall length is often omitted.

Let's begin by retrieving the bracket you drew in Chapter 8.

Continuing with the Bracket Drawing

1. If necessary, start AutoCAD.

2. When the drawing screen appears, type **open** and press Enter to get the Open Drawing dialog box. Alternatively, you can move the cursor to the top line of the screen, pull down the file menu and pick Open.

3. Type the drawing name **Bracket** and press Enter. Alternatively, you can pick the file name from the Open Drawing dialog box, and pick the OK box.

4. When your Bracket drawing appears, give the **Ddedit** command to change the date.

5. If the entire drawing is not visible, give the **z** (for Zoom) command with the **a** (for All) option.

6. Turn off the grid.

Speeding Up Text Regeneration

AutoCAD takes longer to redraw and regenerate text (especially the Complex style) than it does for lines and circles. Since you will not need the information in the title block, you can change it temporarily to make redrawing and regeneration faster. You can do this in one of two ways: by using the Qtext command or by freezing the layer the text is on (TBLOCK in this example). Let's take a look at the Qtext command first.

SPEEDING UP REGENERATION WITH QTEXT

One way to speed up regeneration is to replace each line of text temporarily with a rectangle with the Qtext (Quick text) command. You won't, of course, be able to read your text. However, since you don't need to see the letters in the title block while you are adding dimensions to the drawing, you may wish to trade this inconvenience for speed. Let's try this now.

1. Give the **Qtext** command with the **on** option. (The On option turns on boxes while it turns off text.) Nothing happens yet.

2. Give the **Regen** command. All the text in the drawing is converted to rectangles as shown in Figure 10.1. Notice how quickly the rectangles are drawn.

3. To reverse this effect, give the **Qtext** command again with the **off** option. (Off turns off the rectangles and turns on the original text.) Again, nothing changes on your screen yet.

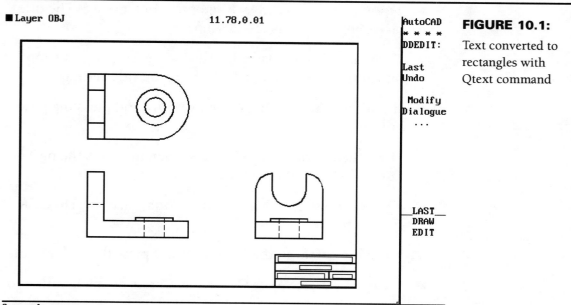

FIGURE 10.1:

Text converted to rectangles with Qtext command

```
Command: regen
Regenerating drawing.
Command:
```

4. Give the **Regen** command. This time, it takes longer to regenerate the screen because the letters have to be drawn.

This time, let's examine another method for speeding up regeneration.

SPEEDING UP REGENERATION BY FREEZING A LAYER

An alternate way to speed up regeneration is to freeze layers you don't need temporarily. Before plotting your drawing, you can turn frozen layers back on. Because your title block text is on layer TBLOCK, it is easy to freeze this text.

1. Give the **Layer** command with the **f** (for Freeze) option.

2. Type the layer name **tblock** and press Enter twice. The title block border and its text disappear.

3. Thaw the TBLOCK layer by moving the cursor to the top line of the screen and picking the menu title Settings.

4. Highlight the menu item Layer Control and press the pick button to get the Layer Control dialog box.

5. Move the cursor to the TBLOCK layer and press the pick button to highlight the line.

6. Check for the letter F after On, showing that the TBLOCK layer is frozen.

7. Move the cursor to the Thaw box and press the pick button.

8. Move the cursor to the OK box and press the pick button to close the Layer Control dialog box.

CHANGING THE FONT WITH THE STYLE COMMAND

When you created the border template, you selected two different fonts—Roman Complex and Roman Simplex. When you selected these typefaces from the dialog box, they were automatically assigned the style names Romanc and Romans. From now on, you can change back and forth between these two with the Style command. Since you used Roman Simplex last, it is still current. You will, however, use Roman Complex for the dimensioning in this chapter. Therefore, change to Roman Complex now.

1. Type the **Style** command with the **?** option and press Enter twice to see the type styles from which you can choose (Romanc, Romans, and Standard).

2. Press **F1** to change back to the graphics screen.

3. Press the spacebar to repeat the Style command.

4. To switch to Roman Complex, type the name **romanc** and press Enter twice.

5. To set the height, type **0.15** and press Enter.

6. Press Enter five more times. *Do not* press **^C** or you will cancel the command prematurely.

Roman Complex is now the default typeface.

Adding Centerlines to the Front View

In this section, you will draw two centerlines on the front using references to the top and right views.

1. Turn on Ortho mode.

2. Turn on the grid.

3. Give the **Layer** command with the **s** (for Set) option or pull down the Layer dialog box to make Layer CEN current. (Remember, you created this layer and set its line type to center in Chapter 8.)

4. Type the layer name **cen** and press Enter twice.

5. Check the top-left corner of the screen to verify that the current layer is CEN.

Now that the center-line layer is current, you can draw two centerlines in the front view. They correspond to a circle in the top view and an arc in the right view. You will therefore reference these lines to the other views with the .X and .Y filters.

1. Give the **L** (for Line) command with the **.x** filter so you can match the X value for the center of the circle in the top view.

2. Type the **cen** Osnap option and press the spacebar.

3. Move to the top view and put the selection box on the edge of the smaller circle (near location **4.5,5.7**). You can also use the larger circle.

4. Press the pick button to specify the X coordinate.

5. Move straight down to the upper edge of the boss, then move up a little. When the Y coordinate readout shows approximately **2.9**, press the pick button to start the centerline. The location does not need to be exact.

6. Move straight down to location **1.4<270** and press the pick button. Because Ortho mode is on, the new line is vertical. (If the coordinates are in rectangular form rather than Polar form, press **^D** twice.)

7. Click the second mouse button to complete the Line command.

8. Make sure the centerlines consist of the alternating long and short dashes. If not, change Ltscale as you did in Chapter 8.

You are now ready to put the centerline on the left edge of the front view.

1. Click the second mouse button to restart the Line command.

2. Type the **.y** filter and press the spacebar so you can match the Y value for the center of the arc in the right view.

3. Type the **cen** Osnap option and press the spacebar.

4. Move to the right view and put the selection box on the circular part of the slot (approximately **8.5,3.0**.)

5. Press the pick button to specify the Y coordinate.

6. Move left to the right edge of the vertical part of the front view. Then move a little more to the right. When the X coordinate shows approximately **3.3**, press the pick button to start another centerline.

7. Move left to location **1.2<180** and press the pick button. Because Ortho mode is on, the new line is horizontal.

8. Press the second mouse button to complete the Line command.

9. Make sure this line consists of alternating long and short dashes.

10. Turn off Ortho mode.

Dimensioning the Front View

AutoCAD can calculate the length of each object or gap in your drawing automatically, and then draw the corresponding information. There are two ways to tell AutoCAD which distance you want to dimension. With the one-point method, you select a point somewhere along a line and AutoCAD calculates the line's length. This method should be used only for well-defined distances such as lines or arcs. Sometimes, however, you will need to dimension an opening or a distance between centerlines. On such an occasion, you must use the two-point method instead. In the two-point method, you select two end points (with an Osnap option) that denote the distance being dimensioned. AutoCAD then calculates the distance between them. We'll start with the simpler one-point method first and then use the two-point method to dimension a gap.

1. Enlarge the front view by giving the **z** (for Zoom) command.

2. Select window corners at **1.2, 5.7** and **7.3,1.5**. The entire front view and part of the top should be visible.

CREATING THE DIM LAYER WITH A DIALOG BOX

You will now create a separate DIM layer for adding dimensions to your drawing. To use the Layer dialog box to create the layer and make it current, follow these steps:

1. Move the cursor to the top line of the screen.

2. When the menu bar appears, highlight the Settings menu.

3. Press the pick button to pull down the Settings menu.

4. Press the pick button to get the Layer Control dialog box.

5. Type the new layer name **dim** but *do not* press Enter.

6. Move the cursor to the New box and press the pick button.

7. Check that the name DIM appears in the table.

8. Move the cursor to the row containing the new layer name DIM and press the pick button. The row becomes highlighted.

9. Move the cursor to the Current box and press the pick button.

10. Move the cursor to the OK box and press the pick button to close the layer dialog box.

11. Look at the upper-left corner of the screen to see that Layer DIM is current.

STARTING THE DIMENSION COMMAND MODE

Normally, when the **Command:** prompt shows on the last line of your screen, you type an AutoCAD command. When you add dimensions to your drawings, however, you change to the Dimension command mode. Then you type commands in response to the **Dim:** prompt.

After you complete each dimension command, you are returned to the **Dim:** prompt automatically, where you can give additional dimension commands. When you have finished giving dimension commands, you return to regular commands by typing **^C** or Exit.

1. Give the **Dim** command.

2. Press Enter to start the dimension options. Notice that the **Dim:** prompt appears on the bottom line instead of the usual **Command:** prompt.

You are now ready to specify your first dimension.

SPECIFYING A VERTICAL DIMENSION

You will start by dimensioning the left vertical edge of the front view.

1. At the **Dim:** prompt, type **ver** (for Vertical dimension) and press the spacebar. AutoCAD expects you to pick the first of two points to be dimensioned by the two-point method.

2. Press the spacebar again to switch to the one-point method. Notice that the cursor changes to a selection box.

3. Move the selection box to the left vertical edge of the front view, near location **2.5,2.5** and press the pick button to select the left edge. The cursor changes back to crossed lines and a "ghostly" image of the dimensions appears.

4. The next prompt asks for the dimension line location. Move the selection box to the left, near location **1.8,3.0** and press the pick button.

5. The **Dimension text <2.00>:** prompt tells you that 2.00 is the calculated value for this dimension. Click the second mouse button to accept this value. The dimension and associated lines are drawn.

If the dimension did not go where you wanted it, type **u** and press the spacebar to remove it so you can do it again. Notice that the Vertical dimension command has been completed. Remember, you will remain in the dimension command mode until you press **^C** to return to the **Command:** prompt.

SPECIFYING A HORIZONTAL DIMENSION

Now let's dimension a horizontal edge.

1. At the **Dim:** prompt, type **hor** (for Horizontal dimension) and press the spacebar.

2. Press the spacebar again to choose the one-point method. As before, the cursor changes to a selection box.

3. Move the cursor to the top line of the front view to location **2.7,4.0** and press the pick button to select this edge. Look for the "ghostly" image.

4. The next prompt asks for the dimension line location. Move the selection box upward to location **2.7,4.3** and press the pick button.

5. The **Dimension text <0.50>:** prompt shows you the value that appears in the dimension. Press the second mouse button to accept this value (0.50). This time, the dimension and the dimension line are placed outside the extension lines because there is not enough room inside.

The remaining dimensions for the front view are on the right edge. Because the dimensions will not fit inside the extension lines, they are placed outside. If you use the one-point method, you have no control on which side. However, if you use the two-point method, you can determine the placement. With the two-point method, the dimension is placed outside the second point you select. Of course, the two points must be selected with Osnaps. To dimension the right edge, follow these steps:

1. Give the 'Osnap transparent command (*do not* forget the apostrophe) with the **endp** option.

2. At the **Dim:** prompt, type **ver** (for Vertical dimension) and press the spacebar.

3. Move the target cursor to the upper-right corner to location **5.5,2.5** and press the pick button.

4. Move the cursor to the lower-right corner to location **0.5<270** and press the pick button. Look for the "ghostly" image.

5. The next prompt asks for the dimension line location. Move down to location **6.2,1.8** and press the pick button.

6. Click the second mouse button to accept the dimension of 0.50. The dimension is placed below the extension lines because you chose the lower corner as your second choice.

To dimension the boss in the front view, follow these steps:

1. At the **Dim:** prompt, type **ver** and press the spacebar.

2. Move the cursor to the upper-right corner to location **5.5,2.5** and press the pick button.

3. Move the cursor to the upper-right corner of the boss (near location **0.46<162**) and press the pick button.

4. The next prompt asks for the dimension line location. Move to location **5.8,3.1** and press the pick button.

5. Press the second mouse button to accept the dimension of 0.10. The dimension is placed above the extension lines because you chose the upper-right corner as your second choice.

6. Compare your drawing with Figure 10.2.

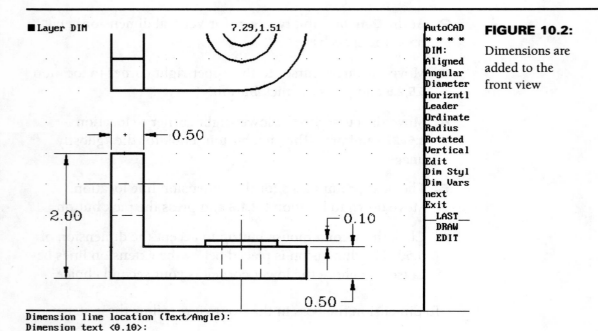

■ Layer DIM   7.29,1.51

AutoCAD
* * * *
DIM:
Aligned
Angular
Diameter
Horizntl
Leader
Ordinate
Radius
Rotated
Vertical
Edit
Dim Styl
Dim Vars
next
Exit
__LAST__
DRAW
EDIT

0.50

2.00

0.10

0.50

Dimension line location (Text/Angle):
Dimension text <0.10>:
Dim:

FIGURE 10.2:

Dimensions are added to the front view

7. Turn off the Endpoint Osnap with **'Osnap** and the **none** option.

Let's do the top view next.

Dimensioning the Top View

You will move to the top view with the Dynamic Zoom command. But before adding any more dimensions, you will enlarge the view with the Zoom command. Remember, you can run the Zoom command from the dimension mode if you preface it with an apostrophe.

DYNAMIC ZOOMING TO THE TOP VIEW

To switch to an enlarged top view, follow these steps:

1. Make sure that the **Dim:** prompt shows on the bottom line.

2. Give the **'z** command (don't forget the apostrophe) and press the spacebar.

3. Type the option **d** (for Dynamic) and press the spacebar. The screen shows the entire drawing with a dotted box around the previous view.

4. Move the cursor and watch a second box, with an X in the center, move on the screen.

5. Move the box over the top view until the X is centered on the circles as shown in Figure 10.3.

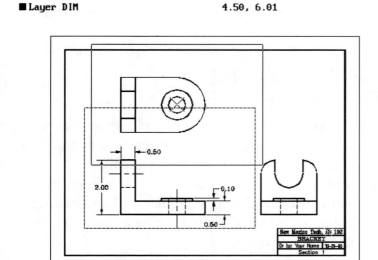

■ Layer DIM   4.50, 6.01

FIGURE 10.3:

The Dynamic Zoom command helps you change views

```
Resuming DIM command.
Dim: 'z
>>Center/Dynamic/Left/Previous/Vmax/Window/<Scale(X/XP)>: d
```

6. When the coordinate readout shows approximately **4.5,6.0** press Enter. The top view now fills the screen.

DIMENSIONING THE TOP EDGE

To dimension the top edge of the top view, follow these steps:

1. Type **hor** (for Horizontal dimension) and press the spacebar.

2. Press the spacebar again to choose the one-point method. The cursor changes to a selection box.

3. Move the cursor to the top edge of the top view to location **3.5,7.0** and press the pick button to select the top edge. Look for the "ghostly" image.

4. The next prompt asks for the dimension line location. Move upward to **3.5,7.5** and press the pick button.

5. The **Dimension text <2.00>:** prompt tells you the value that will appear in the dimension. Press the second mouse button to accept this value.

ESTABLISHING THE FORM OF CROSSED CENTERLINES

The two centerlines you drew in this chapter were not drawn on circles. Because AutoCAD had no way to determine that a centerline was needed, you had to draw the lines on layer CEN that was set for center-line style. However, when you dimension a circle or an arc, AutoCAD determines that the object is circular and automatically chooses the center-line style. Thus, you can draw a centerline on a circle when the DIM layer is current.

As you have seen, centerlines are drawn with alternating long and short dashes. However, when two centerlines cross at the center of a circle, it is customary to place a plus (+) sign at the center. Long dashes are then drawn from the plus sign in all four directions.

Although this is not the default setting, AutoCAD can draw center-lines in this way.

The *Dimcen* variable controls which form will be drawn. When Dimcen is positive (the default), only plus signs are drawn. When Dimcen is negative, however, a pair of crossed centerlines is drawn. When Dimcen is zero, no marks are drawn at all. If you want to dimension concentric circles, you won't want a set of crossed centerlines for each circle. Therefore, when you dimension concentric circles and arcs, set the Dimcen variable to negative for the largest circle or arc. Then set Dimcen to zero for the other concentric circles or arcs.

Dimensioning a Radius

In this section, you will dimension the semicircular arc in the top view of your drawing, and add crossed centerlines. But first you have to set Dimcen to negative.

1. Check that the **Dim:** prompt appears on the bottom line. If the **Command:** prompt is displayed, type Dim and press the spacebar.

2. Type the **dimcen** variable and press the spacebar.

3. Type the value **-0.1** and press the spacebar.

4. To dimension the arc at the right edge of the top view, type **rad** (for Radius) and press the spacebar.

5. The prompt asks you to select an arc or a circle. Move the selection box to the upper-right edge of the arc, near location **5.3,6.6** and press the pick button.

6. The **Dimension text <1.00>:** prompt shows the calculated radius of the outer circle. Click the second mouse button to accept this value. Again, look for the "ghostly" image.

7. Move the cursor upward and right to the approximate location **5.8,6.8** and press the pick button. The value is automatically written with an R prefix to signify a radius. Crossed centerlines are also drawn because Dimcen is negative.

Notice that the radius dimension was drawn near the place where you pick the arc.

Dimensioning Two Diameters

In this section, you will use the Diameter command to dimension the two concentric circles in the top view. As with the previous linear dimensioning, AutoCAD can write the diameter or radius (including the diameter and radius symbols) automatically, and place the dimension line. Because you will not want more crossed centerlines, set Dimcen to zero. Make sure that the **Dim:** prompt appears on the bottom line of the screen.

1. Type the **dimcen** variable and press the spacebar.

2. Type **0** (zero) and press the spacebar. Centerlines will now be drawn for the Diameter command.

3. To dimension the outer circle in the top view, type **dia** (for Diameter) and press Enter.

4. The prompt asks you to select the arc or circle. Move the selection box to the lower-right edge of the larger circle, near location **5.0,5.8**, and press the first mouse button.

5. The **Dimension text <1.10>:** prompt shows the calculated diameter of the circle. Press the second mouse button to accept this value.

6. Move the cursor down and right until it passes the arc and is outside the top view. When the coordinate readout shows approximately **5.7,5.6**, press the pick button. AutoCAD writes the Greek letter *phi,* the diameter symbol, and the value of the diameter.

7. To dimension the inner circle in the top view, type **dia** and press Enter.

8. Move the selection box to the lower-right edge of the inner circle, a little lower this time (near location **4.65,5.74**) and click the first mouse button.

9. The **Dimension text <0.60>:** prompt shows the calculated diameter of the circle. Click the second mouse button to accept this value.

10. Move the cursor down and right until it passes the arc and is outside the top view. When the coordinate is approximately **5.2,5.0**, press the pick button. AutoCAD again writes the Greek letter *phi* and the value of the diameter.

11. Compare your drawing to Figure 10.4.

12. Type **^C** to exit the dimensioning command mode.

EXTENDING THE CENTERLINE

You are now going to extend the horizontal centerline to the left edge of the top view. You will draw the line on the DIM layer, then move it to the CEN layer.

1. Turn on Ortho mode.

2. While still on the Dim layer, give the **L** (for Line) command.

3. Type the **endp** Osnap option and press the spacebar to start the new line.

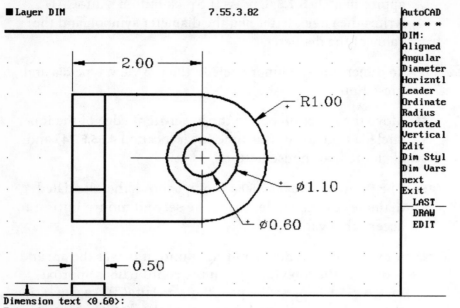

```
Dimension text <0.60>:
Enter leader length for text:
Dim:
```

4. Move the selection box to the left end of the horizontal centerline (near position **3.4,6.0**) and press the pick button. This attaches the new line to the horizontal centerline.

5. Move the cursor left to position **1.4<180** and press the pick button. The location does not have to be exact.

6. Click the second mouse button to complete the Line command. Notice that the new line is continuous rather than dashed because you drew it on the DIM layer rather than on the CEN layer.

7. To move the new line to its proper layer, give the **Chprop** (for Change properties) command.

8. Position the selection box over the new line and press the pick button to select it.

9. Click the second mouse button to complete selection.

10. Type the **La** (for Layer) option and press Enter. The current layer (DIM) is now given.

11. Type **cen** (the layer you want to move the line to) and press Enter twice to complete the Chprop command.

12. Make sure that the line shows the alternating long and short dashes which are characteristic of a centerline.

13. Turn off Ortho mode.

Now let's move on to the right view.

Dimensioning the Right View

Let's use the Dynamic Zoom command to move to the right view, where we will add two dimensions and two centerlines.

1. If the **Command:** prompt does not appear on the bottom line of the screen, type **^C**.

2. Give the **z** (for Zoom) command with the **d** (for Dynamic) option. As before, the screen shows the entire drawing, with a dotted box around the previous view.

3. Move the cursor until the box with an X in it moves to the right view. When the coordinate readout shows approximately **8.5,3.5**, press Enter. The right view fills the screen.

DIMENSIONING THE CORNER

In this section, you will dimension the upper-left arc. But first, make sure that Dimcen is still set at zero so that crossed centerlines will not be drawn.

1. Give the **Dim** command.

2. Type the **dimcen** variable and press the spacebar.

3. Check that the default value is 0. If not, type 0 and press the spacebar.

4. Give the **rad** (for Radius) command and press Enter.

5. Move the cursor to the upper-left arc at coordinate position **7.7,3.8** and press the pick button.

6. Press the second mouse button to accept the value given for the radius (0.50).

7. Move the cursor upward to the left, until the coordinate readout shows **7.5,4.5**, and press the pick button.

ADDING CENTERLINES TO THE SLOT

In this section, you will add crossed centerlines to the circular part of the slot. But first, you must reset Dimcen.

1. Type the **dimcen** variable and press the spacebar.

2. Type the value **-0.1** and press the spacebar.

3. Give the **ce** (for Centerline) option and press Enter so you can draw crossed centerlines.

4. Move to the circular part of the slot at coordinate position **8.5,3** and press the pick button. Crossed centerlines appear in the slot because Dimcen is negative.

5. Give the **'Osnap** command (don't forget the apostrophe) with the **endp** option.

DIMENSIONING THE SLOT

To dimension the slot, follow these steps:

1. At the **Dim:** prompt, type **hor** and press Enter. Because we are dimensioning an opening, there is no object to point to. Therefore, we must use the two-point method.

2. Move the target box to the upper-left opening of the slot (near position **8.0,4.0**) and press the pick button.

3. Move the cursor to the upper-right opening of the slot at coordinate position **1.0<0** and press the pick button.

4. Move the cursor to **9.6,4.4** and press the pick button to select the location of the dimension.

5. The **Dimension text <1.00>:** prompt tells you the value that appears in the dimension. Click the second mouse button to accept this value.

6. Press **^C** to return to command mode.

Notice that the last dimension was placed outside the extension lines on the right side because you picked the right corner of the slot after you had picked the left corner.

EXTENDING THE VERTICAL CENTERLINE

Let's extend the vertical centerline downward, beyond the lower edge of the right view.

1. Turn on Ortho mode.

2. Change to layer CEN by pulling down the Layer dialog box or by giving the **Layer** command.

3. Make sure that the words Layer CEN appear on the top-left corner of the screen.

4. Give the **L** (for Line) command.

5. Move to the bottom end of the centerline at coordinate **8.5,2.9** and press the pick button. This starts the new line at the end of the vertical centerline because the Endpoint option is still on.

6. Move the cursor down below the bottom edge to position **1.2<270** and press the pick button.

7. Click the second mouse button to complete the Line command.

8. Check that the new line has the center-line pattern. If the new line is continuous, give the **Ltscale** command and give a smaller number for the scale.

9. Turn off Ortho mode.

Now, that you have dimensioned the right view of the bracket, compare your screen to Figure 10.5.

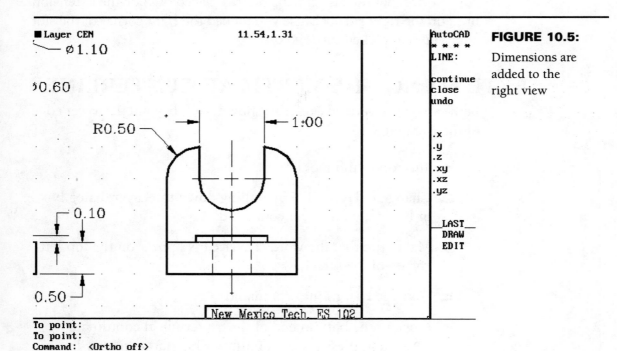

FIGURE 10.5:

Dimensions are added to the right view

COMPLETING THE DRAWING

In this section, you will change back to the OBJ layer. You can make this change either by pulling down the Layer dialog box or by using the Layer command.

1. Give the **z** (for Zoom) command with the **a** (for All) option to see the complete view of the bracket.

2. Give the **La** (for Layer) command with the **s** (for Set) option or pull down the Layer dialog box and make Layer OBJ current.

3. Check the upper-left corner of the screen to verify that layer OBJ is current.

4. Give the **Osnap** command with the **none** option.

Plotting the Drawing

■ Plot your Bracket drawing with its dimensions using the **L** (for Limits) option. If you are a student, turn in your drawing to your instructor.

11 CHAPTER

Dimensioning
the Flange

n this chapter, you will use the methods
learned in Chapter 10 to add dimensions,
centerlines, and a cutting-plane line to the
Flange that you drew in Chapter 9. In addition, you will use the Align method to
dimension at an angle. Finally, you will draw
a section line using the AutoCAD Phantom line type which appears as a sequence
of one long and two short dashes.

The only new dimension subcommand introduced in this chapter is:

■ Align (to orient a dimension at an angle)

Let's begin with the FLANGE drawing.

Dimensioning the Flange Drawing

1. If necessary, start AutoCAD.

2. When the drawing screen appears, type **open** and press Enter to get the Open Drawing dialog box. You can also move the cursor to the top line of the screen, pull down the file menu, and pick Open.

3. Type the drawing name **flange** and press Enter. Or, you can pick the file name from the dialog box, then pick the OK box.

4. When your FLANGE drawing appears, give the **Ddedit** command to change the date.

5. If necessary, turn off the grid.

6. If necessary, turn off Ortho mode.

7. Check the scale of the line type with the **Ltscale** command.

8. Type the value **0.5** and press the spacebar.

9. Give the **La** (for Layer) command with the **m** (for Make) option to create Layer DIM and make it current.

10. Check the top of the screen to see that Layer DIM is current.

11. Give the **Style** command to make Romanc (Roman Complex) current.

12. Set the height to **0.15**. Now, Roman Complex is the default typeface.

13. To reduce the number of displayed digits, give the **Ddunits** command and press the spacebar to get the Units Control dialog box.

14. Click the box below Precision: in the lower-left corner.

15. Click on the row with 0.0.

16. Click the OK box.

17. Check the coordinate display on the status line to see that it shows only one digit past the decimal point.

SPECIFYING A VERTICAL DIMENSION FOR THE FRONT VIEW

You will now dimension a left edge of the front view.

1. Give the **Dim** command and make sure the **Dim:** prompt appears on the bottom line of your screen.

2. Using Figure 11.1 as a guide, dimension the left end of the front view by starting with the **ver** option and pressing Enter.

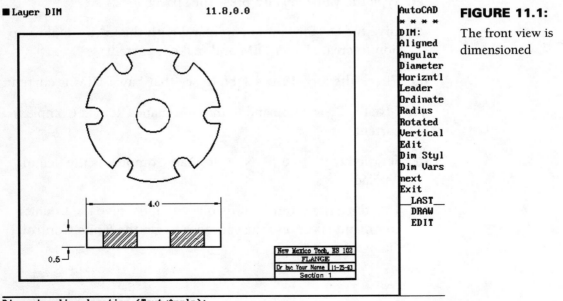

■ Layer DIM   11.8,0.0

AutoCAD
* * * *
DIM:
Aligned
Angular
Diameter
Horizntl
Leader
Ordinate
Radius
Rotated
Vertical
Edit
Dim Styl
Dim Vars
next
Exit
　LAST　
　DRAW
　EDIT

FIGURE 11.1:

The front view is dimensioned

```
Dimension line location (Text/Angle):
Dimension text <4.0>:
Dim:  <Grid on>  <Grid off>
```

3. Type the **endp** Osnap option and press Enter.

4. Move the target box to the upper-left corner at **2.5,2.0** and press the pick button.

5. Type **endp** again and press Enter.

6. Move the target box to the lower-left corner at **0.5<270** and press the pick button.

7. For the dimension line location, move the selection box to the left, to location **2.0,1.8**, and click the left mouse button.

8. Click the second mouse button to complete this step.

Although the Vertical dimension command has been completed, the **Dim:** prompt remains on the bottom line of the screen. You will be working in the dimensioning command mode until you type **^C** or **Exit**.

SPECIFYING A HORIZONTAL DIMENSION FOR THE FRONT VIEW

Next, you will dimension the top edge of the front view.

1. Using Figure 11.1 as a guide, dimension the top of the front view by typing the **hor** (for Horizontal) option.

2. Press the spacebar to choose the one-point method. The cursor changes to a selection box.

3. Move the selection cursor to the center of the top edge of the front view and press the pick button to select the top edge.

4. Move the selection box upward to location **4.5,2.8** and press the left button and then the second mouse button.

5. Press **^G** twice to clean up the screen. Your screen should look like Figure 11.1.

DIMENSIONING THE TOP VIEW

Before we begin with the top view, let's enlarge it.

1. At the **Dim:** prompt, type the **'z** command (don't forget the apostrophe) and press the spacebar.

2. Put the corners of your window at **1.6,7.9** and **8.0,3.0**.

After you have completed the transparent Zoom command, you are returned to the dimension command mode. The top view of your drawing will fill the screen.

Adding Centerlines to One Bolt Slot

In this section, you will add centerlines to the bolt slots in the top view. After you create one crossed pair of centerlines, you will erase the vertical centerline. Then, you will replicate the horizontal line for the remaining slots with the Polar Array command.

1. Make sure that the **Dim:** prompt is displayed.

2. Type the **dimcen** variable and press Enter.

3. Type the value **-0.1** and press Enter.

4. Give the **ce** (for Centerline) command.

5. Move the selection cursor to the arc of the right slot (near location **6.0,5.6**) and press the pick button. A small pair of crossed centerlines appears as shown in Figure 11.2. Notice that there are three segments in each direction. You will now erase the three vertical segments.

6. Type **^C** to exit the dimensioning command mode.

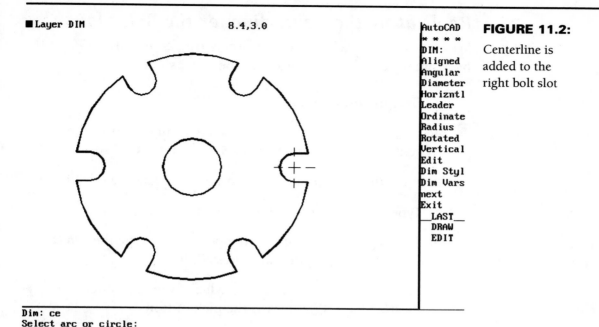

AutoCAD
* * * *
DIM:
Aligned
Angular
Diameter
Horizntl
Leader
Ordinate
Radius
Rotated
Vertical
Edit
Dim Styl
Dim Vars
next
Exit
__LAST__
DRAW
EDIT

FIGURE 11.2:

Centerline is added to the right bolt slot

```
Dim: ce
Select arc or circle:
Dim:
```

7. To remove the three parts of the vertical centerline, give the **e** (for Erase) command.

8. Put your window corners at **6.2,5.9** and **6.3,5.1**.

9. Be sure the three parts of the vertical centerline are spotty. If you selected the polyline perimeter around the top view by mistake, type **r** (for Remove) and press Enter to reverse the selection procedure. Select the polyline again to remove it from the selection set.

10. Click the second mouse button to erase the vertical centerline.

11. Check that the three horizontal parts of the centerline are present.

Replicating the Centerline for the Bolt Slot

We next use the radial option of the Array command to copy the horizontal part of the centerline to the other slots.

1. Give the **Array** command.

2. Put a window around the three horizontal parts of the centerline with corners at **5.7,5.6** and **6.7,5.4**.

3. Press the second mouse button to complete the selection.

4. Type the option **p** (for Polar) and press Enter.

5. To designate the center of the polar array, type the **cen** (for Center) Osnap option and press Enter.

6. Move the target cursor to the edge of the large circle (at location **6.2,6.6**) and press the pick button.

7. At the prompt requesting the number of items, type **6** and press Enter.

8. Press Enter for the next two questions. The centerline is copied to each of the other bolt slots.

Removing Two Horizontal Centerlines

You now need to remove two of the centerlines (those for the left and right slots) because they will be overlapped by the section line you will soon draw.

1. Give the **e** (for Erase) command.

2. Put a long horizontal window around the two horizontal centerlines. Put the corners at locations **2.3,5.6** and **6.7,5.4**.

3. Press **^G** twice to clean up the screen.

Now let's add centerlines to the large circle.

Adding Centerlines to the Large Circle

In this section, you will add a pair of crossed centerlines to the large circle of the top view. You will then delete the horizontal centerline and replace it with a section line.

1. Type the **Dim** command.

2. Type the **cen** (for Centerline) Osnap option and press Enter.

3. Move the selection box to the edge of the large circle at location **6.2,6.6** and press the pick button. Crossed centerlines appear on the top view. (If the crossed centerlines do not appear, change the Dimcen value to −0.1 and try again.)

4. Type **^C** to terminate the dimension subcommand.

5. Give the **e** (for Erase) command so you can erase the three parts of the horizontal centerline.

6. Put a long horizontal window around the three parts of the horizontal centerline. Put the corners at locations **2.3,5.6** and **6.7,5.4**. Be careful not to include any part of the vertical centerline.

7. Press the second mouse button.

Drawing the Bolt-Circle Centerline

We will now draw the centerline for the bolt circle. But first, we need to change to Layer CEN.

1. Give the **La** (for Layer) command with the **s** (for Set) option to make Layer CEN current.

2. Check that Layer CEN shows in the upper-left corner.

3. Give the **c** (for Circle) command.

4. Type the **cen** (for Center) Osnap option and press Enter.

5. Move the selection cursor to the edge of the large circle to location **6.2,6.6** and press the pick button to establish the center.

6. Type **cen** again and press Enter.

7. Move the selection cursor to one of the bolt-slot arcs at location **1.5<0** and click the left mouse button to create a centerline circle with a diameter of 3.5 inches. Because the CEN layer is current, the circle is drawn with alternating long and short arcs.

8. Compare your drawing with Figure 11.3.

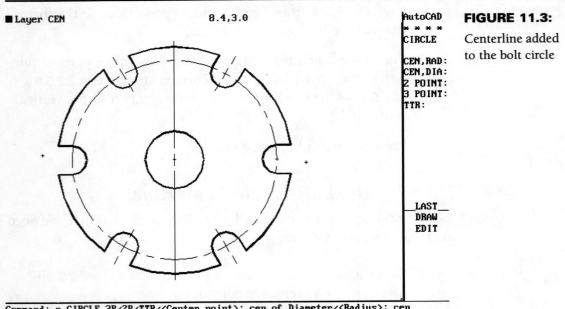

■ Layer CEN   8.4,3.0

AutoCAD
* * * *
CIRCLE

CEN,RAD:
CEN,DIA:
2 POINT:
3 POINT:
TTR:

LAST
DRAW
EDIT

FIGURE 11.3:

Centerline added to the bolt circle

Command: c CIRCLE 3P/2P/TTR/<Center point>: cen of Diameter/<Radius>: cen
of
Command:

Creating a Layer for the Cutting-Plane Line

You need to create a layer for the cutting-plane line and set the line type to Phantom. Phantom lines are drawn with a series of one long and two short segments.

1. Give the **Linetype** command with the **L** (for Load) option.

2. Type **phantom** and press Enter three times to load the Phantom linetype.

3. Move the cursor to the top line of the screen and pick the menu title Settings.

4. Pick Layer Control.

5. When the Layer Control dialog box appears, type the new layer name **phan** but *do not* press Enter.

6. Move the cursor to the New box and press the pick button.

7. Move the cursor to the row containing the new layer name PHAN and press the pick button. The row becomes highlighted.

8. Pick the Current box to make PHAN the current layer.

9. Pick the Set Ltype box to get the Select Linetype dialog box.

10. Move the cursor to the pattern for phantom line and press the pick button.

11. Check that the word Phantom appears in the Linetype box at the bottom of the dialog box.

12. Pick the OK box of the Select Linetype dialog box.

13. Move the cursor to the OK box and press the pick button to close the Layer Control dialog box.

14. Check for the words Layer PHAN on the top line of the screen.

Adding a Cutting-Plane Line

In this section, you will add a cutting-plane line across the middle of the top view. This line marks the cutting plane that matches the adjacent view—in this example, the front. The cutting plane is marked with a wide broken line (one long segment alternating with two short ones). Furthermore, the ends of the cutting-plane line are marked with arrows that point away from the corresponding sectioned view. We will draw the cutting-plane line as a regular polyline. By changing the width, we will create arrows at each end.

1. Turn on the grid.

2. Turn on Ortho mode.

3. Give the **PL** (for Pline) command.

4. Move to the left edge of the top view, then move left and upward to location **2.0,6.0**.

5. Turn on Snap mode and move the cursor so it snaps to the above position.

6. Press the pick button to start the polyline.

7. Type **w** (for Width) and press Enter.

8. Type **0** and press Enter to set the beginning line width (the point of the first arrow).

9. Type **0.12** and press Enter again to set the ending width of the arrowhead.

10. Type the relative distance **@0.2<–90** and press the spacebar to draw the arrowhead.

11. Type **w** (for Width) and press Enter to reset the width.

12. Type **0.03** and press Enter for the beginning width.

13. Press Enter to set the ending width to the beginning width. (The ending width is now 0.03. But because only one digit past the decimal point is showing, all you see is a zero.)

14. Move down to the next grid point that marks the horizontal axis of the top view. When the coordinates show **0.3<270**, click the pick button to establish the next segment.

15. Move right across the center of the top view until you are one grid point past the right edge. The coordinate position shows **5.0<0**.

16. Press the pick button to establish the horizontal segment.

17. Make sure the new line is drawn with an alternating sequence of one long and two short segments.

18. Type the relative distance **@0.3<90** and press the spacebar. (You can also use the .Y filter and the Endpoint Osnap option to match the arrowhead on the left end.)

19. Type **w** (for Width) and press Enter.

20. Type **0.12** and press Enter to set the beginning width of the second arrowhead.

21. Type **0** (zero) and press Enter to set the point of the arrowhead.

22. Move upward to the next grid point and press the pick button to complete the section line.

23. Turn off Snap mode.

24. Turn off Ortho mode.

25. Press Enter to complete the Pline command.

26. Press **^G** twice to clean up the screen.

27. Compare your drawing to Figure 11.4.

28. Change back to Layer DIM, with the Layer command or the Layer dialog box.

29. Make sure that Layer DIM shows on the screen.

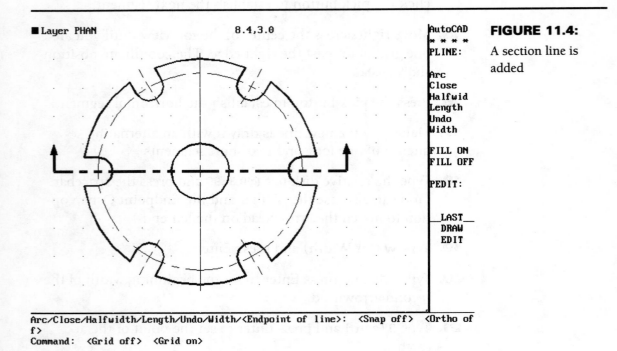

■ Layer PHAN   8.4,3.0

AutoCAD
* * * *
PLINE:

Arc
Close
Halfwid
Length
Undo
Width

FILL ON
FILL OFF

PEDIT:

LAST
DRAW
EDIT

FIGURE 11.4:

A section line is added

Arc/Close/Halfwidth/Length/Undo/Width/<Endpoint of line>: <Snap off> <Ortho of
f>
Command: <Grid off> <Grid on>

Dimensioning a Bolt Slot

We will dimension the upper-right bolt slot next. Because the slot is an opening, we must use the two-point method. Furthermore, we must align the dimension with the angled slot. To see how this will look, review Figure 9.1.

1. Give the **Dim** command to enter dimensioning command mode.

2. Type **align** and press Enter to draw the dimension at an angle. (You can abbreviate the Align command to ali.)

3. Type the **endp** Osnap option and press Enter.

4. Move to the left side of the upper-right slot (near coordinate position **5.3,7.4**) and press the pick button.

5. Type **endp** again and press Enter again.

6. Move to the right side of the slot opening at coordinate position **0.5<330** and press the pick button.

7. Keeping an eye on the "ghostly" image, move upward to location **5.7,7.4** and press the pick button to designate the dimension location.

8. Click the second mouse button to accept the dimension value of 0.5.

Dimensioning the Bolt Circle

We will now dimension the bolt circle. But first turn off the Dimcen variable so that additional crossed centerlines will not be drawn.

1. At the **Dim:** prompt, type the **dimcen** variable and press Enter.

2. Type **0** (zero) and press Enter so centerlines will not be added.

3. Give the **Dia** (for Diameter) command and press Enter.

4. Move the selection box to the lower-right part of the bolt-circle centerline (near location **6.0,4.6**) and press the pick button.

5. Click the second mouse button to accept the value of 3.5. Notice the "ghostly" image of the dimension.

6. Move the cursor outside the flange to location **7.0,4.5** and press the pick button.

7. Compare your drawing to Figure 9.1.

Dimensioning the Inner Circle

1. At the **Dim:** prompt, give the **Dia** command and press Enter.

2. Move the selection box to the upper-right part of the inner circle (near location **5.0,5.7**) and press the pick button.

3. Click the second mouse button to accept the value of 1.0.

4. Move the cursor outside the flange to location **7.0,6.4** and press the pick button. If the leader is dashed, you are not on the DIM layer.

5. Compare your drawing to Figure 9.1.

6. Type **^C** to leave the dimensioning command mode.

7. Give the **z** (for Zoom) command with the **a** (for All) option.

ADDING A CENTERLINE TO THE FRONT VIEW

To add a centerline to the front view:

1. Change to Layer CEN with the Layer command or the Layer dialog box.

2. Make sure that the words Layer CEN appear on the top-left corner of the screen.

3. Turn on Ortho mode.

4. Give the **L** (for Line) command with the **.x** filter and press the spacebar.

5. Type the **cen** Osnap option and press the spacebar.

6. Move the cursor to the edge of the inner circle in the top view. When the position is approximately **4.7,5.0**, press the pick button.

7. Move between the top of the front view and the dimension for this edge. When the approximate location is **4.5,2.5**, press the pick button. You need not be precise.

8. Move down three grid points to the approximate position **1.5<270** and press the pick button. Because Ortho mode is on, the new line is vertical.

9. Click the second mouse button to complete the Line command.

10. Change to Layer OBJ with the Layer command or the Layer dialog box.

Congratulations. You have finally completed the drawing. Compare yours to Figure 9.1.

PLOTTING THE DRAWING

1. Plot your Flange drawing with the **L** (for Limits) option. If you are a student, turn in the drawing to your instructor.

2. Give the **End** command to complete the drawing and quit AutoCAD. Or, if you wish, you can continue on to the next chapter.

12 CHAPTER

FEATURING

Creating four view ports

Moving the coordinate system

Viewing a 3D drawing from different directions

▼

Introduction to Drawing in Three Dimensions

n Chapters 8 through 11, you drew the top, right, and front views of a bracket, and the top and front views of a flange. All these views were two-dimensional and had to be individually drawn. In other words, you had to draw a separate view of the object for each of the viewing directions.

We will now turn to true three-dimensional drawing. With this method, you will be able to draw a three-dimensional object in a single view and, more importantly, view the object from any convenient direction.

In this chapter, you will divide the video screen into four *viewing ports* or windows that will enable you to see your drawing from different directions or *viewpoints*. You will study the *User Coordinate System* (Ucs) and the associated *Ucs Icon* (Ucsicon). (For an example of the Ucs icon, see Figure 2.1.)

When you draw two-dimensional entities such as lines or circles in a three-dimensional drawing, the objects usually appear on the Ucs (X-Y) plane. One exception to this rule is when you use Osnap options to draw lines between objects on different planes. Many three-dimensional commands such as *Box, Cone,* and *Torus* are also oriented with respect to the Ucs.

Initially, the Ucs lies in the *World Coordinate System* (Wcs). This is the X-Y plane you have been using for your two-dimensional drawings. To review, take a look at the Ucs icon in Figure 2.1. Notice that the letter W appears in the icon. This means that the Ucs lies in the Wcs. If you want to draw on a plane oriented at a different angle, you will need to move the Ucs to that plane. If you do so, the letter W will no longer appear in the Ucs icon.

In this chapter, we will introduce the following AutoCAD commands:

- Vpoint (to change the viewpoint)

- Vports (to create four view ports)

- Pan (to move the viewpoint sideways)

- Plan (to change to a plan view)

- Hide (to remove hidden lines)

- Ucsicon (to control display of the coordinate icon)

- Ucs (to change the location and orientation of the coordinate system)

Starting the Cube Drawing

As usual, we will begin the drawing with the border template.

1. If necessary, start AutoCAD.

2. Give the **New** command and press Enter to get the Create New Drawing dialog box.

4. Type the drawing name **cube-ucs** and press Enter.

5. Give the **Ddedit** command to change the drawing title to CUBE-UCS.

6. Change the date.

7. Give the **z** (for Zoom) command with the **a** (for All) option to see all of your drawing.

8. Check that the current layer is OBJ. If not, change to this layer.

9. If necessary, turn on the grid.

10. If necessary, turn on Snap mode.

11. If necessary, turn off Ortho mode.

12. In Chapter 2, you turned off the Ucs icon because it was of little use for two-dimensional drawing. Now it is time to turn it back on. Do so by typing the **Ucsicon** command with the **on** option.

13. Check that the icon appears in the lower-left corner of the screen and that it contains the letter W.

SETTING THE DRAWING LIMITS

In all the previous drawings in this book, the limits check has been turned on, and you defined the drawing limits to be 11, 8.5. Now that you will be drawing in three dimensions, however, you will not be able to draw a torus later in this chapter if the limits check is left on. Therefore, you should check now to make sure that the limits check is *off*.

1. Give the **Status** command and press the spacebar. Your screen should look like Figure 2.5.

2. Check the end of the second line of the status report to make sure the word (Off) is present.

3. Press Enter.

4. Cancel the Status command with ^C.

5. Press **F1** to return to the drawing screen.

6. If the limits check was already off, skip to the next section.

7. On the other hand, if the word On appears at the end of the second line of the status report, it means that the limits check is on and you will not be able to draw the torus in three dimensions. To turn off limits check, give the **Limits** command and press the spacebar.

8. Type **off** and press Enter.

DIVIDING THE SCREEN INTO FOUR VIEWING PORTS

In this section, you will divide your screen into four viewing ports. Your drawing then will appear in four equal-sized rectangles on the screen. Initially, all four ports will show the same view—the conventional view that you have been using thus far. The viewpoint is down the Z axis (showing surfaces in the X-Y plane) which is typical of the top or plan view. You then will change the viewpoint for three of the ports. One port will show the front view (looking down the Y axis to view surfaces in the X-Z plane of the World Coordinate System). The other two views are angled and show surfaces in all three planes.

1. Give the **Vports** command with the **4** option. The screen is divided in half both horizontally and vertically to produce four separate ports as shown in Figure 12.1. Make sure your border drawing appears in each of the four ports.

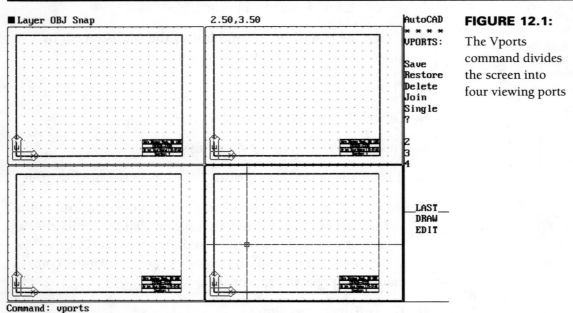

FIGURE 12.1:

The Vports command divides the screen into four viewing ports

```
Command: vports
Save/Restore/Delete/Join/SIngle/?/2/<3>/4: 4 Regenerating drawing.
Command:
```

SETTING GRID AND SNAP IN EACH PORT

Each port can be activated in turn and you can change the Snap and Grid individually.

1. Move the cursor into the upper-left port and press the pick button. Because this is the active port, the cursor is the usual crossed horizontal and vertical lines.

2. Move the cursor to the lower-left port and notice that it changes to an arrow pointing in the upper-left direction.

3. Move the cursor to the lower-right port and observe that the cursor still remains an arrow pointing in the upper-left direction. This is because only one of your four ports is active at any time. The cursor in the active port has the crossed lines, while in the other ports, the cursor is an arrow. In addition, the active port is surrounded by a heavy border.

4. With the cursor in the lower-right port, click the left mouse button. This port now becomes active and the cursor changes to crossed lines.

5. Turn off Snap mode in the lower-right port. (The word Snap should *not* appear in the upper-left corner of the screen.)

6. Turn off the grid. Make sure that the grid disappears from the lower-right port. Notice that the grid still appears in the other ports.

7. Move the cursor to the upper-right port and press the left mouse button to activate the port.

8. The word Snap now shows in the upper-left corner of the screen.

9. Turn off Snap mode in the upper-right port.

10. Turn off the grid in the upper-right port.

CHANGING THE VIEWPOINT IN EACH PORT

One advantage of dividing the screen into several viewing ports is that you can choose a different viewing angle or viewpoint for each port.

1. To change the viewpoint in the upper-right port, give the **Vpoint** command with the coordinates **1,–3,2** (no spaces) and press Enter. Observe that there are three parts to the coordinates—an X, a Y, and a Z direction. This option specifies a viewpoint looking down a line that goes from the origin through the point 1,–3,2. (Notice that the Vports command is plural but the Vpoint command is singular.)

2. Check that your drawing border in the upper-right port is now angled as though you are looking at it from above as shown in Figure 12.2. This will show the front part of your drawing from above.

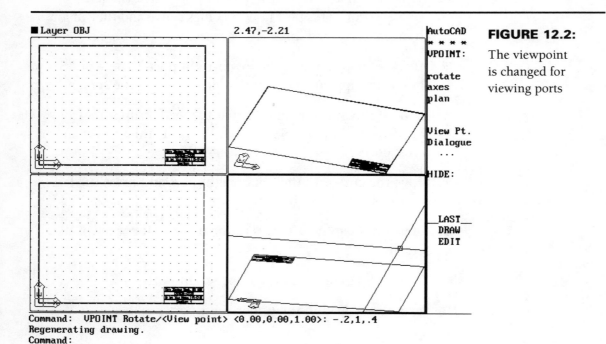

FIGURE 12.2:

The viewpoint is changed for viewing ports

```
Command:  VPOINT Rotate/<View point> <0.00,0.00,1.00>: -.2,1,.4
Regenerating drawing.
Command:
```

3. Check that the Ucs icon is still lying in the plane of the border.

4. Move the cursor to the lower-right port and activate it by clicking the left mouse button.

5. Press the spacebar to repeat the Vpoint command.

6. Type the coordinates **-0.2,1,0.4** (no spaces) and press Enter. This view will show the back side of your drawing from above. Check that your border in the lower-right port is angled, but a little flatter than in the upper-right port, as shown in Figure 12.2.

7. Check that the Ucs icon is still lying in the plane of the border.

8. Move the cursor to the lower-left port and press the left mouse button to activate the port.

9. Turn off Snap mode. Make sure the word Snap disappears from the upper-left corner of the screen.

10. Turn off the grid. Check that the grid disappears from the lower-left port.

11. To change the viewpoint in the lower-left port, give the **Vpoint** command with the coordinates **0,–1,0** (no spaces) and press Enter. This viewpoint is what you see when looking down the Y axis to view objects drawn in the X-Z plane. Your border is shown on edge (and appears as just a line in this view) since it was drawn in the X-Y plane. However, soon you will be drawing in the Z direction (the third dimension) and objects will grow upward in this view.

12. Notice that the Ucs icon in this port has changed. In the two right ports, the icon is angled along with the border. But in this view, the icon would be seen on edge and would be nearly invisible. Therefore, another icon—a broken pencil surrounded by a square—is shown instead of the Ucs icon.

13. Move the cursor to the upper-left port and press the left mouse button to activate it.

Drawing in the Z Direction

You are now ready to draw in three dimensions. You can easily draw solids such as a cube (box), cone, dome, dish (an upside-down dome) and torus (a donut). Unfortunately, these shapes are not built into AutoCAD and, before you can draw them, they must first be loaded via an *Autolisp solids program*. The first time you select a solid from the 3D construction dialog box, the solids program will be loaded. You can also run the 3D Autolisp solids program with the (Load "3D") command.

LOADING THE AUTOLISP SOLIDS PROGRAM FROM THE DIALOG BOX

To load the Autolisp solids program and draw a box, follow these steps:

1. Move the cursor to the top line of the screen.

2. When the menu bar appears, highlight the Draw menu and press the pick button.

3. Highlight the menu title 3D Surfaces and press the pick button to display the next menu.

4. Pick the menu item 3D Objects to get the 3D Objects dialog box as shown in Figure 12.3.

5. Move the cursor to the solid that looks like a cube of butter and press the pick button.

6. Pick the OK box to close the dialog box.

7. Move the cursor to the upper-left port.

8. Click the left mouse button to make this port current if it is not already.

9. Check that the word Snap shows in the upper-left corner of the screen. If necessary, turn on Snap mode.

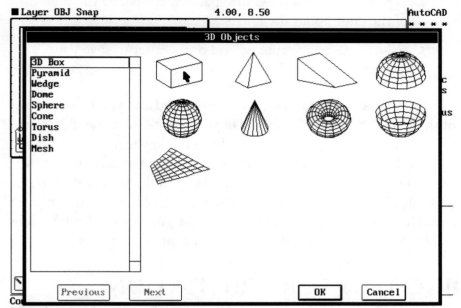

10. If necessary, turn the grid on.

11. Move the cursor to location **3,2** and press the pick button to start the cube at that point.

12. Establish the edge in the X direction by typing the distance **@5<0** (no spaces) and pressing the spacebar. This makes this edge a length of 5.

The three-dimensional rectangular solid called a box is drawn with its base lying in the current X-Y plane. Its height grows in the Z direction. If you want, you can choose X, Y, and Z dimensions that are different. However, we will draw a cube by making all three dimensions the same.

13. Since we want a cube, type the **c** (for Cube) option and press the spacebar. Check the other ports for your cube.

14. Type **0** (zero) and press the spacebar to specify the rotation of the cube about the Z axis.

15. Give the **Qsave** command and press Enter to save your drawing.

The solids program has now been loaded and you can draw any of the items shown in the dialog box—such as the cone, dome, and torus—simply by typing the name from the keyboard.

In the upper-left port, the cube looks like a square because you are looking at it down the Z axis. Similarly, in the lower-left port, the cube also looks like a square since you are looking at it down the Y axis. However, the upper-right and lower-right views definitely show a cube because the viewpoint is not along any of the axes.

ADDING TEXT FOR ORIENTATION

To help with the orientation, put the words Front and Back on the base plane of your border outside the cube. But first, let's create layer TEX for this purpose.

Creating Layer TEX

To create Layer Tex and make it current, follow these steps:

1. Give the **La** (for Layer) command with the **m** (for Make) option.

2. Type **tex** and press Enter twice. Make sure that the words Layer TEX appear on the top line of the screen.

Setting the Text Style

Let's set the typeface to Roman Complex.

1. Give the **Style** command with the **Romanc** option.

2. Type **0.5** and press Enter to set the height.

3. Press Enter five more times. Do *not* press **^C**.

Roman Complex with a height of 0.5 units is now the default typeface.

Writing Text on the New Layer

To write identifying text on the new layer, follow these steps:

1. Give the **Dtext** command and press the spacebar.

2. Type **j** (for justify) and press the spacebar.

3. Type **c** (for Center) and press the spacebar.

4. While still in the upper-left port, move to the bottom of the cube to grid point **5.5,1.0** and press the left mouse button.

5. Press the spacebar or second mouse button to accept zero rotation of the text.

6. Type the word **Front** (with a capital F) and press Enter twice.

7. Turn off Snap mode.

8. Press the spacebar to repeat the Dtext command.

9. Type **j** and press the spacebar.

10. Type **c** and press the spacebar.

11. Type the coordinate **5.5,7.8** (no spaces) and press Enter.

12. Type the angle **180** and press the spacebar to draw the next text upside-down.

13. Type the word **Back** (with a capital B) and press Enter twice to draw the upside-down letters.

Writing Identification Letters at the Corners

For additional help with finding the correct corner of the cube, you will write the letters A–D at the four corners of the cube.

1. Give the **Dtext** command and press the spacebar.

2. To put the letter A near the lower-left corner, type the coordinate position **2.2,1.2** and press Enter.

3. Type **0** (zero) and press Enter to set the angle of rotation.

4. Type the capital letter **A** and press Enter twice.

5. Press the spacebar to repeat the Dtext command.

6. Type the coordinate position **8.3,1.7** (no spaces) and press Enter.

7. Press the spacebar to choose the default rotation of zero.

8. Type the capital letter **B** and press Enter twice.

9. Press the spacebar to repeat the Dtext command.

10. Type the coordinate position **8.8,7.5** (no spaces) and press Enter.

11. Type **180** and press Enter to draw letters upside-down.

12. Type the capital letter **C** and press Enter twice.

13. Press the spacebar to repeat the Dtext command.

14. Type the coordinate position **2.6,7.5** and press Enter.

15. Press the spacebar to choose the default rotation of 180.

16. Type the capital letter **D** and press Enter twice.

17. Compare your screen with Figure 12.4.

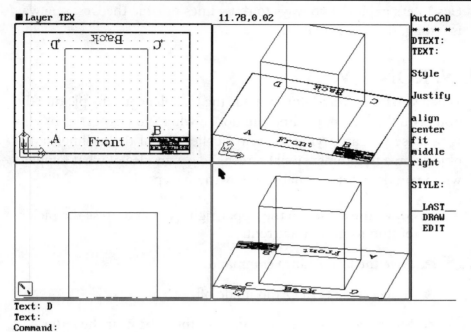

FIGURE 12.4:

Orientation text is drawn on the X-Y plane

Changing Back to the OBJ Layer

1. Give the **La** (for layer) command with the **s** (for Set) option.

2. Type **obj** and press Enter twice to change to Layer OBJ.

3. Check the top-left corner of the screen to make sure that the current layer is OBJ.

Drawing Outside the Plane of the Ucs

Up to now, you have drawn text, lines, circles, and other shapes on the X-Y plane—the plane containing the Ucs. If you want to draw on a different plane, you usually move the Ucs to the new plane. It is possible to draw lines outside the plane of the Ucs. However, you must be careful to use Osnaps. (In that case, it is unnecessary to move the

Ucs.) Let's explore two ways to draw lines outside the Ucs: one way is wrong, the other is right.

THE WRONG WAY

When you try to draw a line outside the Ucs plane just by picking the points on the screen, the line will not go where you expect it to. This is because you are trying to view a collection of three-dimensional objects on a two-dimensional screen. To get an idea of what happens when you do *not* use Osnaps, follow these steps:

1. Move the cursor to the upper-right port and press the pick button to make it current.

2. Give the **L** (for Line) command.

3. If necessary, turn Ortho mode off.

4. Move the cursor to the corner of the cube near the letter A. When you get near position **3,2**, press the pick button to start a line.

5. Move the cursor diagonally up and to the right to the opposite corner of the front face, just above corner B. When you get near coordinate position **7.9<71**, press the pick button to draw a line.

6. Press the second mouse button to complete the line command.

7. Give the **Osnap** command with the **endp** option.

The new line looks correct in the upper-right port, but not in the upper-left port. The line does not go where it appears to go because you did not use an Osnap option. Examine the other three viewing ports and notice that the new line lies only on the X-Y plane and therefore does not rise in the Z direction.

THE RIGHT WAY

The correct way to draw a line outside the Ucs plane is to use Osnaps. If you do, the line will go exactly where you want it to. To see the difference, follow these steps:

1. Type **L** for the Line command.

2. Move the target cursor back to the corner of the cube near the letter A. Then move a little to the right. When the coordinate is about **4,2**, press the pick button to start a second line. This location is exact because you used an Osnap option. (Be careful not to snap to the end of the incorrect line.)

3. Move the target cursor diagonally up and to the right to the opposite corner of the front face again. Then move left along the top edge. When the coordinate is about **7.7<78**, press the pick button to draw a line. (Be careful not to snap to the end of the incorrect line.)

4. Click the second mouse button to complete the line command.

5. Compare your screen with Figure 12.5.

Both the first line and the second line appear to be the same in the upper-right and lower-left ports. Now look for these two lines in the other two ports. You can see that the second line is a diagonal on the front face for the lower-right port. (The second line does not show in the upper-left port because the front face is viewed on edge.)

ERASING THE TWO LINES

Now that you have seen how to draw lines out of the plane of the Ucs, let's erase the two lines you just drew.

1. Move the cursor to the lower-right port and press the pick button to make it current.

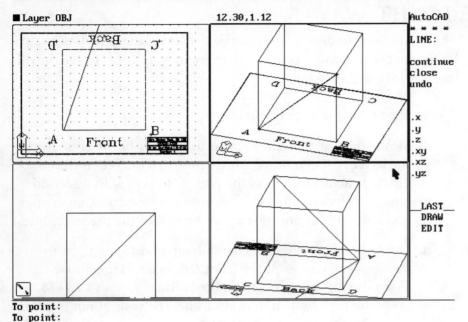

FIGURE 12.5:

Correct and incorrect lines drawn in 3D

2. Give the **e** (for Erase) command.

3. Move the cursor to one of the two new lines and press the pick button.

4. Move the cursor to the other line and press the pick button.

5. When both lines have been selected, click the second mouse button to erase them.

Changing the Location of the Ucs

In the next section, you will draw a circle on the front face of the cube (the X-Z plane). A circle is always drawn in the Ucs plane, but since the Ucs is currently in base plane (the Wcs), you must first move the Ucs to the front plane (World coordinate X-Z).

When you move the Ucs, the Ucs icon moves accordingly. Therefore, you never need to reorient the Ucs icon itself. There are several ways to move the Ucs. The first way involves two steps: first, you will move the origin while keeping the orientation the same. Second, you will rotate the Ucs so that it is parallel to the front face of the cube.

TRANSLATING THE UCS

To move the Ucs to the lower-left corner of the cube (near the letter A), follow these steps:

1. Make the upper-right view port current by moving the cursor there and clicking the left mouse button.

2. Give the **Ucs** command with the **o** (for Origin) option. With this option, simply point to the new location of the origin using an Osnap, and the Ucs moves there automatically.

3. Since the Endpoint Osnap is on, move the target cursor to the corner of the cube near the letter A.

4. Press the pick button to move the Ucs to this corner.

Observe that the Ucs icon did not move. The reason is that the Ucs icon can be positioned at one of two places—the Ucs origin or the lower-left corner of the view (the default position.) Since the Ucs is no longer at the World position, you will notice that the letter W in the Ucs icon has disappeared

MOVING THE UCS ICON
TO THE NEW UCS ORIGIN

■ To make the Ucs icon match the Ucs origin, give the **Ucsicon** command with the **or** (for Origin) option.

(You have already used this command with the Off option to turn off the icon, and with the On option to turn it back on.) The other options are All, Noorigin (the default option), and Origin.

Notice that the icon now appears at the lower corner of the cube, rather than the lower-left corner of the port. Nevertheless, it is still oriented in the base plane. The Ucsicon command with the Origin option only translates the icon to a new location in the same plane.

ROTATING THE
UCS RELATIVE TO THE WCS

In this section, you will rotate the Ucs so it lies in the front face of the cube. Then you can draw on this face.

1. Give the **Ucs** command with the **x** option. This specifies a rotation about the X axis.

You want to rotate the X axis by 90 degrees so the Y axis points upward. You will need to determine whether you want to rotate +90° or −90°. An easy way to do this is by using the "right-hand rule." Imagine you are grasping the X axis with your right hand. You can do this in two ways: with your thumb pointing either towards the positive X direction or towards the negative X direction. First, grab the axis so your thumb points in the positive direction. Then rotate your hand about the X axis the way your fingers are pointing. If this is the direction you want to move, the angle you want is positive. Otherwise, the angle is negative. You want to rotate in the positive direction this time.

2. Type the angle **90** and press the spacebar. Check that the Ucs icon has rotated about the X axis and now lies in the front plane. The Y axis points up in the original Z direction (World) as shown in Figure 12.6.

3. Give the **Osnap** command with the **none** option to turn off Endpoint Osnaps.

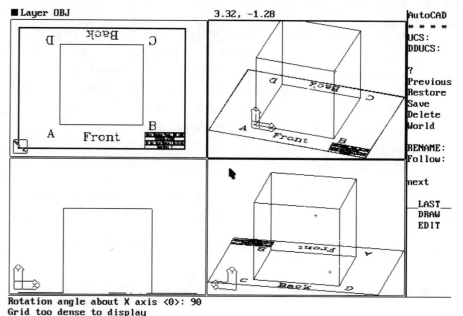

FIGURE 12.6:

The Ucs is aligned with the front plane

Drawing a Circle on the Front Face

Now that you have moved the Ucs and aligned it with the front plane, you can draw on that plane easily. In this section, you will inscribe a circle on the square of the front face (the one between the letters A and B.)

1. Move the cursor to the lower-left port and make it current by clicking the left mouse button.

2. Check that the Ucs icon is aligned with the front face (which appears as a square in this port). This is known as a *plan* view because you are looking down the Ucs Z axis. In this view, the X axis goes to the right and the Y axis points upward as in Figure 12.6.

3. Turn on the grid.

4. Turn on Snap mode.

5. To move the drawing up two grid points in the current port, give the **Pan** command (or the abbreviation **p**) and press the spacebar. (Here, pan is used in its photographic sense—changing the view by moving the viewing port. Magnification stays the same and, as with the Move command, you must give a displacement.) With the Move command, objects are moved relative to the coordinate system. However, with Pan, the objects and coordinate system stay the same.

6. To give the first point of the displacement, put the cursor on any grid point and press the pick button.

7. For the second point, move up two grid points and press the pick button again.

8. To draw a circle on this face, give the **c** (for Circle) command.

9. You want the circle to be centered in the square. Since there is a grid point at the center of the square, we will snap to that point. Move the cursor to position **2.5,2.5** and press the pick button.

10. There are also grid points at the midpoints of the square edges. Move the cursor right to the midpoint of an edge. Check that the circle touches the midpoint of each of the four edges.

11. When the cursor has snapped to the midpoint, press the pick button to complete the circle.

12. Turn off Snap mode.

13. Turn off the grid.

14. Compare your screen with Figure 12.7.

15. Check to see whether the circle has been drawn in the upper-right port as well.

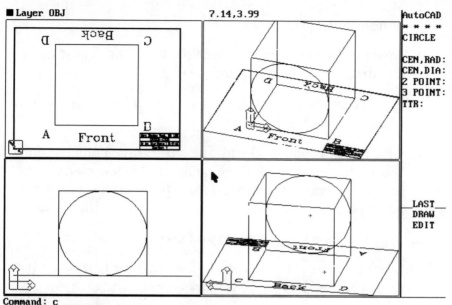

A circle is drawn
on the front face

```
Command: c
CIRCLE 3P/2P/TTR/<Center point>: Diameter/<Radius>:
Command:  <Snap off>  <Grid off>
```

Drawing a Circle and Cone on the Right Face

Next, you will put a circle and a cone on the right face of the cube
(between the letters B and C.) But first you will have to move the Ucs
to the corner marked B and align it with the right (B-C) plane.

MOVING THE UCS TO THE RIGHT FACE

In the previous section, you aligned the Ucs with the front plane in
two steps. First you moved the Ucs origin with one command, then
you rotated it with another. This time you will do both steps at once.

Last time, you drew a circle on a plan view, so the circle had its
normal shape. This time, you will draw a circle on an angled plane,
one that is not a plan view. The circle will then appear as an ellipse
(oval).

1. Move the cursor to the upper-right port and press the pick button to make it current.

2. Give the **Hide** command to hide the back lines of the cube and drawing border (but not the text).

3. Check that the Ucs icon is at corner A and lying in the front plane.

4. Give the **Ucs** command with the **3** (for three-point) option. You now need to mark three points in the new plane in the following order—the new origin, a point on the new X axis, and a point on the new X-Y plane (but not on the X axis.)

5. Type the **endp** Osnap option and press the spacebar.

6. Move the cursor to the cube corner near the letter B and press the pick button. This marks the new origin.

7. Type **endp** and press the spacebar again.

8. Move the cursor to the cube corner near the letter C and press the pick button. This marks the direction of the new X axis.

9. Type **endp** and press the spacebar again.

10. Move the selection cursor straight up to the cube corner above C. (You can also pick the corner above B.) Press the pick button to define the new Ucs.

11. Check that the Ucs icon has moved to corner B and has rotated to align with the right plane as shown in Figure 12.8.

DRAWING A CIRCLE ON THE RIGHT FACE

In this section, you will draw a circle on the right plane. When you drew the previous circle, you snapped to grid points for the center and radius. You can also inscribe a circle on the right face the same

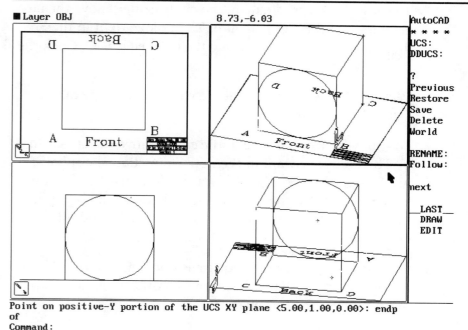

FIGURE 12.8:

The Ucs is aligned with the right face

```
Point on positive-Y portion of the UCS XY plane <5.00,1.00,0.00>: endp
of
Command:
```

way. This time, however, to introduce a different method, you will use the .X filter and osnaps instead.

1. Check that the upper-right port is current and that the Ucs icon is aligned with the right face, which appears as a parallelogram in this view.

2. To draw a circle on this face, give the **C** (for Circle) command.

3. You want the circle to be centered in the square. Therefore, we will take the X coordinate from the midpoint of the bottom edge of the square and the Y coordinate from the midpoint of the right edge of the square. Type the **.x** filter and press the spacebar.

4. Type the **mid** Osnap option and press the spacebar.

5. To show the X coordinate of the circle center, move the target cursor to the Ucs icon at B. Then move right in the X direction about half-way along the cube edge B-C. Click the left mouse button.

6. When AutoCAD asks for the YZ coordinates, type **mid** again and press the spacebar.

7. To show the Y coordinate of the circle, move the cursor to C. Then move upward in the new Y direction about half-way along the cube edge. Click the left mouse button. You have now defined the circle center. There should be a plus mark (+) to show the center, and the circle should fill the cube face.

8. Since the midpoint of the square is one point on the circumference, we can use that location to fix the circle size. Type **mid** and press the spacebar.

9. With the cursor still on one edge of the square, press the pick button to complete the circle. Compare your screen with Figure 12.9.

10. Check the lower-right port to see that the circle has been drawn there too.

The new circle is not visible in the other two ports because it is viewed on edge in these views.

DRAWING A CONE ON THE RIGHT FACE

In this section, you will draw a cone on the right face of the cube. The cone is one of the solids that was loaded into AutoCAD along with the cube earlier. To draw a cone, you need to specify the location of the center, base radius, top radius, height, and the number of surface segments.

1. Check that the upper-right port is still current.

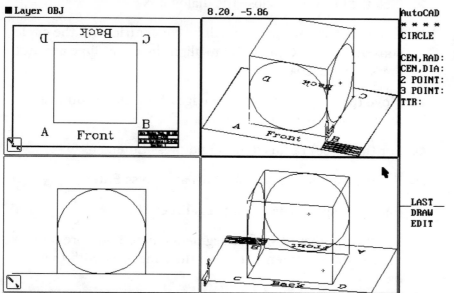

```
CIRCLE 3P/2P/TTR/<Center point>: .x of mid of (need YZ): mid of Diameter/<Radius
> <2.50>: mid of
Command:
```

2. Move the cursor to the top line of the screen to get the menu bar with its menu titles.

3. Move the cursor to highlight the menu title Draw and press the pick button to pull down the menu. If two menus appear, press the pick button and skip to step 6 below.

4. Highlight the menu item 3D Surfaces and press the pick button to display the next menu.

5. Pick the menu item 3D Objects to get the 3D Objects dialog box as shown in Figure 12.3.

6. Move the cursor to the cone icon and press the pick button.

7. Pick the OK box to close the dialog box.

8. Since the base of the cone will be concentric with the circle, you can use the Cen Osnap to align the cone. Type **cen** and press the spacebar.

9. Move the target cursor to the edge of the circle you just drew and press the pick button.

10. For the (base) radius, type **1** and press Enter.

11. For the top radius, type **0** (zero) and press Enter.

12. For the height, type **2** and press Enter.

13. For the number of surface segments, type **8** and press Enter. (The surface segments connect the cone apex with the base.)

14. Check each port for your cone.

15. Give the **Hide** command.

16. Move the cursor to the lower-right port and press the pick button to make it active.

17. Give the **Hide** command again.

18. Compare your screen with Figure 12.10.

The cube and cone you drew are formed by a polygon mesh (which looks a little like a wire frame model) which enables you to see through such solids. However, using the Hide command, you can hide (remove) those line or wires that are in the back part of the solid. This process is called *hidden-line removal*.

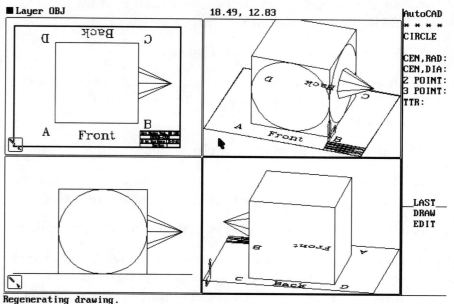

FIGURE 12.10:
The cone and cube with hidden lines removed

Drawing a Torus on the Back Plane of the Cube

In this section, you will draw a torus on the back side of the cube (between the letters C and D.) We will use the lower-right port because the back face is nearly plan view there. Before starting, you will have to move the Ucs to this face.

MOVING THE UCS TO THE BACK PLANE

To move the Ucs to the back plane, follow these steps:

1. If necessary, move the cursor to the lower-right port and press the pick button to make it current.

2. Give the **Ucs** command with the **3** (for three-point) option.

3. Type the **endp** Osnap option and press the spacebar.

4. Move the target cursor to the cube corner near the letter C and press the pick button to mark the new origin.

5. Type **endp** and press the spacebar again.

6. Move the target cursor right to the cube corner near the letter D and press the pick button. This marks the direction of the new X axis.

7. Type **endp** and press the spacebar again.

8. Move the target cursor to corner D. Then move up the edge to the top. Press the pick button to define the new Ucs.

9. Give the **Ucsicon** command with the **or** (for Origin) option.

10. Check that the Ucs icon has moved to corner C and rotated to align with the back plane. The icon will not move if there isn't room. If the icon has not moved, give the **Zoom** command with the **0.9x** option.

DRAWING THE TORUS

1. Check that the lower-right port is still current.

2. Turn on Snap mode.

3. Move the cursor to the top line of the screen to get the menu bar with its menu titles.

4. Move the cursor to highlight the menu title **Draw** and press the pick button to pull down the menu.

5. If two menus appear with 3D Objects highlighted in the lower menu, click the left mouse button to get the 3D Objects dialog box directly. Otherwise, pick 3D Surfaces and 3D Objects.

6. Move the cursor to the torus icon.

7. Press the pick button.

8. Pick the OK box to close the dialog box.

9. Move the cursor to the center of the back face C-D. When the cursor snaps to point **2.5,2.5**, press the pick button to define the center of the torus.

10. Turn off Snap mode.

11. For the torus radius, type **2** and press Enter.

12. For the tube radius, type **0.3** and press Enter.

13. For the number of tube segments, type **16** and press Enter.

14. For the number of torus segments, type **8** and press Enter.

15. Check each port for your torus and compare to Figure 12.11.

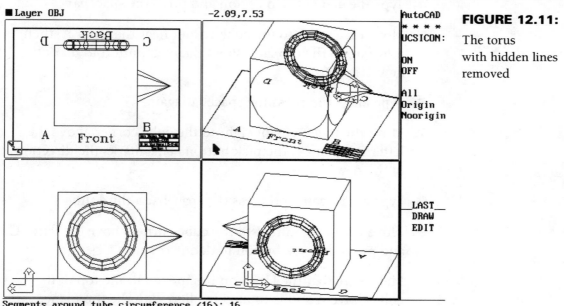

FIGURE 12.11:

The torus with hidden lines removed

```
Segments around tube circumference <16>: 16
Segments around torus circumference <16>: 8
Command:
```

Drawing a Dome on the Top of the Cube

In this section, you will draw a dome (hemisphere) on top of the cube. But first, we'll move the Ucs and change the view point.

MOVING THE UCS TO THE TOP OF THE CUBE

1. Move the cursor to the upper-right port and press the pick button to make the port current.

2. Give the **Hide** command.

3. Give the **Ucs** command with the **3** (for three-point) option.

4. Type the **endp** Osnap option and press the spacebar.

5. Move the cursor to the cube corner near the letter A, then move up to the top face. Press the pick button to mark the new origin.

6. Type **endp** and press the spacebar again.

7. Move the target cursor right to the cube corner above the letter B and press the pick button. This marks the direction of the new X axis.

8. Type **endp** again and press the spacebar a third time.

9. Move the target cursor to the cube corner above the letter C and press the pick button to define the new Ucs.

10. Make sure that the Ucs icon has moved to the top of the cube above A and is rotated to align with the top plane.

DRAWING THE DOME

1. Check that the upper-right port is still current.

2. Move the cursor to the top line of the screen to get the menu bar with its menu titles.

3. Move the cursor to highlight the menu title Draw and press the pick button to pull down the menu.

4. If two menus appear with 3D Objects highlighted in the lower menu, press the left mouse button to get the 3D Objects dialog box directly. Otherwise, pick 3D Surfaces and 3D Objects.

5. Move the cursor to the icon that looks like a dome or upside-down bowl (in the upper right corner of the dialog box) and press the pick button.

6. Pick the OK box to close the dialog box.

7. Turn on Snap mode.

8. Move the cursor to the center of the top face. When the cursor snaps to coordinate point **2.5,2.5**, press the pick button to define the center of the dome.

9. Turn off Snap mode.

10. For the dome radius, type **1** and press Enter.

11. For the number of longitudinal segments, type **8** and press Enter.

12. For the number of latitudinal segments, type **6** and press Enter.

13. Check each port for your dome and compare to Figure 12.12.

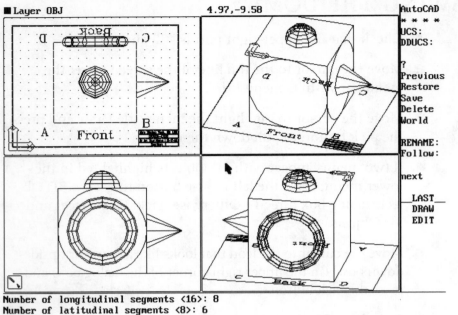

■ Layer OBJ   4.97,-9.58

AutoCAD
* * * *
UCS:
DDUCS:

?
Previous
Restore
Save
Delete
World

RENAME:
Follow:

next

___LAST___
DRAW
EDIT

FIGURE 12.12:
The dome is
drawn on the
cube top

```
Number of longitudinal segments <16>: 8
Number of latitudinal segments <8>: 6
Command:
```

Returning to World Coordinates

You have moved the coordinates several times so you could draw on different planes. Now let's move them back to the World coordinate position.

1. Give the **Ucs** command and press the spacebar.

2. Press Enter to accept the default of world coordinates.

3. Check the upper-right port to see that the Ucs icon has moved back to the World position.

4. Give the **QSave** command.

COMPLETING THE DRAWING

When you have more than one viewing port on the screen, the Plot command will print from the current port. In addition, you must specifically select the plot option to remove hidden lines, whether or not the view on the screen has hidden lines removed. You will make two plots of your work, one of the upper-right port and one of the lower-right port.

1. Move the cursor to the upper-right port and press the pick button to make it current.

2. Give the **Plot** command to get the Plot Configuration dialog box.

3. Move to the Additional Parameters area and pick the Hide Lines check box.

4. Pick the Full radio box in the Preview region.

5. Pick the Preview box to see what your drawing will look like.

6. To move the Plot Preview dialog box out of the way, move the cursor over the words Plot Preview, hold the left mouse button down, and move the mouse to the right. Release the left button when the dialog box is out of the way.

7. Pick End Preview.

8. If you are plotting to a file, pick the File Name box and change the name to **Cube1**.

9. Pick the OK box to start the plot.

10. Make the lower right view port current.

11. Give the **Plot** command again and change the file name to **Cube2**.

12. Pick the OK box to start the second plot.

13. If you are a student, turn in the drawings to your instructor.

14. Give the **End** command.

Paper Space: Separating the Model from the Drawing

FEATURING

Inserting one drawing into another

Changing from model to paper space

Plotting four views at once

▼

n this chapter, we will explore the AutoCAD feature known as *Paper Space*. The Paper Space feature enables you to separate the three-dimensional model from the design and plotting of the two-dimensional drawing of the model.

Until now, you have been working exclusively in *Model Space*, where you drew objects, borders, and title blocks. It is possible, though, to draw the object in Model Space and then switch to Paper Space to design the plot. Paper Space is where you will place the border, title block, and other things that are not part of the solid model. In addition, you can arrange several view ports on Paper Space so they can be plotted together.

In Chapter 12, you divided the screen into four contiguous viewing ports so you could view your object from different angles. You then made separate plots from two of the ports. With Paper Space, you can arrange viewing ports in a variety of ways and they need not be contiguous. You can hide the port boundaries so only the objects themselves are visible and you can freeze layers in some view ports but not in others.

Until now, you have drawn objects that were small enough (when drawn full scale) to fit into the drawing boundary of 11, 8.5. But with Paper Space, you can maintain two scales—one for Model Space and one for Paper Space. This feature allows you to draw a large object full scale in Model Space and then create a drawing in Paper Space scaled to the plotter size.

Let's begin with a copy of the Cube-Ucs drawing you made in Chapter 12. You will erase the border and title block from this drawing and create a layer for the Paper Space borders. You can change from Model Space to Paper Space by turning off the Tilemode variable (1 = on, 0 = off). Because Paper Space is a different framework from the usual Model Space, you will also need to set the units, limits, grid, and snap as you did in Chapter 2.

By inserting your border drawing into Paper Space, you avoid having to draw the border and title block again. You will create a view port in Paper Space to show your cube drawing from different directions. To get different views of the drawing, you copy the first view port to make four versions. After changing back to Model Space, you will change the viewpoint in three of the ports to match those you used in Chapter 12. Finally, you will switch back to Paper Space, hide the port boundaries, and plot the drawing to show four views at once.

New AutoCAD commands introduced in this chapter are:

- Insert (to insert one drawing into another)

- Mview (to create Paper Space view ports)

- Mspace (to change to Model Space)

- Vplayer (to hide layers on one view port)

- Pspace (to change to Paper Space)

Starting the Combined Model Space, Paper Space Drawing

To begin the new technique, follow these steps.

1. If AutoCAD is running, go on to step 2. If not, start AutoCAD as usual.

2. Type the **New** command to get the Create New Drawing dialog box.

3. Type the drawing name **cubepapr=cube-ucs** and press Enter. Your new drawing will now begin with a copy of the previous one. *Do not* change the title and date at this time—we will erase them a little later.

4. If there is only one view port on the screen, skip to step 8.

5. Move the cursor to the upper-left port and press the pick button to make it current.

6. Turn off Grid, Snap, and Ortho if they are on.

7. Give the **Vports** command with the **si** (for Single port) options. The screen changes to show a single view port as shown in Figure 13.1.

8. If the Ucs icon does not show, give the **Ucsicon** command with the **On** option.

9. If the viewpoint of your drawing does not look like Figure 13.1, give the **Vpoint** command with the coordinates **0,0,1**.

10. If the entire border is not visible, give the **z** command with the **a** (for All) option.

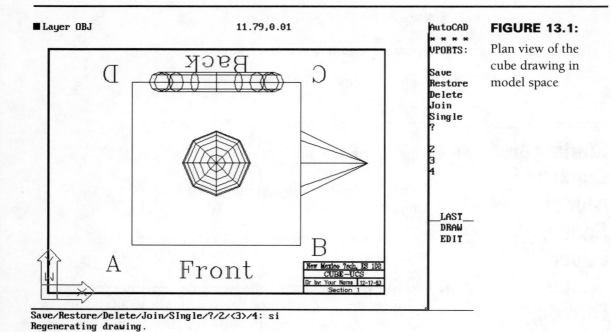

Save/Restore/Delete/Join/SIngle/?/2/<3>/4: si
Regenerating drawing.
Command:

FIGURE 13.1:

Plan view of the cube drawing in model space

ERASING THE BORDER AND TITLE BLOCK FROM MODEL SPACE

You are currently in Model Space, AutoCAD's default. You will now erase the border and title block so you can draw them in Paper Space later.

1. Give the **e** (for Erase) command.

2. Move the selection cursor over the border and press the pick button. The border becomes spotty.

3. Put a regular window around the title block to add it to the selection set. Put the corners at **7.8,1.6** and **10.7,0.3**.

4. Press the second mouse button to erase the border and title block.

CREATING A LAYER FOR DRAWING IN PAPER SPACE

In this section, you will create a new layer for drawing in Paper Space. Then you will change its color to yellow and make it current.

1. Move the cursor to the top line of the screen.

2. When the menu bar appears, highlight the Settings menu.

3. Press the pick button to pull down the Settings menu.

4. Move the cursor down the menu to highlight the item Layer Control.

5. Press the pick button to get the Layer dialog box.

6. Type the name **paper**, but don't press Enter.

7. Pick the New box and check that the name PAPER appears in the table.

8. Move the cursor to the PAPER layer in the table and press the pick button to highlight it.

If you don't have a color screen, skip to step 14.

9. In the next few steps, you will change the color of lines on the Paper layer to yellow. Pick the Set Color box to get the Select Color dialog box.

10. Move the cursor to the small yellow box at the top of the dialog box and press the pick button.

11. Look at the bottom of the Set Color dialog box to see that the color yellow has been selected.

12. Pick the OK box to close the Select Color dialog box.

13. Look at the COLOR layer in the table to see that its color is yellow for Layer PAPER.

14. Move the cursor to the Current box and press the pick button.

15. Move the cursor to the OK box and press the pick button to close the Layer dialog box.

16. Look at the upper-left corner of the screen to see that Layer PAPER is current and a yellow box appears.

17. Check that the Ucs icon has its usual shape, and that the letter W is displayed.

Changing to Paper Space

The AutoCAD variable Tilemode controls whether view ports behave as they did in previous chapters (where they are simply borders around your drawing), or whether they are separate entities, as in Paper Space. Your work in previous chapters was done with Tilemode on. When you created the four view ports in Chapter 12, they lay side by side (like tiles) because you were drawing in Model Space. In contrast, turning the Tilemode variable off (changing it to 0), switches you to Paper Space, where you can open viewing ports to look at your model.

To change to Paper Space, follow these steps:

1. Give the **Tilemode** command and press the space bar.

2. Type **0** (zero) and press the space bar. The screen becomes blank as it is switched to Paper Space.

3. Compare your screen to Figure 13.2. Notice that the top-left corner of the screen shows the letter P because Paper Space is current. Also observe that the Ucs icon has changed shape. In Model Space, the icon had two arrows, one

pointing in the X direction and one in the Y direction. The Paper Space icon, however, is a drafting triangle. An X in the right corner points in the X direction and the letter W indicates World coordinates. Furthermore, the box in the lower-left corner of the icon shows that we are looking down the Z axis.

The screen is blank because you have not designated anything to be plotted yet.

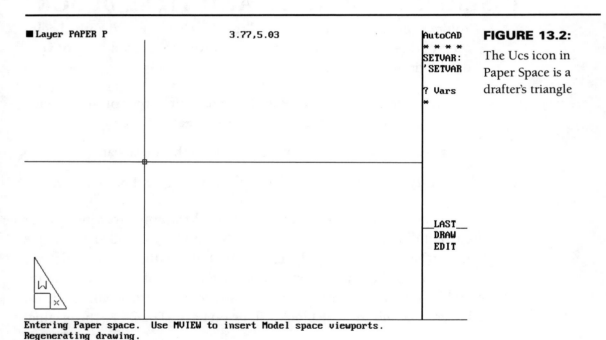

FIGURE 13.2: The Ucs icon in Paper Space is a drafter's triangle

ADJUSTING PAPER SPACE

Because Paper Space has its own scale and drawing limits, you must establish these before continuing.

1. Give the **Limits** command.

2. Press the space bar to accept the lower-left limits of 0,0.

3. Type the coordinates **11,8.5** (no spaces) and press Enter to establish the upper-right limits. These just happen to be the same limits you chose for the drawing in Model Space. Of course, these two limits can be different.

4. Give the **z** (for Zoom) command with the **a** (for All) option to make your Paper Space drawing screen match the limits.

INSERTING A BORDER AND TITLE BLOCK

You now could draw a border and title block as you did at the beginning of this book. It will be easier, however, to insert a copy of your Border drawing instead.

1. Check for the letter P in the upper-left corner of the screen to ensure that you are currently in Paper Space.

2. Give the **Insert** command and press the space bar.

3. Type ***border** (*do not* forget the asterisk) and press Enter.

The Insert command allows you to add another drawing to your current drawing. Normally, the inserted drawing is added as a single entity. Then you cannot change any part of it without first exploding it. But by placing the asterisk at the beginning of the name, the individual entities are retained. In this case, the border will reside on Layer BOR and the title block will be on Layer TBLOCK, the original layers.

4. Type **0,0** (two zeros) and press Enter to designate the insertion point of the border.

5. Press Enter to accept a scale factor of one.

6. Press Enter to accept zero rotation. Your border and title block should now be in their usual place as shown in Figure 13.3.

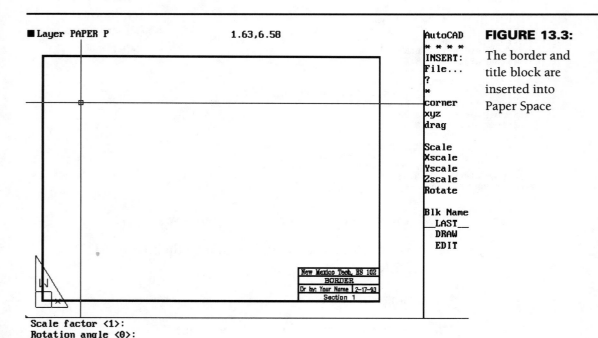

■ Layer PAPER P   1.63,6.58

AutoCAD
* * * *
INSERT:
File...
?
*
corner
xyz
drag

Scale
Xscale
Yscale
Zscale
Rotate

Blk Name
__LAST__
DRAW
EDIT

New Mexico Tech, ES 102
BORDER
Dr by: Your Name | 2-17-93
Section 1

Scale factor <1>:
Rotation angle <0>:
Command:

FIGURE 13.3:

The border and title block are inserted into Paper Space

7. To check the drawing border, give the **List** command and press the space bar.

8. Move the selection cursor to the border and press the pick button. The border becomes spotted.

9. Press the second mouse button to complete the selection.

10. Check the information about the border to make sure that it is located in Paper Space as shown in Figure 13.4.

11. Press Enter to see the rest of the information.

12. Press **F1** to return to the drawing screen.

```
              POLYLINE  Layer: BOR
                        Space: Paper space
           Closed
starting width      0.03
   ending width     0.03

              VERTEX    Layer: BOR
                        Space: Paper space
           at point, X=     0.50  Y=     0.50  Z=     0.00
starting width      0.03
   ending width     0.03

              VERTEX    Layer: BOR
                        Space: Paper space
           at point, X=    10.50  Y=     0.50  Z=     0.00
starting width      0.03
   ending width     0.03

              VERTEX    Layer: BOR
                        Space: Paper space
           at point, X=    10.50  Y=     8.00  Z=     0.00
starting width      0.03
-- Press RETURN for more --_
```

FIGURE 13.4:

The List command shows the drawing border located in Paper Space

13. Zoom on the title block with a window.

14. Give the **Ddedit** command to change the title to CUBE PAPER.

15. Change the date.

16. Give the **z** command with the **a** option.

Adding View Ports to Paper Space

When you changed from Model Space to Paper Space, the cube model disappeared because you had not yet defined viewing ports in Paper Space.

In this section, you will create or "open" viewing ports in Paper Space so you will be able to see your model from different directions. You can have top, front, side and angled views, but for each one, you must create a view port.

1. Check that the Paper Space icon appears in the lower-left corner of the screen. If you are not in Paper Space, give the **Pspace** command.

2. Turn on the paper-space Grid.

3. Turn on Snap mode.

4. Give the **Mview** (for Make view) command. You can see from the prompt that there are several options. However, we will simply mark two opposite corners to define a window for the view port, the default response.

5. Define the upper-left corner of the port by moving the cursor to location **1.5,7.5** and pressing the pick button.

6. Define the lower-right corner by moving the cursor to location **5.0,5.0** and pressing the pick button.

7. Compare your screen to Figure 13.5. The top view of the cube should be visible through the view port.

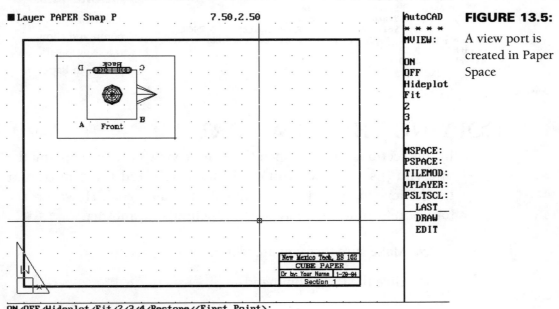

FIGURE 13.5:

A view port is created in Paper Space

CHECKING THE NEW VIEW PORT

You now have one view port and can see your model. If you have a color screen, the view-port border is yellow. Let's explore the first view port with the List command.

1. Give the **List** command.

2. Move the selection cursor to the view-port border (not the drawing border) and press the pick button.

3. Press the second button to complete the List command and to see a description of the view-port border as shown in Figure 13.6.

4. Press **F1** to return to the drawing screen.

```
        VIEWPORT  Layer: PAPER
                  Space: Paper space
                  Status: On and Active
                  Scale relative to Paper space:    0.2940xp
    center point, X=     3.25  Y=     6.25  Z=     0.00
      width        3.50
     height        2.50

Command: _
```

FIGURE 13.6:

The List command shows the view-port border in Paper

COPYING THE VIEW PORT

In this section, you will open three more view ports by copying the one you just created. You could have selected the 4 option at the Mview command to accomplish the same goal. However, the four ports would then have been touching one another.

1. Make sure that you are still in Paper Space.

2. Give the **Copy** command.

3. Move the cursor to the view-port border (not to the drawing border) and press the pick button. The view-port border becomes spotty.

4. Press the second mouse button to complete the selection step.

5. At the **<Base point or displacement>/Multiple:** prompt, give the option **m** (for Multiple copies) and press the space bar.

6. For the first point of the displacement, move the cursor to the upper-left corner of the port at location **1.5,7.5** and press the pick button.

7. For the location of the upper-right port, move the cursor to the right to coordinate position **4.5<0** and press the pick button. A second view port is drawn to the right of the first.

8. To create the lower-left port, move the cursor below the original port to coordinate position **3.0<270** and press the pick button. A third view port is drawn under the original.

9. For the lower-right port, move the cursor below the upper-right port to coordinate position **5.41<326** and press the pick button. A fourth view port is drawn.

10. Press the second mouse button to complete the copy command.

11. Turn off Snap mode.

12. Turn off the paper-space grid. Your screen should look like Figure 13.7, with all ports showing the same view.

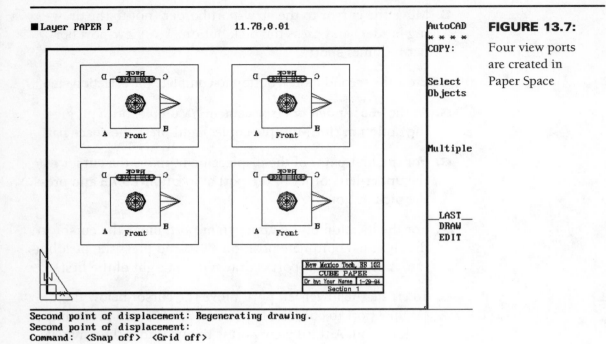

FIGURE 13.7:

Four view ports are created in Paper Space

Changing the Viewing Direction for the New Ports

In this section, you will change the viewpoint or viewing direction in the new view ports. To do this, you first need to change back to Model Space.

1. Give the **Mspace** command.

2. Make sure that the Paper Space icon and the letter P on the status line have disappeared, indicating that you are now in Model Space.

3. Check that the Model Space icon appears in the lower-left corner of each of the four view ports.

4. Move the cursor and check that it is an arrow pointing in the upper-left direction (except when the cursor is in the current view port.)

CHANGING THE VIEWING DIRECTION FOR THE UPPER-RIGHT PORT

Now let's change the viewing direction for the upper-right port.

1. Move the cursor into the upper-right view port and press the pick button to make this port current. The cursor changes to crossed lines. Notice, however, that the lines of the cursor stop at the view-port border. They no longer extend to the edges of the drawing screen.

2. Give the **Vpoint** command with the coordinate **1,–3,2**.

3. Give the **z** command with the **a** option.

4. To center the cube, give the **p** (for Pan) command. (As you learned in Chapter 12, the Pan command moves the viewpoint sideways.)

5. Move the cursor to the middle of the cube and press the pick button.

6. Move the cursor to the middle of the port and press the pick button again.

7. Give the **Hide** command to hide the details on the back side of the model (but only in the active view port.)

CHANGING THE VIEWING DIRECTION FOR THE LOWER-RIGHT PORT

1. Move the cursor into the lower-right port and press the pick button to make this port current. The cursor changes to crossed lines.

2. Give the **Vpoint** command with the direction **–0.2,1,0.4**, as you did in Chapter 12.

3. If necessary, give the **Pan** command to center the cube in the port.

4. Give the **Hide** command to hide the details on the other side of the model.

CHANGING THE VIEWING DIRECTION FOR THE LOWER-LEFT PORT

1. Move the cursor into the lower-left view port and press the pick button to make this port current.

2. Give the **Vpoint** command with the **0,–1,0** coordinate.

3. Give the **z** command.

4. Type the option **0.9x** (don't forget the x) and press Enter. This reduces the image 10 percent.

5. If necessary, give the **Pan** command to center the cube in the port.

6. Give the **Hide** command to hide the details (the torus) on the backside of the model.

7. Compare your screen with Figure 13.8.

8. Notice that there is a line on either side of the cube near the bottom. These lines are the identifying letters A–D as viewed on edge. To turn off these letters (just in this view), give the command **Vplayer** (for View port layer) and press the space bar.

9. Type the option **f** (for Freeze) and press the space bar.

10. Type the layer name **tex** and press the space bar.

11. Press Enter twice to freeze the TEX layer on the current port only.

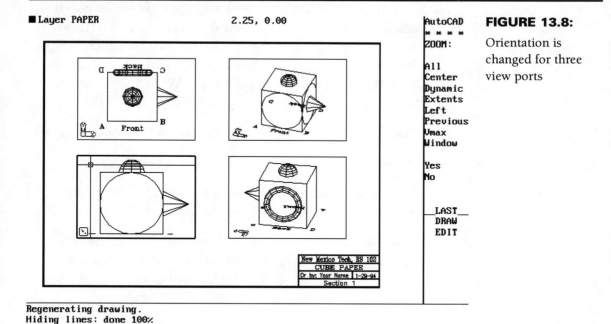

Resizing and Deleting a View Port

As you have seen, when you are in Paper Space, each view port is a separate entity. Let's switch back to Paper Space so you can resize and then remove the lower-left port.

1. Change back to Paper Space by typing the **Pspace** command.

2. Make sure that you are in Paper Space by looking for the P in the upper-left corner and for the triangular Ucs icon.

3. Give the **Stretch** command with the **c** (for Crossing window) option.

4. Move the cursor to the lower-right corner of the lower-left port. Then move a little up and to the right and press the pick button.

5. Move the cursor to the lower-left corner of the lower-left port. Then move a little farther down and to the left. When the lower part of the port is enclosed, press the pick button. The entire port boundary becomes spotted. The model in the port is not part of this operation. What you are doing is changing the viewing port that is used to look at the model.

6. Press the second mouse button to complete selection.

7. Turn on Snap mode.

8. Press the pick button to mark one point of the displacement. (It doesn't matter where the cursor is.)

9. Move the cursor down one grid point and press the pick button to enlarge the port. Observe that the model in the port did not change, only the port boundary.

10. Turn off Snap mode.

11. Give the **e** (for Erase) command.

12. Move the selection cursor to the border of the lower-left port and press the pick button.

13. Press the second mouse button to erase the border and remove the view. Of course, the model is not affected by this operation.

14. Give the **U** command to restore the erased lower-left view.

Plotting the Paper Space Drawing

Before plotting your drawing, you will mark two of the ports for hidden-line removal. You will also turn off the view-port borders so they won't show.

HIDING DETAILS IN TWO PORTS

When you made your plot in Chapter 12, you selected the Remove hidden lines option to remove *all* the hidden lines. In Paper Space, however, you have more control. You will now hide parts of only the upper-right and lower-right ports.

1. Make sure you are in Paper Space.

2. Give the **Mview** command.

3. Type the option **h** (for Hide) and press the space bar.

4. Give the **on** option.

5. Move the selection cursor to the border of the upper-right view port and press the pick button to select it.

6. Next, move the cursor to the border of the lower-right view port and press the pick button to select it.

7. Press the second mouse button to complete selection.

Now the hidden lines of these ports will be removed when plotted, even though you will later select the option not to remove hidden lines.

HIDING THE PORT BOUNDARIES

In this section, you will freeze the port boundaries so they will not appear in the plot.

1. Pull down the Layer dialog box.

2. Pick layer OBJ to highlight it.

3. Pick the Current box to make OBJ the current layer.

4. Pick layer OBJ again to remove the highlighting.

5. Pick layer PAPER to highlight it.

6. Pick the Freeze box to freeze the Paper layer.

7. Pick the OK box to close the dialog box.

8. Check the upper-left corner of the screen to make sure that Layer OBJ is current.

9. Check that the view-port boundaries do not show on the screen.

10. Give the **Qsave** command to save your drawing.

Previously, you moved, resized, and deleted a view port by selecting the port boundary. Unfortunately, when the boundary layer is frozen, you cannot do any of these things.

PLOTTING THE DRAWING

Congratulations! You've just created a Paper Space drawing starting with the three-dimensional model you drew in Chapter 12. Let's plot it.

1. Plot the drawing in the usual way for a planar drawing. In other words, use the options from Chapters 2-11, *not* those from Chapter 12. For example, pick the **Limits** radio box and remove the X from the Hide Lines check box.

2. Compare your plot to Figure 13.9.

3. If you are a student, turn in your plot to the instructor.

The lessons in this book have covered the most important features of AutoCAD Release 12. There are, however, many additional features you might wish to explore. One of the best ways to find out about these additional features is by using the Help command. In addition, you may also find the book *Mastering AutoCAD Release 12* from SYBEX to be helpful.

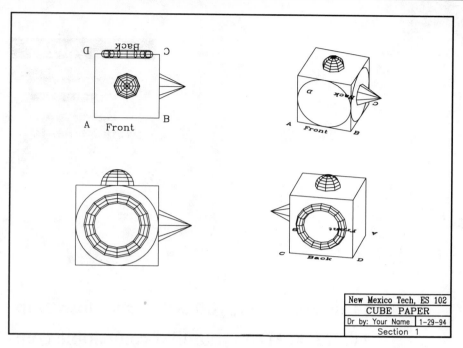

New Mexico Tech, ES 102
CUBE PAPER
Dr by: Your Name | 1-29-94
Section 1

FIGURE 13.9:

Paper Space plot of the cube

Installing
AutoCAD

n this appendix, you will learn how to install AutoCAD on your IBM-compatible computer. You will go through the process of starting your computer and setting it up for AutoCAD. You will then run the AutoCAD installation program. Do not try to copy Auto-CAD from the original disks to your computer, because it is not in usable form on the original disks. Finally, you will start Auto-CAD and configure it for your hardware.

But before installing AutoCAD, let's go over the equipment you will need in order to run AutoCAD Release 12.

Required and Optional Equipment to Run AutoCAD

- IBM or compatible computer with an 80386 or 80486 CPU

- A minimum of 4M bytes of memory, but 8M bytes is recommended

- Hard disk with a minimum of 20M bytes of memory (50M bytes of memory are recommended)

- One high-density floppy disk drive

- Mouse, tablet, or other input device

- A math coprocessor

- Graphics video screen or XGA (Hercules or EGA are not satisfactory)

- PC-DOS or MS-DOS (version 3.3 or later)

In addition, the following additional equipment is recommended, but not essential:

- 4MB or more of expanded or extended memory

- Dot-matrix or laser printer

- Plotter

- Surge suppressor

Configuring Your Computer for AutoCAD

The following section gives directions for turning on and configuring your computer for AutoCAD. Follow these steps to turn on your computer:

1. Make sure that there is no floppy disk in the disk drives.

2. Check that the main switches on the computer and the screen are turned on.

3. Turn on the surge suppressor switch (if you have one) to start up the computer. (If you do not have a surge suppressor, consider buying one to protect your computer and your data.)

REMOVING THE EXTENDED MEMORY MANAGER

Each time your computer is turned on, the disk file named CONFIG.SYS is automatically read for instructions. You must remove certain instructions from this file because they interfere with AutoCAD Release 12. AutoCAD's extended memory manager is incompatible with the DOS extended memory manager. Therefore, you have to remove the extended memory manager (if it is present) from the CONFIG.SYS file.

1. To check the CONFIG.SYS file for the memory manager, give the command **type config.sys** and press Enter.

2. Look at the display on your monitor. If the lines

DOS=HIGH
DEVICE=C:\DOS\himem.sys
DEVICE=C:\DOS5\smartdrv.sys
DEVICE=C:\DOS5\ramdrive.sys

appear, you must remove them or AutoCAD will not work properly. (If none of these lines is present, skip ahead to the next section.) Use your editor program to remove the above lines from a copy of your CONFIG.SYS file. If you do not know how to use the editor program, you will need to rename the CONFIG.SYS file.

3. To rename the file, type **ren config.sys *.old** and press Enter.

This changes the name CONFIG.SYS to CONFIG.OLD. You may have to change CONFIG.OLD back to the original when not running AutoCAD.

A better solution is to replace the DOS memory manager HIMEM.SYS with Quarterdeck's QEMM386, which is compatible with AutoCAD.

Running the AutoCAD Installation Program

Your AutoCAD program is contained on many 5¼-inch or 3½-inch disks. To install the complete AutoCAD package, you need 25M bytes of free space on your hard drive. You can, however, install a limited version of AutoCAD in only 11M bytes. (You can rerun the installation program later to install more of the program.) If there is insufficient room on your disk, the installation program will tell you and then terminate. To install AutoCAD, follow these steps:

1. Put the disk labeled Executables 1 in drive A.

2. Type **a:** and press Enter.

3. At the **A:\>** prompt, type **install** and press Enter.

4. Press Enter at the first screen. A screen requesting information appears as in Figure A.1.

5. Fill in the requested items using at least *four* characters for each entry.

6. After providing the required information, press Enter.

7. When asked for verification, check the information and type **y** if it is correct. The information is then written onto the first disk.

8. After reading the next two screens of information, press Enter.

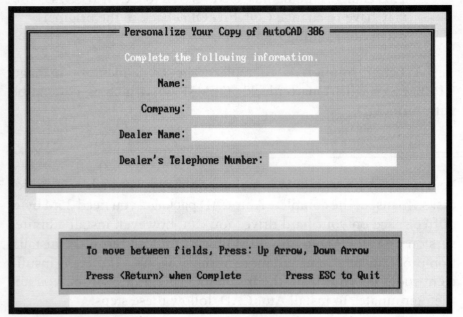

FIGURE A.1:

The AutoCAD Owner Information screen

9. The next screen shows the various parts of AutoCAD that can be installed as in Figure A.2. The default is everything which requires 25M bytes of hard disk space. Move the cursor up or down with a cursor arrow and press the space bar to select or unselect an item.

10. The Select Drive screen appears, showing which drives are available for AutoCAD installation. Use an up or down cursor arrow to select the drive (normally C) and press Enter.

11. The Select Directory screen appears as in Figure A.3, suggesting the directory name for AutoCAD installation. If you currently have another version of AutoCAD installed, use the cursor keys to change the directory name so you can still run your old version (for example, ACAD2). If you have no other copy of AutoCAD, press Enter to accept the suggested name of \ACAD.

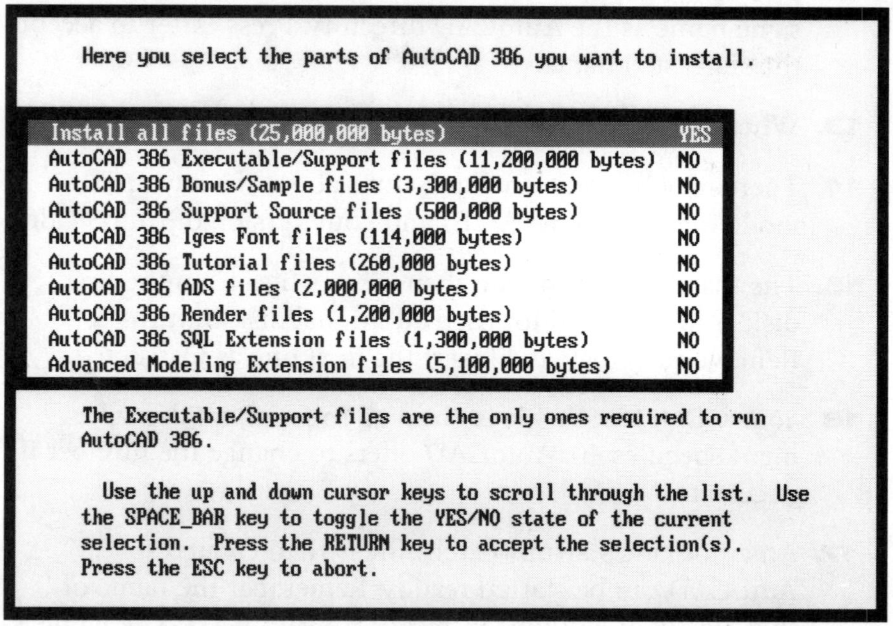

```
Here you select the parts of AutoCAD 386 you want to install.

Install all files (25,000,000 bytes)                    YES
AutoCAD 386 Executable/Support files (11,200,000 bytes)  NO
AutoCAD 386 Bonus/Sample files (3,300,000 bytes)         NO
AutoCAD 386 Support Source files (500,000 bytes)         NO
AutoCAD 386 Iges Font files (114,000 bytes)              NO
AutoCAD 386 Tutorial files (260,000 bytes)               NO
AutoCAD 386 ADS files (2,000,000 bytes)                  NO
AutoCAD 386 Render files (1,200,000 bytes)               NO
AutoCAD 386 SQL Extension files (1,300,000 bytes)        NO
Advanced Modeling Extension files (5,100,000 bytes)      NO

The Executable/Support files are the only ones required to run
AutoCAD 386.

    Use the up and down cursor keys to scroll through the list.  Use
the SPACE_BAR key to toggle the YES/NO state of the current
selection.  Press the RETURN key to accept the selection(s).
Press the ESC key to abort.
```

FIGURE A.2:

The screen to select parts to be installed

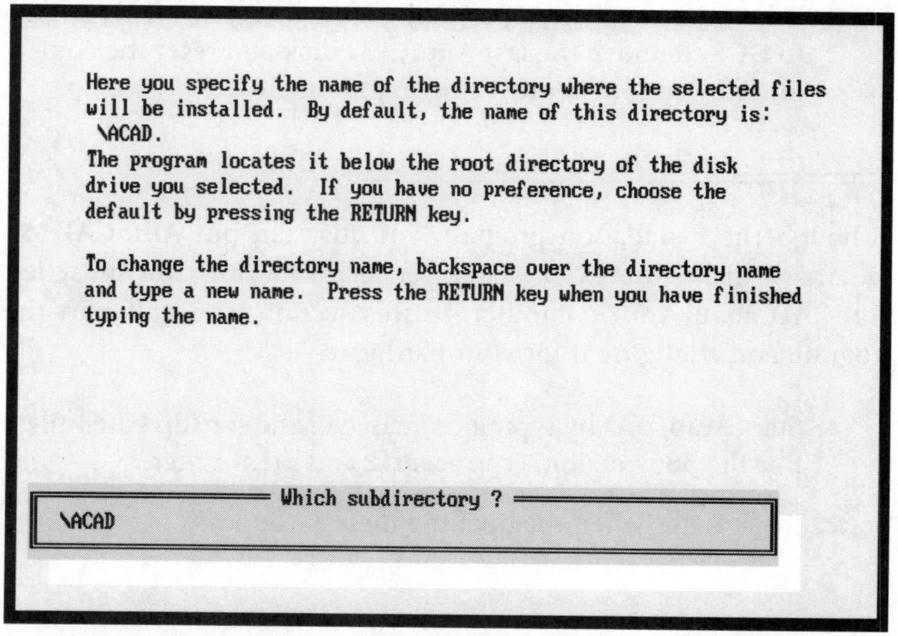

```
Here you specify the name of the directory where the selected files
will be installed.  By default, the name of this directory is:
 \ACAD.
The program locates it below the root directory of the disk
drive you selected.  If you have no preference, choose the
default by pressing the RETURN key.

To change the directory name, backspace over the directory name
and type a new name.  Press the RETURN key when you have finished
typing the name.


======= Which subdirectory ? =======
\ACAD
```

FIGURE A.3:

The Select Directory screen

12. The Select Support Directory screen appears, suggesting the same name as the AutoCAD directory. Press Enter to accept the suggested name.

13. When you have made your selection, press Enter.

14. There may be additional questions about the advanced modeling extension (AME) and your version of AutoShade.

15. The installation program then creates files from the first disk. You are asked for each additional disk in turn. Remove each disk and insert the next one as instructed.

16. Your CONFIG.SYS file is checked to see that Files statement specifies 40. AutoCAD offers to change the number if necessary.

17. An automatic startup (batch) file is then created so AutoCAD can be started readily. Remember the name of this file—you will type it to start up AutoCAD. The name is ACADR12.BAT.

18. When the installation program is finished, you are returned to DOS. Remove the last AutoCAD disk and reset the computer by simultaneously pressing Ctrl-Alt-Del.

Configuring AutoCAD for Your Computer

Although the installation program you just ran put AutoCAD on your hard disk, AutoCAD is not yet ready to run. You must tell AutoCAD about your computer. In this section, you will start the program and configure it for your hardware.

1. Start AutoCAD by typing the name of the startup batch file. For the 386 version, type **acadr12** and press Enter.

2. Press Enter when the opening message appears.

3. The next screen appears with the message

> **AutoCAD is not yet configured**
> **Press RETURN to continue**

Press Enter.

4. Several questions about your screen appear. These deal with the aspect ratio (whether circles are out of round) and what colors you want. Press Enter for each question to accept the default value. Later, you can reconfigure AutoCAD to change these items.

5. The next screen gives a list of digitizers (mice). Type the corresponding number and press Enter.

6. Press Enter for each question to accept the default value.

7. Next, a list of plotters is given. Type the corresponding number and press Enter.

8. The next questions are about the default plot options. Choose the default options for now, except for rotation of the plot. Choose 90°. You can change these options later when you plot a drawing.

9. Continue with the default responses until you are given the AutoCAD drawing screen.

AutoCAD is now ready to use.

AutoCAD Commands

This appendix lists some of the most important AutoCAD commands that can be typed from the keyboard or selected from the various menus. To see a *complete* list of AutoCAD commands, just type **help** or **?,** press Enter, and pick the index box.

Commands beginning with an apostrophe are called *transparent* commands and have the same function as the command without the apostrophe. The difference is that they can be used while another command is running. Abbreviations are shown in parentheses.

ARC (A)	BHATCH	CHPROP
AREA	BREAK	CIRCLE (C)
ARRAY	CHANGE	'COLOR

COPY	INSERT	PLINE (PL)
DDEDIT	'LAYER	PLOT
DIM	'LIMITS	POINT
'DIST	LINE	POLYGON
DONUT	'LINETYPE	PSPACE
DOUGHNUT	LIST	PURGE
DTEXT	LOAD	QSAVE
DVIEW (DV)	'LTSCALE	QTEXT
EDGESURF	MINSERT	QUIT
ELEV	MIRROR	REDO
ELLIPSE	MOVE (M)	'REDRAW (R)
END	MSPACE	'REDRAWALL
ERASE (E)	MULTIPLE	REGEN
EXPLODE	MVIEW	REGENALL
EXTEND	NEW	'REGENAUTO
'FILES	OOPS	RENAME
'FILL	OPEN	REVSURF
FILLET	'ORTHO	ROTATE
'GRID	'OSNAP	RULESURF
'HELP or '?	'PAN (P)	SAVE
HIDE	PEDIT	SAVEAS
'ID	PLAN	SCALE

SELECT	TABLET	'VIEW
'SETVAR	TABSURF	VIEWPORTS
SHADE	TEXT	VIEWRES
SHAPE	'TIME	VPLAYER
SHELL/SH	TRACE	VPOINT
SKETCH	TRIM	VPORTS
'SNAP	U	WBLOCK
SOLID	UCS	'ZOOM (Z)
'STATUS	UCSICON	3DFACE
STRETCH	UNDO	3DMESH
'STYLE	'UNITS	3DPOLY

INDEX

A

a (Add) option, 75
absolute Cartesian references, 5
ACADR12.BAT file, 296
accuracy, display, 12, 219–220
active ports, 238
Add option, 75
advanced modeling extension
    (AME), 296
Align dimension command, 231
aligning
    dimensions, 230–231
    Ortho mode for, 38–39
angle brackets (<>), values in, 15
angled lines, 54, 57–59
angled planes, circles on, 255
angles
    for arcs, 122
    for polar arrays, 117
    for polar notation, 7
    for rotating, 41, 91
apostrophes ('), 206–207, 298
Arc command, 121
architectural drawings, 2,
    194–195
arcs
    center lines for, 132
    converting circles to, 93,
        172–176

dimensioning, 208
drawing, 118–122
replacing, 125–126
for rounded corners, 151–154
Array command, 33, 116–118,
    126–129
arrow keys, 51–52
arrowheads
    on cutting-plane lines, 168
    on dimension lines, 194
aspect ratio, 297
at signs (@) for relative
    references, 7
attached line segments, 56–57
Autolisp solids program, 242–244
automatic saving, 63
AutoShade, 296

B

^B command, 16
Backspace key, 39, 51
base points
    for moving objects, 91
    for rotating objects, 90, 110
    for stretching objects, 112
batch files, 296
Bhatch command, 187
bolt slots
    centerlines for, 214, 222–226

dimensions for, 214–215,
230–232
drawing, 170–182
border template, 9–10, 25
for bracket drawing, 132
company name in, 38–40
for cube drawing, 236
dates in, 43–44
drawing border for, 19–22
for flange drawing, 168
layers for, 26–28
names in, 42–43
plotting, 45–47
for pulley drawing, 103
saving, 24
titles in, 28–35, 40–42
updating, 135–136
widening lines for, 22–23
borders
drawing, 19–22
erasing, 272
in Paper Space drawings,
276–278
for title blocks, 30–32
boss in bracket drawing
dimensioning, 205–206
drawing, 139–140, 143–144,
149–151
boundaries
hiding, 287–288
trim, 94–96
Boundary Hatch dialog box,
187–189
bracket drawing, 130–131
centerlines in, 199–201

dimensioning the front view,
201–206
dimensioning the right view,
213–217
dimensioning the top view,
206–213
drawing front view, 141–144,
155–157, 199–201
drawing right view, 157–158,
160–162
drawing top view, 136–141,
163–164
hidden lines in, 154–158
line types for, 132–136
opening, 195–196
plotting, 165–166
starting, 132
widening object lines in,
159–165
Break command, 93–94, 98–100

C

c (Circle) command, 62–63
c (Close) command, 22
c (Cube) option, 243–244
^C for terminating commands, 11
Cartesian notation, 5–7
cen (Center) Osnap option, 79,
89, 91
centering text, 40–41
centerlines, 132
for bolt slots, 214, 222–226
in bracket drawing, 199–201
for circles, 132, 225

with dimensions, 208–209
extending, 211–213, 215–216
as extension lines, 195
in flange drawing, 232–233
layer for, 133–134
line type for, 134–135
removing, 224
centers
of circles, 79–80, 208
dashes and dots for, 132
Change command, 27–28, 82–85
Change Layer dialog box, 154
Change-point option, 85
Choose Hatch Pattern dialog box, 187
Chprop command, 212
Circle command, 62–63
circles
in bracket drawing, 136
breaking, 93, 98–100
centerlines for, 132, 225
centers of, 79–80, 208
concentric, 114–115, 139–140
connected, 103–105, 173–174
converting, to arcs, 93, 172–176
dimensioning, 208
drawing, 62–63
in flange drawing, 169–180
polygons for, 113
selecting, 64
tangent, 115–116
in three-dimensional drawings, 253–258
trimming, 100–101, 138–139, 175–176

widening lines for, 164–165
Close command, 22
color
of lines, 273–274
setting up, 297
Command: prompt, 11, 21
commands
dynamic, 118–119, 206–207, 298
help for, 2–3
list of, 298–300
terminating, 11
undoing, 59–61, 79
commas (,) in coordinate systems, 5
company name in title blocks, 38–40
concentric circles, 114–115, 139–140
cones, drawing, 258–261
CONFIG.SYS file, modifying, 291–293
configuring with AutoCAD, 291–293, 296–297
connecting objects
circles, 103–105, 173–174
Osnap options for, 31, 86–87
construction lines, 120
erasing, 124–125
for flange, 177–182
for mirroring objects, 124
context-sensitive help, 3
converting
circles to arcs, 93, 172–176

lines to polylines, 22–23, 159–165

polylines to lines, 146–147

coordinate icon, 18–19, 235

coordinates

Cartesian notation for, 5–7

and drawing limits, 13–15

polar notation for, 6–8

readout for, 4–5, 12

for three-dimensional drawings, 235

coprocessor requirements, 291

Copy command, 88–89, 280–282

copying

lines, 140

objects, 33, 88–89, 116–118, 123–124

viewing ports, 280–282

wedges, 126–129

corners

dimensions for, 213–214

rounded, 152–154

correcting text, 39

Create New Drawing dialog box, 49

crossing polygon windows, 78–79

crossing windows

default selections for, 126

selecting objects with, 71, 76–77

cube drawing

circles on, 253–258

cones on, 258–261

domes on, 264–266

drawing limits for, 236–237

orientation text in, 244–247

outside Ucs plane, 247–250

plotting, 267–268

starting, 236

torus on, 261–263

Ucs location in, 250–253

viewing ports for, 237–239

viewpoints in, 239–241

z direction in, 242–247

current layer, 29–30

cursor with Snap mode, 16–17

cutting-plane lines, 168

adding, 228–230

layers for, 227–228

cutting planes, 167–168

D

dashes

for crossing windows, 77, 126

for cutting-plane lines, 168

for hidden lines, 132

dates, 26

changing, 50–52

in title blocks, 43–44

Ddedit command, 51–52

Ddunits command, 12, 219–220

default layer, 27

Delete key, 51

deleting

centerlines, 224

construction lines, 124–125

hidden lines, 260–261

selection set objects, 73–74

viewing ports, 285–286

deselecting objects, 73–74

dia (Diameter) dimension command, 210–211
digitizers, selecting, 297
digits, setting, 12, 219–220
dim layer, 202
Dim: prompt, 202
Dimcen variable, 209–210
Dimension command mode, 202–203
dimension lines, 194
dimensions, 193
  aligning, 230–231
  for bolt slots, 214–215, 230–232
  for bracket drawing, front view, 201–206
  for bracket drawing, right view, 213–217
  for bracket drawing, top view, 206–213
  for corners, 213–214
  for diameters, 210–211
  for flange drawing, 218–219
  for flange drawing, front view, 220–221
  for flange drawing, top view, 222–232
  horizontal, 204–206, 221
  layers for, 202
  principles of, 194–195
  for radii, 209–210
  vertical, 203–204, 220–221
directories for AutoCAD installation, 294–296
disks
  plotting to, 45

requirements for, 291, 293
displacement
  in copying objects, 88–89
  with panning, 254
Display option in plotting, 45
displayed digits, setting, 12, 219–220
domes, drawing, 264–266
Donut command, 139
DOS requirements, 291
dots. *See* grid system
drawing area, setting up, 11–15
drawing cursor, 4–5
drawing editor screen, 4–5, 11
drawing limits
  checking, 14, 237
  for cube drawing, 236–237
  for Paper Space drawings, 275–276
  in plotting, 45
  setting, 13–15
drives for AutoCAD installation, 294
Dtext command, 35, 38–39
duplicating. *See* copying
dynamic commands, 118–119, 206–207, 298

E

e (Erase) command for selected objects, 78
Edit Text dialog box, 51–52
editor for text, 51–52
ellipses, 255

elongating objects, 110–112
End command, 24
End key, 52
end points for lines, 5
endp (Endpoint) Osnap option,
    66–67, 86–87, 93
engineering drawings, 2, 194–195
enlarging drawings, 19, 32, 52–53,
    113–114, 118–119, 206–208
equipment, required, 290–291
Erase command for selected
    objects, 78
erasing
  borders and titles, 272
  centerlines, 224
  construction lines, 124–125
  lines, 59–61
expanded memory requirements,
    291
Explode command, 146–147
Extend command, 97–98,
    174–175
extended memory, 291–293
extending centerlines, 211–213,
    215–216
extension lines, 195

F

F1 key, 4, 12
F3 (Grid) key (Sun), 15–16
F4 (Ortho) key (Sun), 39
F5 (Snap) key (Sun), 16
F7 (Grid) key, 15–16
F8 (Ortho) key, 39

F9 (Snap) key, 16
Fence option for selecting objects,
    75–76
Fillet command, 152–154
filters, point, 41
Fit option for text, 38
five-pointed star, drawing,
    118–129
flange drawing, 167
  dimensions for, 218–219
  dimensions for front view,
    220–221
  dimensions for top view,
    222–232
  drawing front view, 182–189,
    232–233
  drawing top view, 169–182,
    189–191
  starting, 168
floppy disks, plotting to, 45
fonts, 35–38, 42, 198–199
"found" messages, 67–68
freezing layers, 197–198, 284
front view
  of bracket drawing, dimension-
    ing, 201–206
  of bracket drawing, drawing,
    141–144, 155–157, 199–201
  of flange drawing, centerlines
    for, 232–233
  of flange, drawing, 182–189
  of flange drawing, dimension-
    ing, 220–221
front views, 2
full scale drawings, 12

G

^G command, 15–16
graphics screen requirements, 291
Grid command, 16–17
grid system
  Snap mode with, 16–17
  spacing for, 17–18
  turning on, 15–16
  in viewing ports, 238–239

H

hard disk requirements, 291, 293
hardware, required, 290–291
Hatch Options dialog box, 187
hatch patterns, 167
  layers for, 186–187
  for section lines, 187–189
height
  of drawings, displaying, 14
  of text, 39
Help command, 2–3
Help dialog box, 2–3
Help Index dialog box, 2
hemispheres, drawing, 264–266
hidden lines
  in bracket drawing, 154–158
  dashed lines for, 132
  layer for, 133–134
  line type for, 134–135
  in Paper Space drawings, 287–288

removing, 260–261
Hide command, 256, 260
HIMEM.SYS memory manager, 293
Home key, 52
hor (Horizontal) dimension option, 204, 221
horizontal dimensions, 204–206, 221
horizontal lines, 55–56, 84–85

I

icons, coordinate, 18–19, 235
index, help, 2
information, drawing screen, 13
Inquiry menu, 13
Insert command, 276–278
install program, 293–296
installing AutoCAD, 290–297
int (Intersection) Osnap option, 94, 98–99
interior lines
  in flange drawing, 183–186
  in title block, 32–35
Intersection Osnap option, 94, 98–99

J

j (Join) command, 23
justifying text, 38

L

L (Last) option for selecting
  objects, 70
Layer command, 27, 197
Layer Control dialog box, 29–30
layers
  creating, 26–27
  current, 29–30
  for cutting-plane lines, 227–228
  for dimensions, 202
  freezing, 197–198, 284
  for hatch patterns, 186–187
  for line types, 133–134
  moving to, 27–28
  for Paper Space drawings,
    273–274
  for text, 244
  for title block, 28–29
leaders, 195
lettering. *See* text
levels. *See* layers
limits. *See* drawing limits
Limits command, 14, 237
Limits option in plotting, 45
Line command, 19–22, 53–57
line segments, drawing, 56–57
line types
  for bracket drawing, 132–136
  layers for, 133–134
  scale of, 158
lines
  angled, 54, 57–59
  in bracket drawing, 136–138,
    140–143, 148–149

color of, 273–274
construction, 120, 124–125,
  177–182
converting to polylines, 22–23,
  159–165
converting from polylines,
  146–147
copying, 140
drawing, 19–22, 53–57
end points for, 5
erasing, 59–61
extending, 97–98, 174–175
in flange drawing, 183–186,
  189–191
hidden. *See* hidden lines
Ortho mode for, 55–56, 84–85
rotating, 178–179
tangent, 106–108
trimming, 95–97
width of, 22–23, 159–165,
  189–191
Linetype command, 133
List command, 67, 71, 147
Ltscale command, 158

M

magnifying drawings, 19, 32,
  52–53, 113–114, 118–119,
  206–208
marking points, 19–20
Mastering AutoCAD Release 12, 288
math coprocessor requirements,
  291
maximum coordinates, 13

memory
  extended memory managers for,
    292–293
  requirements for, 291
menus, 4
mid (Midpoint) Osnap option,
    41, 80, 86
minimum coordinates, 13
Mirror command, 123–124
Model Space, 14, 269–270
Move command, 91–92, 254
moving
  to layers, 27–28
  objects, 91–92
  Ucs, 251–252, 261–262
Mspace command, 282
Mview command, 279, 287

N

names
  in border templates, 42–43
  for drawings, 13, 136
  for layers, 27
  verifying, 50
nea (Nearest) Osnap option, 34
networks
  plotting on, 45
  starting AutoCAD on, 10
new drawings, 49–50

O

^O command, 39
object lines

for visible edges, 132
  widening, 159–165
Object Snap menu, 86
objection selection target, 64
objects
  connecting circles, 103–105,
    173–174
  connecting Osnap options for,
    31, 86–87
  copying, 33, 88–89, 116–118,
    123–124
  elongating, 110–112
  moving, 91–92
  removing sections of, 93–94,
    98–100
  rotating, 89–91, 109–110
  selecting. See selecting objects
  trimming, 94–97, 100–101,
    138–139, 175–176
  zooming, 113–114
one-point dimensioning method,
    201
open command, 195
Open drawing dialog box, 195
options
  selecting, 17
  undoing, 59, 61
orientation of plotting, 45–46
orientation text for cube drawing,
    244–247
origins
  in Cartesian notation, 5
  displaying, 14
  of Ucs, 251–252

Ortho mode
  for lines, 55–56, 84–85
  setting, 38–39
orthogonal axes, 5
orthographic projections, 2
Osnap cursor menu, 87
Osnap options, 31
  connections with, 86–87
  for drawing outside Ucs plane,
    247–249
Osnap screen menu, 86–87
ovals, 255
overlays. *See* layers
Owner Information screen, 294

P

P (Previous) option for selecting
    objects, 69–70
Pan command, 254
Paper Space drawings, 269–270
  borders and titles in, 276–278
  changing to, 274–275
  drawing limits for, 275–276
  layers for, 273–274
  plotting, 286–289
  starting, 271–272
  viewing ports for, 270, 278–
    282, 285–286
  viewpoints for, 282–285
parentheses () for graph points, 5
Partial option in plotting, 46
parts, exploding, 146–147
Pedit command, 22, 159

per (Perpendicular) Osnap
    option, 31
perimeter lines in bracket
    drawing, 136–138, 142–143
phantom lines, 227–228
plan views, 253
Pline command, 30
Plot command, 45
Plot Configuration dialog box,
    45–46, 267
Plot dialog box, 45–46
Plot Preview dialog box, 267
Plot Rotation and Orientation
    dialog box, 45–46
plotters, selecting, 45, 297
plotting
  border template, 45–47
  bracket drawing, 165–166
  Paper Space drawings, 286–289
  three-dimensional drawings,
    267–268
plus symbols (+)
  for circles, 62, 208
  for lines, 54
pointing, selecting objects by,
    67–69
points
  changing location of, 85
  coordinates for, 5–8
  filters for, 41
  marking, 19–20
Polar arrays, 33, 117–118
polar notation, 6–8
Polygon command, 144–145
polygon windows, 78–79

polygons for circles, 113
polylines
  converting lines to, 22–23, 159–165
  exploding, 146–147
  width of, 22–23
positioning points, 16–17, 85
PostScript printers, 45
precise connections, Osnap options for, 31, 86–87
precision, display, 12, 219–220
Preview Effective Plotting Area dialog box, 46
previewing plotting, 46, 267
Previous option for selecting objects, 69–70
printer requirements, 291
processor requirements, 291
prompts, 4, 11, 202
properties
  changing, 85, 212
  for layers, 28
proportional typefaces, 35
Pspace command, 278
pulley drawing, 102
  arcs in, 118–122
  from border template, 103
  concentric circles for, 114–115
  connected circles for, 103–105
  copying objects in, 116–118
  elongating objects for, 110–112
  rotating, 109–110
  tangent circles for, 115–116
  tangent lines for, 105–108
  wedges in, 122–129
  zooming objects in, 113–114

Q

QEMM386 memory manager, 293
Qsave command, 24
qtext, 196–197
qua (Quadrant) Osnap option, 89–91
question marks (?) for help, 2

R

r (Redraw) command, 97
r (Remove) option, 73
rad (Radius) dimension command, 209
radial distances, 7
radii
  of circles, 62
  dimensions for, 209–210
  for Fillet, 153
radio buttons, 45
Radius dimension command, 209
raised areas in bracket drawing
  dimensioning, 205–206
  drawing, 139–140, 143–144, 149–151
rectangles for qtext, 196–197
rectangular arrays, 33–34
Redo command, 61, 79
Redraw command, 97
regen (Regenerate) command, 113, 172
regeneration of text, 196–198
regular polygon windows, 78–79

regular windows
  default selections for, 126
  selecting objects with, 71–73
relative references, 7, 21
Remove option, 73
removing
  centerlines, 224
  construction lines, 124–125
  hidden lines, 260–261
  selection set objects, 73–74
  viewing ports, 285–286
replicating. *See* copying
right-hand rule, 252
right views of bracket drawing
  dimensioning, 213–217
  drawing, 130–131, 157–158,
    160–162
Roman typefaces, 35–37
Rotate command, 89, 109–110,
  178–179
rotating
  lines, 178–179
  objects, 89–91
  plotting, 45–46
  pulley drawing, 109–110
  text, 41
  Ucs, 252
rounded corners, 152–154
rubber-band line, 21

S

Save Drawing As dialog box, 136
Saveas command, 136
savetime system variable, 63

saving
  automatic, 63
  border template, 24, 135–136
  views, 176–177
scales
  adjusting, 19
  of line types, 158
  for Paper Space, 270
  selecting, 12
screen, viewing ports on, 237–239
section lines, hatch patterns for,
  187–189
section planes, lines for, 132
sectional views, 167
Select Color dialog box, 273
Select Directory screen, 294–295
Select Drive screen, 294
Select Linetype dialog box,
  134–135
Select objects: prompt, 67
Select Support Directory screen,
  296
Select Text Font dialog box,
  36–37, 39, 42
selecting objects, 48, 64–66
  with crossing windows, 71,
    76–77
  by pointing, 67–69
  with polygon windows, 78–79
  previously drawn, 70
  previously selected, 69–70
  with regular windows, 71–73
selection cursor, 22
selection sets
  adding objects to, 68, 75–76

removing objects from, 73–74
serif fonts, 35
setting up drawing area, 11–15
Settings menu, 28
shape descriptions, 193
size
  of circles, 62
  of drawing area. *See* drawing
    limits
  of Regular windows, 72
  of text, 39
  of viewing ports, 285–286
Size A drawings, 13
slots. *See* bolt slots
Snap mode, 16–17
  spacing in, 18
  in viewing ports, 238–239
spacing
  for grid system, 17–18
  for Snap mode, 18
squares, drawing, 144–146
starting AutoCAD, 10–11
startup files, 296
Status command, 13–15, 50
status line, 4
Steel hatch pattern, 189
Stretch command, 110–112
style
  of lines, 132
  of text, 198–199, 244–245
Style command, 198–199
Sun computers
  function keys on, 15–16, 39
  screens on, 4
surge supressors, 292

symbols, fonts for, 37
system plotters, 45

T

tan (Tangent) Osnap mode,
    105–108
tangent circles, 115–116
tangent lines, 106–108
targets, 64
templates. *See* border template
temporary construction lines, 120
  erasing, 124–125
  for flange, 177–182
  for mirroring objects, 124
terminating commands, 11
text
  changing, 50–52
  dimension, 203
  fonts for, 35–38, 42, 198–199
  layers for, 244
  for orientation, 244–247
  qtext, 196–197
  regeneration of, 196–198
  style of, 244–245
  in title blocks, 28–32, 38–44
Text command, 35
text screen, 4, 12–13
thickness of lines, 132
3D construction dialog box, 242
3D Objects dialog box, 242–243,
    259
3D Surfaces command, 242, 259
three-dimensional drawings, 2,
    234. *See also* Paper Space

drawings
  circles on, 253–258
  cones on, 258–261
  coordinate systems for, 235
  domes on, 264–266
  drawing limits for, 236–237
  orientation text in, 244–247
  outside Ucs plane, 247–250
  plotting, 267–268
  torus on, 261–263
  Ucs location in, 250–253
  viewing ports for, 237–239
  viewpoints in, 239–241
  z direction in, 242–247
three-point break method, 93, 98
Tilemode system variable, 270, 274
Time command, 26
titles and title blocks, 40–42
  changing, 50–52
  company name in, 38–40
  creating, 30–32
  dates in, 43–44
  enlarging, 31
  erasing, 272
  interior lines for, 32–35
  layer for, 28–29
  names in, 42–43
  in Paper Space drawings, 276–278
To Point: prompt, 21, 56
toggle keys, 16
top views, 2
  of bracket drawing, 130–131

of bracket drawing, dimensioning, 206–213
or bracket drawing, drawing, 136–141, 163–164
of flange drawing, dimensioning, 222–232
of flange drawing, drawing, 169–182, 189–191
torus, drawing a, 261–263
translating Ucs, 251
transparent commands, 298
triangles on menus, 36
trim boundaries, 94–96
Trim command, 94–97
trimming, 94
  in bracket drawing, 138–139
  circles, 100–101, 138–139, 175–176
  lines, 95–97
two-point break method, 93
two-point dimensioning method, 201
typefaces, 35–38, 42, 198–199

U

U command, 59–61
Ucs. *See* User Coordinate System (UCS)
Ucs command, 266
Ucs icon, 18–19, 235
Ucsicon command, 19, 75, 251
undoing commands, 59–61, 79
Units Control dialog box, 12, 219
user coordinate icon, 18–19, 235

User Coordinate System (UCS), 235
  drawing outside of plane for, 247–250
  location of, 250–253
  moving, 251–252, 261–262
  returning to, 266
  rotating, 252

V

vectors
  in copying objects, 88–89
  with panning, 254
ver (Vertical) dimension option, 203, 220
verifying names, 50
vertical dimensions, 203–204, 220–221
vertical lines, 56–57
View command, 176–177
viewing ports, 235
  copying, 280–282
  dividing screen into, 237–239
  for Paper Space drawings, 270, 278–282, 285–286
  viewpoints in, 239–241
viewpoints, 235
  for Paper Space drawings, 282–285
  in viewing ports, 239–241
views, 2
Vplayer command, 284
Vpoint command, 239–241, 283–284

Vports command, 238

W

w (Window) option, 71
wedges, drawing, 122–129
width
  of drawings, displaying, 14
  of lines, 22–23, 159–165, 189–191
Window option
  in plotting, 45
  in selecting objects, 71
Window polygon option, 78
windows. *See also* viewing ports
  default selections for, 126
  selecting objects with, 71–73, 76–77
wire frame models, 260
World Coordinate System (WCS), 235, 266
World icon, 19
Wp (Window polygon) option, 78

X

X-axes, 5
.x command, 41

Y

Y-axes, 5

Z

z (Zoom) command, 19, 32,
    52–53, 113–114, 118–119,
    206–208
z direction, drawing in, 242–247
zigzag lines, 54

YOUR GUIDE TO DOS DOMINANCE.

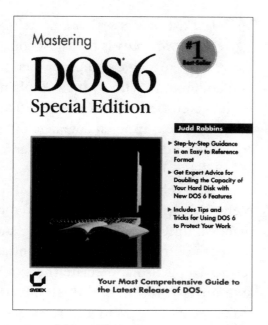

999 pp. ISBN: 1236-6

DOS 6 can save you hundreds of dollars in hardware and software purchases. *Mastering DOS 6 (Special Edition)* shows you how.

Whether you're a beginner or expert, whether you use DOS or Windows, *Mastering DOS 6 (Special Edition)* will help you make the most of the new DOS 6 utilities. Find out how to protect your computer work with Backup, Undelete and Anti-Virus. Get a complete overview of disk caching and disk defragmenting. Discover the secret of automatically expanding your memory by typing a single command.

You'll even find out about the new DOS utility DoubleSpace that will double the available space on your hard disk.

SYBEX. Help Yourself.

POCKET-SIZED PC EXPERTISE.

550 pp. ISBN: 756-8.

2021 Challenger Drive
Alameda, CA 94501
1-510-523-8233
1-800-227-2346

SYBEX

YES, YOU *CAN* DO WINDOWS.

WINDOWS HAS NEVER BEEN CLEARER.

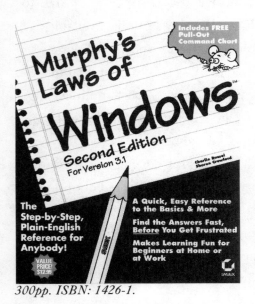

300pp. ISBN: 1426-1.

Even though Windows has done so much to make computers easier to use, you can still run into trouble. That's why you need *Murphy's Laws of Windows*.

Whether you're new to computers or just new to Windows, you'll get a gold mine of problem-solving information you can use. You'll learn how to avoid problems with Windows, correct Windows mistakes, and more.

You'll get all of this and more in an entertaining and easy-to-reference format. Thanks to this book, you'll never again have to say, "I don't do Windows."

SYBEX. Help Yourself.

2021 Challenger Drive
Alameda, CA 94501
1-510-523-8233
1-800-227-2346

SYBEX

YOUR GUIDE TO DOS DOMINANCE.

1000 pp. ISBN:1442-3

SYBEX

YOUR GUIDE TO A WORLD OF CONVENIENCE.

THE BEST BET FOR dBASE BEGINNERS.

MAKE A GOOD COMPUTER EVEN BETTER.

SYBEX

FREE BROCHURE!

Complete this form today, and we'll send you a full-color brochure of Sybex bestsellers.

Please supply the name of the Sybex book purchased.

_____

How would you rate it?

_____ Excellent _____ Very Good _____ Average _____ Poor

Why did you select this particular book?

_____ Recommended to me by a friend
_____ Recommended to me by store personnel
_____ Saw an advertisement in _____
_____ Author's reputation
_____ Saw in Sybex catalog
_____ Required textbook
_____ Sybex reputation
_____ Read book review in _____
_____ In-store display
_____ Other _____

Where did you buy it?

_____ Bookstore
_____ Computer Store or Software Store
_____ Catalog (name: _____)
_____ Direct from Sybex
_____ Other: _____

Did you buy this book with your personal funds?

_____ Yes _____ No

About how many computer books do you buy each year?

_____ 1-3 _____ 3-5 _____ 5-7 _____ 7-9 _____ 10+

About how many Sybex books do you own?

_____ 1-3 _____ 3-5 _____ 5-7 _____ 7-9 _____ 10+

Please indicate your level of experience with the software covered in this book:

_____ Beginner _____ Intermediate _____ Advanced

Which types of software packages do you use regularly?

_____ Accounting	_____ Databases	_____ Networks
_____ Amiga	_____ Desktop Publishing	_____ Operating Systems
_____ Apple/Mac	_____ File Utilities	_____ Spreadsheets
_____ CAD	_____ Money Management	_____ Word Processing
_____ Communications	_____ Languages	_____ Other _____

(please specify)

Which of the following best describes your job title?

_____ Administrative/Secretarial   _____ President/CEO

_____ Director   _____ Manager/Supervisor

_____ Engineer/Technician   _____ Other _____

(please specify)

Comments on the weaknesses/strengths of this book: _____

_____

_____

_____

_____

Name _____

Street _____

City/State/Zip _____

Phone _____

PLEASE FOLD, SEAL, AND MAIL TO SYBEX

-- --

SYBEX, INC.
Department M
2021 CHALLENGER DR.
ALAMEDA, CALIFORNIA USA
94501

SYBEX

SEAL

Selecting a Text Font with a Dialog Box

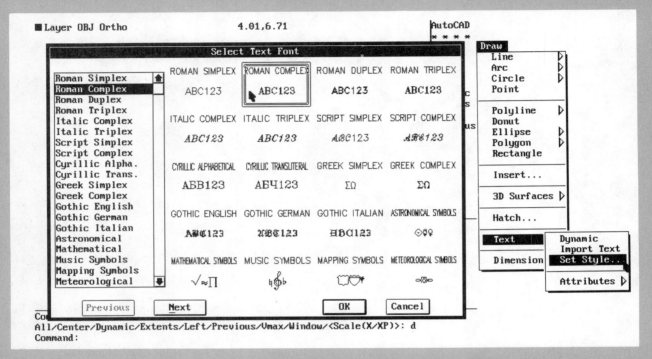

1. Move the cursor to the top of the screen. When the menu bar appears, highlight the menu title Draw and press the pick button to pull down the menu.

2. Move the cursor down the menu to highlight Text and press the pick button.

3. Highlight Set Style and press the pick button.

4. You can now choose a font from the options displayed, or pick Next to see more options.